Teacher as a

Decision Maker

CURRICULUM

Jerry A. Redman & Mary G. Anderson

great river learning

All images are Shutterstock.com, unless otherwise indicated.
Cover image © iStock/Thinkstock

great river learning

Text + website ISBN 978-1-68075-214-4
Text ISBN 978-1-68075-534-3

Printed in the United States of America

Contents

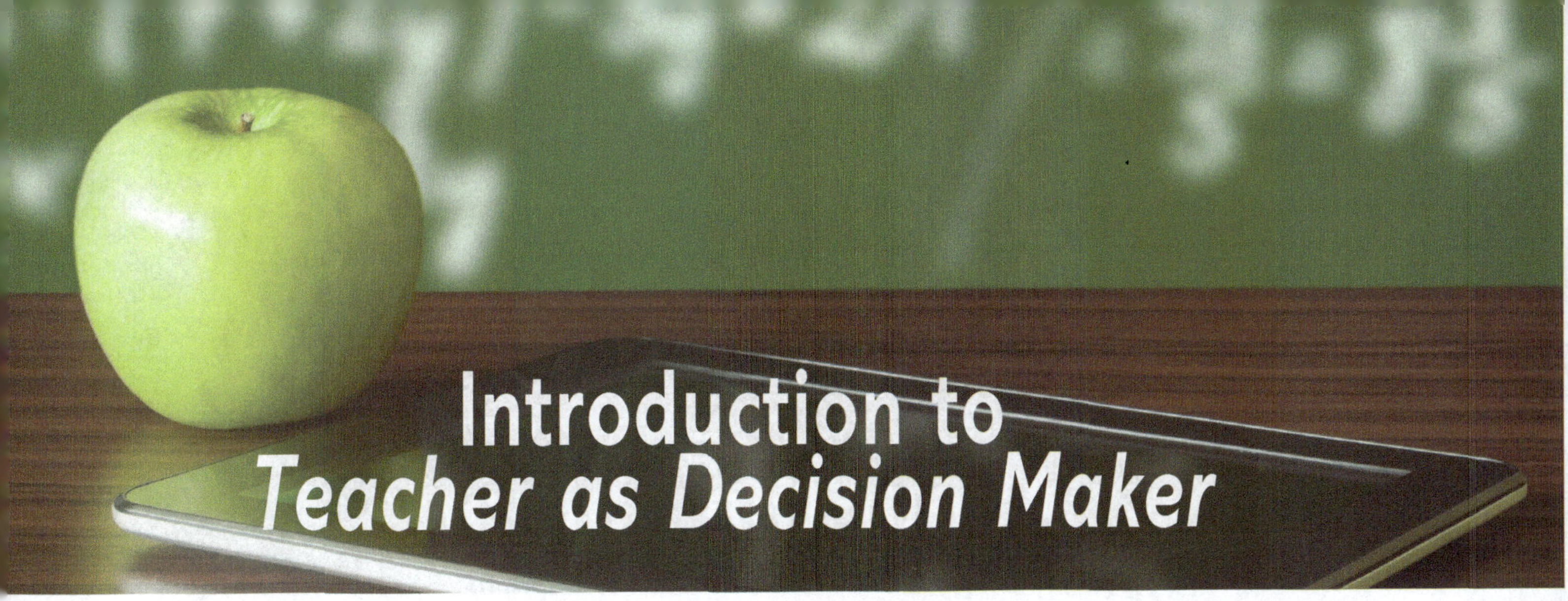

Introduction to *Teacher as Decision Maker*

Every person's work is a portrait of himself or herself! An excellent teacher is an excellent decision maker. Excellent teachers make decisions based on attaining the most positive results for their students, demonstrate flexibility in dealing with change, influence others by their actions, create a synergy among colleagues, and build consensus through teamwork. Excellent teachers develop caring, contributing, responsible, and academically successful students.

Excellent teachers have a clear vision of teaching and learning, which is like a good road map. Without a good road map it is difficult to determine where you are going and impossible to know when you have arrived. *Teacher as Decision Maker: Curriculum, Teacher as Decision Maker: Instruction, and Teacher as Decision Maker: Assessment* are designed to help teacher candidates develop their vision in the three areas of curriculum, instruction, and assessment.

These books are intended to develop an understanding of curriculum content, instructional strategies and resources, and techniques of evaluation as identified through research and demonstrated by effective school practitioners. The topics and concepts presented will promote an awareness of the essential role of the teacher in creating and sustaining a learning environment, which meets the needs and interests of all grade levels. The books are also purposefully planned to model effective teaching strategies and practices that are exhibited in 21st century classrooms.

About the Authors

Dr. Jerry Redman is an Associate Professor and Director of Center of Assessment and Accreditation at Winona State University and CEO of Redman and Associates, LLC. Dr. Redman has been a science teacher; curriculum, instruction and assessment coordinator; instructional services director; and an assistant administrator. He has worked at various levels of education ranging from middle secondary schools to technical colleges to intermediate educational agencies to the university. Dr. Redman loves teaching and contributing to the growth and development of our next generation of educators.

Dr. Mary Anderson is an Assistant Professor at Winona State University in the College of Education. Prior to her years at WSU, Dr. Anderson has dedicated over 35 years to making elementary learning environments engaging, joyful, fun, and productive for all. She has been an elementary principal, an executive director, an elementary teacher, and a special educator. During her career, she has provided leadership in many types of elementary school structures including multi-age, grades 3-5, birth to grade 6, K-5, public, and charter. Dr. Anderson loves to inspire and be inspired by students of all ages and by educators who love to teach and learn.

Collectively the authors have worked with over 80 different school districts and have hosted a range of teacher professional development on the topics of curriculum, instruction and assessment. They have also collectively taught over 20 different courses at the university level.

Dr. Redman and Dr. Anderson's hope is that these books turn your vision of teaching excellence into a reality in your own classroom!

Tell me, I forget. Show me, I remember. Involve me, I understand.

Chapter 1
Creating Good Schools

> "Insanity is doing the same thing over and over again and expecting a different result."
> Albert Einstein

Anticipatory Set: The Good, the Bad, and the Ugly

DIRECTIONS: *We have all seen productive and counterproductive things happen with respect to the teaching/learning process in the classroom. This activity allows you to draw on your own experiences. Think of your own experiences being the lead instructor or being a student participant in the instructional process. What emotions do you recall? Do you recall any personal teaching/learning experiences that you had that caused you to want to succeed, or do you recall a class that was a negative experience? In either case, what were your feelings? Briefly describe those experiences by answering the questions in the table. You will share your experiences with a partner in the next class, using the strategy* ***think-pair-share****. This strategy is a collaborative learning strategy in which students work together to solve a problem or answer a question about an assigned reading. This technique requires students to first think individually about a topic or answer to a question and then share ideas with a designated partner. This allows each student to fully answer and think about the questions.*

Good	Bad
One good experience you've had in the teaching/learning process. What made it "good?"	One bad experience you've had in the teaching/learning process. What made it "bad?"
What happens to students when classroom instruction is done well?	What happens to students when classroom instruction is done poorly?
What does "done well" look like?	What does "done poorly" look like?

Chapter Overview

What is a good school? What elements compose a good school? What characteristics are associated with a good school? In this chapter, you will investigate a wide range of educational topics that will cause you to reflect upon your beliefs pertaining to good schooling. First you will define essential learnings and examine differing educational philosophies. Then you will investigate learning concepts such as constructivism, contextual learning, and 21st century skills. Finally, you will explore culturally relevant teaching practices, funds of knowledge skills, and the role of caring in education. As you read and analyze each topic, reflect on your role as instructional designer and decision maker. The nature of decision making and the theme of teacher as decision maker will be expanded and explored throughout this book.

Performance Expectations

DIRECTIONS: *How well do you know the performance expectations? Rate your knowledge of each expectation using this Likert scale. You will rate yourself again at the end of the chapter. This is for your information to assess your own learning. Visit the online book to record your answers.*

1 = I do not have any knowledge of this concept.
2 = I have minimal knowledge of this concept.
3 = I have some understanding of this concept.
4 = I have a satisfactory understanding of this concept.
5 = I am confident in my understanding of this concept.

This chapter should prepare you to:

Rating	#	Performance Expectations
	1.	Discuss the concepts of good schools and teacher as decision maker.
	2.	Explain the concept of essential learnings.
	3.	Define and cite examples of educentrism.
	4.	Compare and contrast essentialism, perennialism, progressivism, and reconstructionism.
	5.	Discuss the four major trends cited by Willard Daggett that greatly impact our country and its educational system today.
	6.	Cite examples of 21st century skills in four broad categories.
	7.	Develop a working definition of constructivism and contextual learning.
	8.	Differentiate between asset and deficit building educational models.
	9.	Develop a working definition of culturally relevant teaching and funds of knowledge.
	10.	Explain the statement: "Effective teachers care about their students."
	11.	Discuss the McREL report on What Matters the Most.
	12.	Develop a teaching tool kit of curriculum, instruction, and assessment concepts and strategies.

1.1 Good Schools

An old African proverb states, "It takes a whole village to educate a child." Education is integral to maintaining the cultural and structural stability of society. Throughout the new millennium, national and state attention has been directed toward the quantity and quality of our public educational system. Public demands for higher standards and more accountability are ever increasing. Most of this attention is justifiable because good schools are the foundation for a strong community and a compassionate society. Good schools produce responsible citizens, informed consumers, skilled workers, inspired leaders, and life-long learners. Good schools develop caring, contributing, responsible, and academically successful students. Our role as educators and stakeholders in the educational process is to create and maintain good schools that house our nation's future.

Good schools, however, don't just happen! Good schools happen when educators reinvent themselves by adopting new ways of thinking and acting that take advantage of new research and the best we know about the profession and our professional role as educational decision makers. Good teaching requires translating the effective schools research into a vehicle for student learning and achievement. Since its legislated establishment in 1858 to "prepare teachers for the common schools of the state," Winona State University's rich heritage of educating and preparing quality teachers and other educational professionals to create good schools continues today. If every state's educational system is to truly rise to the challenge of every student achieving educational success, then every classroom must be led by an effective teacher and every school must be led by an effective leader!

1.2 Data-Driven Decision Making

Today's school reform movement is based on a need to facilitate and sustain profound improvement in student achievement through a vision of excellence in teaching and learning. Public demands for accountability, ranging from governmental mandates to school report cards and accreditation requirements, are motivating increased awareness of the need to provide evidence of a school's or college's effectiveness in achieving its vision. Administrators and faculty need to collect, analyze, and interpret data to determine how both their students and programs are doing and then take action based on their findings if needed.

The major theme that permeates this textbook is "**teacher as decision maker**." Charlotte Danielson (1996) once stated, "The complexity of teaching is well recognized; a teacher makes over 3000 decisions daily. It is useful to think of teaching as similar to not one but several other professions, combining the skills of business management, human relations, and theater arts" (p. 2). Teachers are designers and decision makers—they make planning decisions on curriculum, they make implementation decisions on instruction, they make evaluation decisions on learning achievement and grading, and they make decisions about classroom management. Another source states, "The average classroom teacher will make 1,500+ educational decisions every school day. In a 6-hour school day, that's more than four decisions every minute" (Teach Thought, 2016).

What tools do teachers use to make the many decisions that they face on a day-to-day basis? In this book, teachers will build a "tool kit" of ideas, strategies, and resources to assist with this decision-making process. In each chapter of the text, you will explore a plethora of tools and techniques on curriculum, instruction, and assessment that can be used in the decision-making process. You will be asked to become a reflective practitioner, analyzing the strengths and limitations of each practice and determining where and when that practice would work best for you and your students. At the end of the three books, you will have increased confidence, knowing that you have enhanced your teaching capability and performance in these three vital areas of study.

1.3 Essential Learnings

Good schools are about continuous school improvement and about becoming an effective learning organization. Peter Senge, founder of the Center for Organizational Learning at MIT's Sloan School of Management and author of the best-selling book, *The Fifth Discipline*, (2006) defines a learning organization as ". . . an organization that is continually expanding its capacity to create its future" (p. 3). Senge is a big proponent of systems thinking, which is the fifth discipline and structured around personal mastery, mental models, shared vision, and team learning. School improvement and student success are about becoming an effective learning organization that employs system thinking principles and practices. The focus of school improvement is to create a comprehensive learning organization that understands, cares about, and works for students. It takes time to identify what is important for students to know and be able to do, care about, and then to represent it accurately in words. Defining and describing a student's essential learnings is often considered the most important element in understanding and increasing student achievement.

Essential learnings are derived from the district's mission, vision, and beliefs. These statements drive the curriculum, assessment, and instructional strategies that prepare students for life-long learning and future careers. Essential learnings provide criteria by which the school evaluates its success, and statements of what the school wants its graduates to know, to do, and to be like as they leave school. They are used to determine what will best prepare the students for the future and to shape the future. Identifying essential learnings is critical to building a continuum of learning that makes sense for preparing students for the world they will face when they are on their own (Bernhardt, 2000). The authors of this text endorse essential learnings that make students both "good and smart" and involve educating both the "head and heart."

Synonyms for Essential Learnings

- **Learning targets**
- **Power standards**
- **Priority standards**
- **Enduring understandings**

It is often stated that it takes about five years from the time a school starts to rebuild to the time it will see substantial increases in student achievement directly attributed to school improvement efforts. In an increasingly complex and challenging world, students need greater knowledge and skills to live productive, enjoyable lives. While this greater need increases the effort expected of students, it also increases the pressure on teachers and administrators to provide an education that will deliver this necessary preparation. Limits in time and revenue—to name just two constraints—require that schools examine their practices for the effectiveness of teaching and learning. In effect, these new challenges and continuing constraints require that you work "smarter" rather than work "harder," focusing your educational efforts and more closely scrutinizing the outcomes.

1.4 Educentrism

In the face of change, however, many people still believe that schools should remain familiar and predictable. According to Schwahn and Spady (1998), in their book *Total Leaders*, "this acceptance and advocacy of the prevailing paradigm of education reflects thinking that is neither critical in an analytical sense nor systematic in an organizational sense" (p. 14). Educational leaders must lead amidst the enormous inertia (inertia described as educentrism) surrounding the basic structures, processes, roles, practices, and institutional forms that constitute public education. For example, how many classrooms are structured with the teacher's desk in the front and all the student desks in rows facing the teacher? In how many classrooms does the textbook still dictate the curriculum or lecture dominate the pedagogy? Why are most school schedules still based on the agrarian calendar? This educentrism inertia is embedded in the laws and regulations that define education; institutionalized in the structures, cultures, and practices of public education; and ingrained in the minds of all who have spent their youth (and adulthood) in schools.

Another good example of educentrism is exemplified by the question, "Are readiness for college and readiness for work the same or different?" For decades it has been a commonly held belief that high school students planning to attend college need to take more rigorous coursework than those going directly into the workforce. Today, however, many employers are convinced that in an expanding global economy, entry-level workers need much the same knowledge and skills as college-going students. In Daggett and Pedinotti's (2014) study, *Reading Skills and the Career Readiness Gap*, there is clear evidence that required reading for entry-level jobs is significantly higher than the required reading in high school textbooks and higher than many college textbooks. ACT (2006) researchers have also engaged in several empirical studies that examined the relationship between college readiness and workforce readiness. Specifically, the researchers sought to:

- Identify the level of reading and mathematics skills students need to be ready for entry-level jobs that require less than a bachelor's degree, pay a wage sufficient to support a family, and offer the potential for career advancement;
- Compare student performance on ACT tests that measure workforce readiness with those that measure college readiness; and
- Determine if the levels of performance needed for college and workforce readiness are the same or different.

The findings of these studies have important implications for American high school education. It suggests that all high school students should be educated according to a common academic expectation that prepares them for both postsecondary education and the workforce. This means that all students should be ready and have the opportunity to take a rigorous core preparatory program in high school, one that is designed to promote readiness for both college and workforce training programs. Results of this new ACT study provide empirical evidence that, whether planning to enter college or workforce training programs after graduation, high school students need to be educated to a comparable level of readiness in reading and mathematics. Graduates need this level of readiness if they are to succeed in college-level courses without remediation and to enter workforce training programs ready to learn job-specific skills. Only then—whether they are among the two-thirds who enter college directly after graduation or those who enter workforce training programs—will they be ready for life after high school.

1.5 Philosophies of Education

Along with essential learnings and the educentrism debate, another significant factor that must be considered in the good schools reform discussion is the school district's philosophy or belief system. The Oxford English Dictionary defines philosophy as "the love, study, and pursuit of wisdom." Philosophers are usually concerned with questions such as: What is the purpose of life? What is good? and What is truth? (Henson, 2001). We might focus these questions on schooling and ask: What is the purpose of education? What is the purpose of good schools? and What course of study makes schools effective?

For many centuries, scholars and educators have grappled with many of these questions. These efforts have led to the development of several philosophical orientations and belief systems, such as essentialism, perennialism, progressivism, and reconstructionism. Each philosophy reflects a unique view of what is good and what is important (Armstrong, 1989).

Essentialism is one of the most widely accepted of all the philosophies. Organized by William Bagley, essentialists believe that "the purpose of schools is to stabilize society by teaching knowledge that is essential"

(Henson, 2001). Essentialists believe that there is some basic knowledge and information that all learners should know. They focus on subject matter and believe students need practical knowledge to function as productive and contributing members of society. Essentialists would require mastery of subjects such as reading, writing, arithmetic, and history. The curriculum for all subjects would be organized from simple to complex and concrete to abstract. Essentialists promote the transmission of cultural heritage and believe that education is preparation for life (Olivia, 1988).

Perennialism assumes that a limited number of common themes have challenged humans throughout the ages. Robert Hutchins and Mortimer Adler introduced perennialism as a way "to teach students how to think" (Henson, 2001). Perennialists view the goals of education as disciplining the mind, the development of the ability to reason, and the pursuit of truth (Olivia, 1988). They would argue that the best method of achieving these goals is through studying the humanities (e.g., great books, modern languages, and logic) in combination with the 3Rs (reading, "riting," and "rithmetic"). For perennialists, the purpose of schooling is to bring learners into contact with the great thinking of the past. They favor having all students engage in a curriculum drawn heavily from literature, humanities, fine arts, and the classics. The perennialist, like the essentialist, believes education is preparation for life, but if taken seriously, they would view education as being the most suitable for only those individuals who possess high verbal and academic aptitudes (Olivia, 1988).

Progressivism is also an American structure and almost the opposite view of essentialism and perennialism. Also known as pragmatism, progressivism was advocated by John Dewey, William Kilpatrick, and Boyd Bode (Olivia, 1988). These theorists believed that students learn best through an activity-based or project-centered curriculum. Progressivists believe that yesterday's answers have very little to offer people confronting today's problems. They emphasize the needs of the student and support the idea that students should be allowed to make some personal choices as they progress through a program of study (Armstrong, 1989). Content from the social and natural sciences and concepts such as democracy and the scientific method are advocated by progressivists as they provide learners with the opportunity to develop problem-solving and reflective thinking skills. To the progressivist, education is not a product to be learned, but a process that continues as long as one lives. Progressivists believe in "learning by doing" and that "education is life" (Olivia, 1988).

Reconstructionism is a belief that supports rebuilding society along a more humanistic line. Reconstructivists believe that schools should be framed and organized to remove cultural crises such as AIDs, poverty, world hunger, racism, pollution, crime, and war. Contributors such as George Counts (1932), in his book, *Dare the Schools Build a New Social Order*, believed that the "mission of the school's curriculum was to redesign a society that has become inequitable" (Henson, 2001). This philosophy implies a need to raise a student's level of social conscience, question unfair practices, and support learner activism positively. Curricular emphasis is placed on the behavior sciences and students are taught to influence the community and society. Reconstructionism with its heavy emphasis on controversial social issues and the need to make schools its primary agent for social change has not made great inroads with the largely middle-class centrists school in the United States (Olivia, 1988).

"Philosophy has entered into every important decision that has been made about curriculum and teaching in the past and will continue to be the basis of every important decision in the future . . . There is rarely a moment in a school day when a teacher is not confronted with occasions where philosophy is a vital part of action" (Hopkins, 1941, pp. 198–200). Curriculum developers need to be aware of philosophical differences. Philosophers would not tell us what values the curriculum should support, but they would remind us to think about the role that philosophy plays in the curriculum development process (Henson, 2001). For example, what effect, if any, does having an LGBT club in high school have on student values? Philosophy helps curriculum developers and instructional leaders to "(1) indicate in general what we mean; (2) make what we mean more specific and definite; and (3) develop what we mean into a useful construct" (Doll, 1989, p. 32).

Philosophies of Education

- **Essentialism = Focus on subject matter**
- **Perennialism = Focus on student thinking**
- **Progressivism = Focus on learning by doing**
- **Reconstructivism = Focus on social issues**

Check for Understanding: Philosophies of Education

DIRECTIONS: *Complete the* ***comparison matrix*** *that compares and contrasts the four major philosophies of education. For each philosophy, describe the primary belief upon which that philosophy is based, identify the major component that advocates of that philosophy view as the primary source of need, list curriculum priorities, and cite key historical educators who have contributed to that belief system. Visit the online book to view the video. Have the chart completed for the next class.*

Video: Changing Paradigms

DIRECTIONS: *View the 11-minute YouTube video on Changing Paradigms by Sir Ken Robinson. For the next class, be prepared to "table talk" to your classmates about the effects of economics and culture on education and educational change. How have industrial age, standardization, and ADHD influenced schools?* ***Table talk*** *is a technique where every student within a small group must share an answer/opinion/thought. When all students in the group have contributed, conversation then can freely flow.*

1.6 21st-Century Skills

Willard Daggett, President of the International Center for Leadership in Education, has also studied education, its history, and the change process. According to Daggett (2005), the changing nature of work, technology, and competition in the global job market has far outpaced what the U.S. education system provides for students, despite the ongoing efforts of educators and communities to improve schools. He identifies four major trends—globalization, changing demographics, technology, and changing values and attitudes—impacting our country in general, and our students in particular, which must be addressed to ensure our nation and our students are prepared for the challenges of the near and distant futures. He concludes that to meet these challenges, schools need to be restructured and educators need to provide all students with an academically rigorous and relevant education for them to compete and excel in the global society.

Article: Preparing Students for the Future

DIRECTIONS: *The article "Preparing Students for the Future" by Willard Daggett outlines four mega trends that our nation must address if we are to successfully meet the challenges of the 21st century. After reading the article, be prepared to discuss the four trends using the* ***Muddiest Point*** *strategy. In this strategy, each student will discuss the most difficult or confusing part of the four trends.*

Former Secretary of Education, Richard Riley, once said, "We are currently preparing students for jobs that don't yet exist . . . using technologies that haven't yet been invented . . . in order to solve problems we don't know are problems yet" (Trilling & Fadel, 2009, p. 3). Four powerful forces—knowledge work, thinking tools, digital lifestyle, and learning research—are converging and leading us toward new ways of learning for life in the 21st century. Additionally, these four forces are simultaneously supplying the tools, environments, and guiding principles required to support 21st-century learning practices.

We need a different skill set today than we did in the 20th century, and educational institutions have a critical role to play in developing those skills. But by and large, primary and secondary schools have not kept pace with the changing skill sets that students need to succeed. Today's curriculum does not fully prepare students to live and work in an information age society. What type of knowledge, skills, understandings, and dispositions are required for 21st-century learning? The Assessment and Teaching of 21st-Century Skills (ATC21S) Project (2012), which started with a group of more than 250 researchers across 60 institutions worldwide, categorized 21st-century skills into four broad categories:

- **Ways of Thinking** = Creativity, critical thinking, problem solving, decision making, and learning;
- **Ways of Working** = Communication and collaboration;
- **Tools for Working** = Information and communications technology (ICT) and information literacy; and
- **Skills for Living in the World** = Citizenship, life and career, and personal and social responsibility.

The Partnership for 21st-Century Skills (P21) (2009) has also developed a unified, collective vision for 21st-century learning that can be used to strengthen American education. The key elements of 21st-century learning are represented in the graphic and descriptions in the link at the end of this paragraph. The graphic represents both 21st-century skills student outcomes (as represented by the arches of the rainbow) and 21st-century skills support systems (as represented by the pools at the bottom). The knowledge, themes, and skills of the Partnership for the 21st-century learning rainbow offer a memorable image of what students will need to learn to be successful in the 21st century. They include the (1) Core Subjects and 21st-Century Themes; (2) Learning and Innovation Skills; (3) Information, Media, and Technology Skills; and (4) Life and Career Skills. The 21st century support systems include standards and assessments, curriculum and instruction, professional development, and learning environments. The support systems are critical to ensuring student mastery of the 21st century outcomes.

Article: P21 Framework

To further examine the P21 Framework, read the following article. Visit the online book to read a 2-page synopsis of P21.

To help make all of the essential 21st-century skills of the P21 framework even more memorable, Trilling & Fadel (2009) condensed the skill sets into seven lists, all beginning with the letter "C":

- Critical thinking and problem solving;
- Creativity and innovation;
- Collaboration, teamwork, and leadership;
- Cross-cultural understanding;
- Communication, information, and media literacy;
- Computing and ICT literacy; and
- Career and learning self-reliance.

Thus, if we take the basic "3Rs" skills of Reading, "Riting," and "Rithmetic" and multiple them by the 7Cs, we now have a handy formula for successful learning in the 21st century: 3Rs × 7Cs = 21st-Century Learning.

Video: Did You Know 2016?

Directions: *View the video "Did You Know 2016." After you have watched the fast- paced video, list five things that surprised you. You will* ***share the surprises*** *in class with a small group. Your group will also discuss how the surprises will affect you as a teacher.*

1.7 Constructivism and Contextual Learning

Now that we know what knowledge and skills (i.e., essential learnings) are required in the future, let's talk a minute about restructuring our schools and the teaching and learning process. Instructional practices need to be grounded in what is known about how children learn. Author Combs (1981), a noted humanistic philosopher once said, "Learning is the personal discovery of meaning." Current research suggests that students learn best when they are actively engaged in hands-on authentic exercises that promote experiential learning. Research has also shown that we learn best when we are able to connect our prior knowledge and use it to construct new meaning and understanding (Henson, 2001). Learners gain understanding when they construct their own knowledge and develop their own cognitive maps of the interconnections among facts and concepts (Shepard, 1991).

Constructing their own knowledge is known as constructivism. **Constructivism** is a theory of knowledge that argues that humans generate knowledge and meaning from an interaction between their experiences and their ideas. Constructivists believe that true understanding happens only when we connect new information to previously acquired understanding and that it is the teacher's responsibility to make this happen. Constructivists also believe that learning happens best when learners work with their peers and help one another. Russian psychologist Lev Vygotsky called this process of learning together "socially negotiating meaning." By 2000, 80 percent of American teachers reported they worked with small groups of students at least twice a week (Henson, 2001).

An old Chinese proverb states: "Tell me, I forget. Show me, I remember. Involve me, I understand." **Contextual learning** is defined as processing new information in such a way that it makes sense to the learners in their frame of reference (Hull, 1993). This approach to teaching and learning assumes that the mind naturally seeks meaning in context or the environment where the person is located. The mind searches for relationships that make sense and appear useful. Contextual learning focuses on the multiple aspects of the learning environment and students are constantly discovering meaningful relationships between abstract ideas and practical applications in the context of the real world.

A key skill for the future is teaching students how to learn. Good schools have teachers who employ constructivist and contextual learning concepts and principles. They plan, develop, implement, and evaluate the impact of learning activities that model constructivism and contextual learning.

Article: But That's Just Good Teaching!

DIRECTIONS: *You will read "But That's Just Good Teaching! The Case for Culturally Relevant Pedagogy" by Gloria Ladson-Billings. While this article was written in 1995, it is pertinent today. This should be read prior to reading 1.8. Visit the online book to read the article.*

1.8 Culturally Relevant Teaching

Culturally relevant teaching is a term created by Gloria Ladson-Billings (1994) to describe "a pedagogy that empowers students intellectually, socially, emotionally, and politically by using cultural referents to impart knowledge, skills, and attitudes." Making sure all students can be successful means understanding students' cultural backgrounds, beliefs, and practices. By engaging in culturally responsive practices, teachers are demonstrating the importance of understanding the values, beliefs, and behaviors of people from other cultures.

Nationally, race has been a predictor of success in schools. Data on academic achievement, discipline, and graduation rates indicate that students of color have statistically significant lower rates of success as compared to their white peers. Often referred to as the "achievement or equity gap," many states have tried to address the long-standing inequities in our educational system. Part of the solution in helping students overcome these challenges means that educators need to understand and apply culturally relevant teaching practices.

Geneva Gay (2010), in her landmark book, *Culturally Responsive Teaching: Theory, Research, and Practice*, expanded the traditional view of culture beyond race and ethnicity. She wrote, "Even without being consciously aware of it, culture determines how we think, believe, and behave." Culture is a student's beliefs, motivations, and even social groups and norms. Strategies for designing curriculum, instruction, and assessment activities for culturally diverse students are similar to those same strategies that are used for differentiating instruction. In other words, a culturally responsive teacher uses differentiated instruction to tailor learning to every aspect of a student's learning and culture. Research on culturally responsive teaching has found that students both are more engaged in learning and learn more effectively when the knowledge and skills taught are presented within a context of their experience and cultural frames of reference (Gay, 2010; Ladson-Billings, 1995).

Funds of knowledge refers to the "historically accumulated and culturally developed bodies of knowledge and skills essential for household or individual functioning and well-being" (Moll, Amanti, Neff, & Gonzalez, 1992, p. 133). Simply put, funds of knowledge is the practical and intellectual knowledge and skills found among the social networks in students' homes and communities. Funds of knowledge can serve as an Asset Building Model. In 1990, Search Institute released a framework of assets, which identifies a set of skills, experiences, relationships, and behaviors that enable young people to develop into successful and contributing adults (Search Institute, 2016). This set of skills is relevant today. The educational process can be greatly enhanced when teachers learn about the everyday contexts of their students' lives.

How do teachers integrate the funds of knowledge concept in their classrooms? First, they must get to know their students—their background and neighborhoods, their needs and interests, and their strengths and weaknesses. Teachers then contextualize their content and curriculum in the student's frame of reference. Teachers build upon the student's strengths (i.e., their assets)—success breeds success. Finally, teachers employ differentiated instructional strategies for implementing curriculum, instruction, and assessment. Funds of knowledge provides culturally responsive and meaningful lessons that tap into a student's prior knowledge, family background, and social experiences. By getting to know your students, contextualizing the information from their frame of reference, building upon their strengths, and differentiating instruction teachers can provide culturally responsive and meaningful lessons that enhance a student's learning.

Principles of Learning

- **21st-Century Learning = 3Rs × 7Cs**
- **Constructivism = Connecting new learning to previous understanding**
- **Contextual = Seeking meaning in the student's frame of reference**
- **Culturally Relevant = Culturally responsive teaching practices**
- **Funds of Knowledge = Knowledge and skills found among the student's social network**

Video: Ubuntu

DIRECTIONS: View the video of Nelson Mandela discussing the concept of "ubuntu." Ubuntu is a word from the Southern regions of Africa. While it appears to have a range of meanings, is commonly used to reflect having the consciousness of one's whole team, group, society, or humanity in general, rather than simply one's self in isolation. Focusing on what a group has in common and how they can work together is at the core. Another necessary implication may be recognizing and appreciating the value of each human being. For the next class, be prepared to share with a classmate about how Mandela's concept of ubuntu relates to culturally relevant teaching and funds of knowledge. You will be using the strategy ***I Think—We Think****. In I Think—We Think students use a two-column sheet of paper to record (1) individual ideas prior to pairing and (2) then formulate ideas that encapsulate how the pair thinks collectively. Visit the online book to view the video.*

1.9 The Role of Caring

Most recent educational research on good schools and teacher effectiveness concentrates on relating teaching behaviors and student achievement. Studies suggest that instructional and management processes are key to effectiveness (Stronge, 2002). Some studies, however, suggest that the teacher's affective behaviors, more than the pedagogical practices, are the keys to effectiveness.

Effective teachers care about their students. Several studies (Stronge, 2002; Good and Brophy, 1997; Cotton, 2000; National Association of Secondary School Principals, 1997) explore what makes a good teacher and show the importance of caring in the eyes of students, colleagues, and supervisors. Caring, in and of itself, is a broad encompassing term. Specific teacher attributes that demonstrate caring include listening, understanding, encouragement, and overall love for children. Caring teachers know their students—their learning styles and needs, likes and dislikes, and their personal and home situations that may affect behavior and performance. Caring teachers also actively listen to their students, ask for feedback, and are honest in their reflections. Children want to be nurtured and they value teachers who are kind, gentle, and encouraging. Knowing your students, being available to your students, and showing concern and empathy for your students all contribute to enhancing the learning process. According to Zakrzewski (2012), science has found that students who have caring relationships with teachers are academically more successful and show greater "pro-social" (or kind, helpful) behavior. A caring teacher can transform the school experience especially for students who face enormous difficulties, such as dropping out or dysfunctional home lives.

1.10 What Matters the Most

Bryan Goodwin (2010), the author of "*Changing the Odds for Student Success: What Matters Most*," a McREL study, believes that America's goal should be to change the odds for all kids to make it out of poverty and be successful. This McREL report identifies principles and practices that can be employed right now to change the odds in favor of students. In preparing the report, Goodwin has tried to go beyond simply "what works" to a framework of "what matters" the most.

In Goodwin's article, he identifies five components that, when addressed properly, are most likely to have positive effects on student success. The five components are:

- Guarantee challenging, engaging, and intentional instruction;
- Ensure curricular pathways to success;
- Provide whole child student supports;
- Create high-performance school cultures; and
- Develop data-driven and high-reliability systems.

What makes a teacher effective? In short, decades of research suggest three behaviors that distinguish highly effective teachers. Highly effective teachers (1) challenge their students, (2) create positive classroom environments, and (3) are intentional about their teaching. Simply put, highly effective teachers challenge and engage their students and are intentional in their planning, implementation, and assessment. They provide instruction that develops higher order thinking and use a repertoire of instructional strategies to help their students accomplish their learning goals. Good teachers also develop positive and genuine relationships with their students.

Chapter Summary

As noted previously in this chapter, Peter Senge (2006) defines a learning organization as "... an organization that is continually expanding its capacity to create its future." School improvement is about becoming an effective learning organization; in essence a good school! In order for schools to become true learning organizations, they must put into place a leadership infrastructure and strategic planning initiatives that allow necessary improvements to be made from within the organization and to be supported outside of the organization. The focus of school improvement is to create a comprehensive learning organization that understands, cares about, and works for students. Collectively, all educational stakeholders can and must build a school improvement system that successfully meets the challenge of improving 21st-century learning and performance for this nation's most precious resource—its children!

A Fable: The Last Day of School

DIRECTIONS: *In your small group during class, read the Curriculum Fable. What is the connection between the fable and good schools? Come to* **consensus** *on the moral of the fable. Be prepared to share your answers. Visit the online book to read the article.*

Check for Mastery: Performance Expectations

DIRECTIONS: *You rated yourself on performance expectations at the start of this chapter. Have you now mastered each performance expectation? Rate yourself using the Likert scale online. Compare this to how you rated yourself at the beginning of this chapter. If you do not know an expectation, go back to the text and reread the information.*

Summary Learning Activity: What Is the Best Teaching Scenario?

DIRECTIONS: *Rank the following scenarios as to which best teaching is taking/has taken place from one to six. Use* (1) *for the scenario in which the best admirable teaching and learning has taken place and use* (6) *for the scenario in which the least admirable teaching and learning has taken place. After you do your individual ranking, you will be working in small groups in the next class to persuade others of your ranking. Therefore, as you do your ranking you should be thinking about the principles that inform your ranking and how you will explain and defend them to others.*

_____ A. Frank has been taking golf lessons for six months. His pro is famous for basing his instruction on four key principles. Frank knows these principles by heart. In fact, he's so good at explaining them to others that his playing companions feel that they are getting the benefit of professional advice without having to pay for it. However, Frank isn't always able to put these principles into practice. Sometimes everything clicks for a hole or two but rarely for more than that. Frank scored in the low 90s when he began his lessons, and he typically scores in the low 90s now.

_____ B. Maria has completed her dissertation and has just accepted a job in the Department of History in a major research university. As she packs up her apartment, she finds herself thinking about the course that started her on her way, an introductory course on 19th-century European history. Although she doesn't remember much about the specific content and has rejected the type of historiography her professor did, she does remember the passion that Professor Neal displayed in her teaching, and the profound conviction she expressed that "doing history" matters. That was the first time Maria thought that studying history could make a difference and that being a historian was a worthwhile pursuit.

_____ C. Peter recently moved with his two small children to a house in the city on a street far busier than the one they lived on in the suburbs. Peter explained to his kids, ages two and three, that they must never walk in the street because cars were dangerous. One day he was raking leaves while the kids were playing. He turned his back for a minute or two and looked back, horrified to see his kids jumping in the leaves he had raked into the street. He ran to the kids and slapped their hands, the first time he had ever physically disciplined them. The children were shocked and burst into tears. Neither child ever went in the street again.

_____ D. As Jude looks back on high school, she realizes that her favorite class was sophomore English. It was different from any other class she had ever taken—maybe it was this uniqueness that made it powerful and special for her. In this class, there were no formal assignments. Her teacher, Mr. James, began the year by soliciting topics from the class that were of interest to them and that were also of social significance. He then brought a wide variety of materials in on these topics—ranging from articles and videos to classic pieces of literature. He also encouraged them to find their own information. Students spent almost all of their time reading and thinking about these issues, usually on their own. Each week, discussions and debates would be held in small groups. At the end of each quarter, groups formed and created "knowledge documents." They were free to choose their topics and their projects. During the year, Jude had participated in creating a museum display, a video documentary, a hypermedia document, and an informational Web site. Each quarter ended with a "Family and Friends Night" where these projects were shared. Though Jude couldn't remember Mr. James ever actually instructing her in any way, she had never read so much or been so motivated to learn. And though she couldn't really name what she'd learned, she knew it had to do with asking questions, working alone, and working with others.

_____ E. Tom has a piano competition coming up soon. His teacher has gone through Tom's piece with him several times, note by note, explaining every detail. His teacher has also recorded the piece the way it should be played. Tom listens to it all the time; he even falls asleep with his ear buds listening to the piece. Tom practices hours every day until he plays the piece exactly the way his teacher did. At the competition, Tom plays the piece just as he had hoped and he wins first place. His parents have never been so proud.

_____ F. Arlene is working this summer with her uncle, who is an electrician. He insists that she know how to do everything, and that she understands why they do things the way they do. It is hard, frustrating, challenging, but fun—and she feels like she is learning a lot. Her uncle often tells her: "I want to help you understand electricity the way electricians AND physicist understand it." To this end, they began playing with batteries, conducting wire, and light bulbs to make different kinds of circuits. Her uncle then asked her to articulate rules of electrical circuits. He then took what she thought and set up experiments that contradicted what she thought. He often said to her: "Observe, explain, and observe again!" Her uncle would ask her to explain problems that she observed on the job. Soon after that, he let her do her own work, under his careful eye, and then allowed her to work on her own. Arlene felt like she really knew about electricity and that every day she knew a little bit more that built on what she knew before. Still, this kind of learning took a long time, and there were still things she didn't understand and that her uncle wouldn't let her do.

Supplemental Learning Exercises

Source: J. Redman

1. Think back to some of your favorite teachers. What characteristics did you like about them? What influenced you to become a teacher? What are the attributes of an effective teacher? In small groups, design the effective educator. Identify your "Top Ten Attributes" and write them on the body of the teacher in the portrait. Share your ideas with the class and then try to reach consensus. Key characteristics can be summarized on the limbs.
2. Policy makers and curriculum designers have varying views about what priorities should be reflected in their educational programs. Examine the brief excerpts below from four separate policy statements. For each, which philosophical position is reflected? What might be important subjects and/or courses in that setting?
   A. We need to raise the learners' level of social conscience. Today's answers fail to serve even today's needs. Schools need to become the agents for social change. When a problem develops in society, we need to turn to the school systems to solve those problems.
   B. We believe that the process of education continues as long as one lives. Schools need to advocate for learning by doing and teach problem-solving skills that students will need to engage in life's challenges. Yesterday's answers have little to offer people confronting today's problems. In essence, education is life.
   C. We believe that there is basic, practical knowledge and information that is needed to function as a productive member of society. Schools should emphasize mastery of the 3Rs and the transmission of cultural heritage. In essence, education should be preparation for life.
   D. We believe that new problems encountered by society today are really variations on themes that have dominated human affairs for centuries. The purpose of schooling is to bring learners in contact with the classics and the great thinkers of the past. Exposure to these ideas will prepare them well to deal with the challenges of the future. Learners are the best judges of what they should take away from their educational experiences.
3. Culturally relevant teaching is a term created by Gloria Ladson-Billings (1994) to describe "a pedagogy that empowers students intellectually, socially, emotionally, and politically by using cultural referents to impart knowledge, skills, and attitudes." Funds of knowledge refers to the practical and intellectual knowledge and skills found among the social networks in students' homes and communities. Participating in culturally relevant teaching and employing the funds of knowledge essentially means that teachers create a bridge between students' home and school lives, while still meeting the expectations of the district and state curricular requirements. Both of these concepts utilize the backgrounds, knowledge, and experiences of the students to inform the teacher's lessons and methodology. When this knowledge is used to plan and deliver instruction, it becomes valuable resource for teachers to enhance student learning and achievement.

Create a school profile in which you:

A. Describe the community that the school serves. Include in your discussion factors such as location, population (rural, suburban, or urban), topography, climate, primary industries, and challenges or issues the residents are facing.

B. Describe your school. Name the school, cite the grade levels it serves, and state its enrollment. Discuss the school's demographic data profile. Are there school climate and culture-like issues that affect the school?

C. Describe one of your student's and his or her family background. Cite one example of how your PLC will utilize the concepts of culturally relevant teaching and funds of knowledge to inform and design your curriculum, instruction, and assessments.

4. Assignment for the duration of the semester: tool kit creation! You will be expected to have 80+ strategies in at least three categories. Strategies should be categorized for easy use. Examples of categories are: ways to group students, greetings, graphic organizers, and how to get students' attention.
Assignment: Each pre-teacher is expected to create a "tool kit" as a class requirement.

Visit the online book to view a power point with more information and examples on tool kits. Also included is a rubric for assessing the tool kit assignment.

Final Test

DIRECTIONS: *Read each question or statement below. Select the appropriate answer or write the correct answer in the blank provided.*

____ 1. What is the major theme that permeates this textbook?
- A. Use both your head and heart to teach.
- B. Teacher as decision-maker.
- C. It takes a village to educate a child.
- D. Design with the end in mind.

T F 2. Many of a school's essential learnings today are found in local, state, and/or national standards.

____ 3. Which of the following is ***false*** about educentrism inertia?
- A. Educentrism is embedded in the laws and regulations that define education.
- B. Educentrism is ingrained in the minds of all who spent their youth in schools.
- C. Educentrism forces a paradigm shift and promotes school and social change.
- D. Educentrism is institutionalized in the structures, cultures, and practices of public education.

____ 4. What educational philosophy emphasizes the basics skills of reading, writing, and arithmetic?
- A. Essentialism
- B. Perennialism
- C. Progressivism
- D. Reconstructionism

____ 5. Which of the following themes would a progressivist *most* likely support?
- A. Transmission of cultural heritage
- B. Education is preparation for life
- C. Agents for social change
- D. Learn by doing

______ 6. What type of curriculum would the perennialist prefer?
   A. Issues-based topics and themes
   B. Activity-based coursework
   C. Great books and the classics
   D. Vocational and technical courses

______ 7. Which of the following is ***not*** a major trend cited by Willard Daggett for greatly impacting today's school system?
   A. Changing technology
   B. Changing marketplace (globalization)
   C. Changing demographics
   D. Changing climate

T F 8. Funds of knowledge is defined as the practical and intellectual knowledge and skills found among the social networks in student's homes and communities.

______ 9. Which of the following strategies would ***not*** be supported when implemented the Funds of Knowledge concept and Culturally Relevant Teaching methods?
   A. Build upon the weaknesses or deficits exhibited by the student in order to improve those skill areas (e.g., if he/she is weak in math, give them more math).
   B. Explain concepts in a contextual manner or in terms of the student's frame of reference.
   C. Get to know each of their students—their strengths and weaknesses, their needs and interests, their backgrounds and learning styles, etc.
   D. Provides differentiated and meaningful lessons that tap into a student's prior knowledge, family background, and social experiences.

______ 10. According to the Effective Schools Research, what term *best* describes the set of soft skills that "good" or successful teachers possess?
   A. Organizers
   B. Innovative
   C. Flexible
   D. Caring

DIRECTIONS: *Write a brief response.*

1. What is your "working definition" for the term Twenty-first Century Skills (P21)? Cite some examples.
2. Differentiate between constructivism and contextual learning. Discuss how curriculum, instruction, and assessment would be structured based on constructivist and contextual learning principles.

Works Cited and Suggested Readings

ACT (2006). *College and Workforce Readiness, Ready for College, Ready for Work: Same or Different?* Iowa City, IA: ACT, Inc.

Armstrong, David. (1989). *Developing and Documenting the Curriculum.* Needham Heights, MA: Allyn and Bacon.

Bernhardt, Victoria. (2000). Intersections. *Journal of Staff Development*, National Staff Development Council, *21*(1), 23–36.

Brooks, Martin & Grennon Brooks, Jacqueline. (1999). The Constructivist Classroom: The Courage to be Constructivist. *Education Leadership, 57*(3), 18–24.

Coffee, Heather. (2015). *Culturally Relevant Teaching*. LEARN, NC (A Program of the UNC School of Education).

Combs, Arthur. (1981). Humanistic Education: Too Tender for a Tough World. *Phi Delta Kappan, 62*(6), 446–449. Retrieved from: http://www.jstor.org/stable/20385941.

Cotton, Kathleen. (2000). *Schooling Practices That Matter the Most*. Portland, OR: Northwest Regional Educational Laboratory and Alexandria, VA: Association for Supervision and Curriculum Development (ASCD).

Counts, George. (1932). *Dare the Schools Build a New Social Order*. New York, NY: John Day.

Daggett, Willard R. (2005). *Preparing Students for Their Future*. Rexford, NY: International Center for Leadership in Education, Model Schools Conference.

Daggett, Willard R. (2005). *Achieving Academic Excellence through Rigor and Relevance: What Defines Academic Excellence*. Rexford, NY: International Center for Leadership in Education, Model Schools Conference.

Daggett, Willard R. & Pedinotti, Jerry Jr. (2014). *Reading Skills and the Career Readiness Gap: A Study of High School Students' Preparedness for College and Career*. International Center for Leadership in Education.

Darling-Hammond, Linda & Bransford, John (Eds.). (2005). *Preparing Teachers for a Changing World: What Teachers Should Learn and Be Able to Do*. San Francisco, CA: John Wiley & Sons, Inc.

Danielson, Charlotte. (1996). *Enhancing Professional Practice: A Framework for Teaching* (2nd ed.). Alexandria, VA: Association for Supervision and Curriculum Development (ASCD).

Discovering What Kids Need to Succeed. Search Institute. (2016). *Discovering What Kids Need to Succeed*. Retreived from: www.search-institute.org.

Doll, Ronald C. (1989). *Curriculum Development: Decision Making and Process* (7th ed.). Boston, MA: Allyn and Bacon.

Esteves, Jose. (2016). *Did You Know 2016*. (Based on the original by Karl Fisch, Scott McLeod, and Jeff Brenman. Retrieved from https://www.youtube.com/watch?v=uqZiIO0YI7Y.

Gay, Geneva. (2010). *Culturally Responsive Teaching: Theory, Research, and Practice* (2nd ed.). New York, NY: Teachers College Press.

Good, Thomas & Brophy, Jere. (1997). *Looking in Classrooms* (7th ed.). New York, NY: Addison-Wesley.

Goodwin, Bryan. (2010). *Changing the Odds for Student Success: What Matters Most*. (A Special Issue of "Changing Schools"). *Mid-continent Research for Education and Learning (McREL).*

Goodwin, Bryan. (2011). *Simply Better: Doing What Matters Most to Change the Odds for Student Success*. Copyright by McREL. Alexandria, VA: Association for Supervision and Curriculum Development (ASCD).

Grennon Brooks, Jacqueline & Brooks, Martin. (1993). *In Search of Understanding: The Case for Constructivist Classrooms*. Alexandria, VA: Association for Supervision and Curriculum Development (ASCD).

Griffin, Patrick, McGraw, Barry, & Care, Esther (Eds.). (2012). *Assessment and Teaching of 21st Century Skills (Educational Assessment in an Information Age)* (2012 ed.). Dordrecht, Netherlands: Springer.

Henson, Kenneth. (2001). *Curriculum Planning Integrating Multiculturalism, Constructivism, and Educational Reform* (2nd ed.). New York, NY: McGraw-Hill Higher Education.

Heritage, Margaret. (2010). *Making Use of Assessment Information: Challenges and Prospects*. Chicago, IL: Localizing the Common Core State Standards Conference, Learning Point Associates.

Hopkins, Thomas L. (1941). *Interaction: The Democratic Process*. Boston, MS: Heath.

Hull, Dan. (1993). *Opening Minds, Opening Doors: The Rebirth of American Education*. Waco, TX: Center for Occupational Research and Development (CORD).

Ladson-Billings, Gloria. (1995). Toward a Theory of Culturally Relevant Pedagogy. *American Research Journal, 32*(3), 465–491.

Ladson-Billings, Gloria. (1994). *The Dreamkeepers: Successful Teaching for African-American Students*. San Francisco, CA: Jossey-Bass.

Moll, Luis, Amanti, Cathy, Neff, Deborah, & Gonzalez, Norma. (1992). Funds of Knowledge for Teaching: Using a Qualitative Approach to Connect Homes and Classrooms. *Theory Into Practice*, *XXXI*(2), 132–141.

National Association of Secondary School Principals (NASSP). (1997). Students Say: What Makes a Good Teacher? *Schools in the Middle*, *6*(5), 15–17.

Olivia, Peter F. (1988). *Developing the Curriculum* (2nd ed.). *Statesboro, GA:* Georgia Southern College.

Partnership for 21st Century Skills. (2009). *A Framework for 21st Century Learning*. Washington, DC: Author.

Saylor, Galen J., Alexander, William M., & Lewis, Arthur J. (1981). *Curriculum Planning for Better Teaching and Leaning* (4th ed.). New York, NY: Holt, Rinehart and Winston.

Pink, Daniel. (2009). *Drive: The Surprising Truth About What Motivates Us*. New York, NY: Penguin Group.

Schwahn, Charles J. & Spady, William G. (1998). *Total Leaders: Applying the Best Future-Focused Change Strategies to Education.* Arlington, VA: American Association of School Administrators.

Schwahn, Charles J. & Spady, William G. (2010). *Total Leaders: 2.0: Leading in the Age of Empowerment.* Lanham, MD: R and L Education.

Senge, Peter. (1990, revised 2006). *The Fifth Discipline: The Art and Practice of the Learning Organization*. New York, NY: Doubleday.

Shepard, Lorrie. (1991). Psychometricians' Beliefs About Learning, *Educational Researcher*, *20*, 2–16.

Stronge, James. (2002). *Qualities of Effective Teachers*. Alexandria, VA: Association for Supervision and Curriculum Development (ASCD).

Teach Thought. (2016). *A Teacher Makes 1500 Educational Decisions a Day.* Retreived from: www.teachthought.com.

Trilling, Bernie and Fadel, Charles (2009). *21st Century Skills: Learning for Life In Our Times*. San Francisco, CA: Jossey-Bass.

Winona State University, College of Education. (2011). *WSU Unit's Conceptual Framework*. Winona, MN: WSU (Approved by TEA 9/1/11 and APA 9/6/11).

Zakrzewski, Vicki. (2012). *Four Ways Teachers Show They Care.* Retreived from: http://greatergood.berkeley.edu/article/item/caring_teacher_student_relationship.

Source: Shutterstock.com

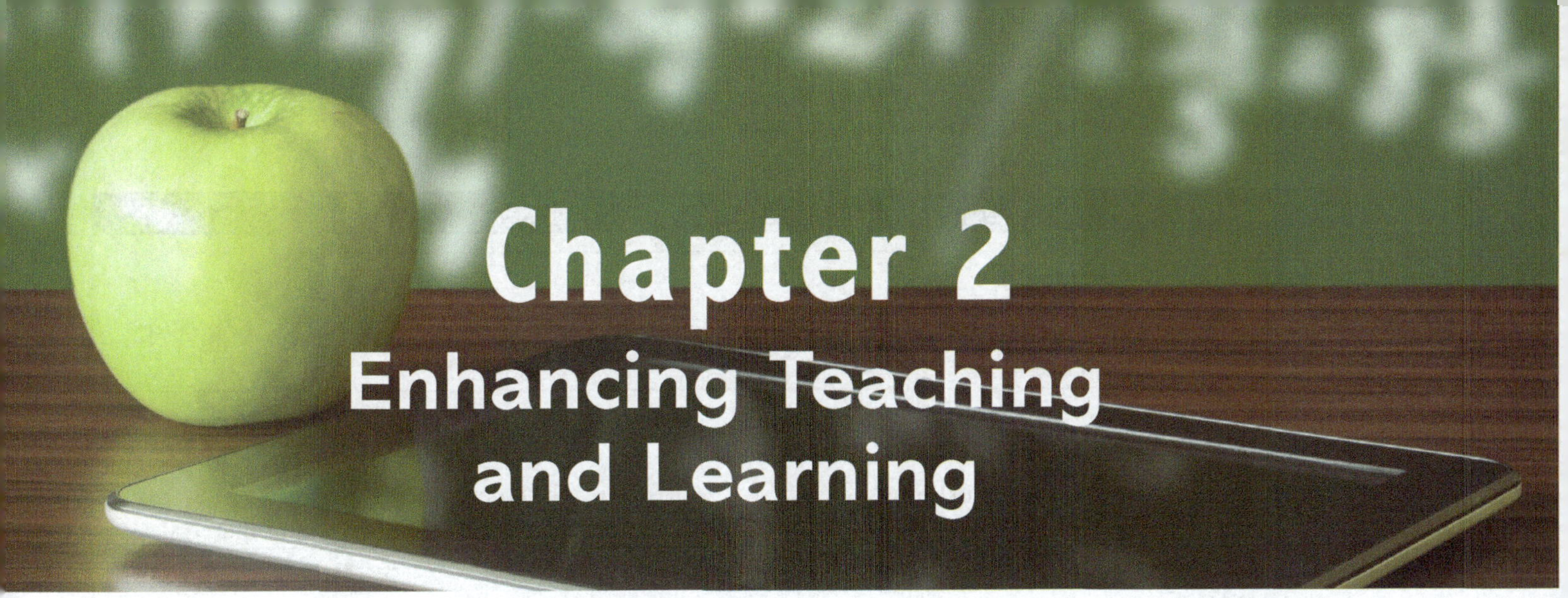

Chapter 2
Enhancing Teaching and Learning

"The mediocre teacher tells. The good teacher explains.
The superior teacher demonstrates. The great teacher inspires."

William Arthur Ward

Video: Keynote Speech to Educators

DIRECTIONS: *View the YouTube video, Dalton Sherman's Keynote Speech. What message is ten-year old Dalton Sherman conveying to a group of Dallas educators? What impact would his message have on you if you were a teacher at that opening day in-service? Be prepared to share with a partner in class. To find a partner, each student will receive a "**partners that go together**" card and then find the classmate with the matching card (Batman and Robin, Tarzan and Jane, and Thelma and Louise). Visit the online book to view the video.*

Anticipatory Set: PBI Self-Assessment

DIRECTIONS: *Reflect and think about a classroom you have been in as a student or a preservice teacher. Was that classroom based more on traditional or performance-based instructional practices? Use this self-assessment to review the teaching practices associated with the Performance-Based Instruction (PBI) Model. Read through each of the characteristics and place a mark or move the cursor on the PBI continuum to indicate how you would describe your current teaching practice in that area: Not PBI, Moderately PBI, or Highly PBI.*

Source: Shutterstock.com

Element	Teaching Practices
WHO *is the focus of your curriculum?* ***(Focus)***	Not PBI — Moderately PBI — Highly PBI Not PBI: • Curriculum centers on what the TEACHER will do Highly PBI: • Curriculum centers on how LEARNERS will do
WHAT *will learners learn?* ***(Curriculum)***	Not PBI — Moderately PBI — Highly PBI Not PBI: • Based on textbooks • Emphasizes facts and information Highly PBI: • Based on a needs assessment • Emphasizes application of material
How will you know **WHEN** *learners have learned?* ***(Assessment)***	Not PBI — Moderately PBI — Highly PBI Not PBI: • Relies on pencil/paper testing • Focuses on retention of facts • Ambiguity about what will be evaluated • Allows for averaging of grades Highly PBI: • Relies on performance of the skills • Focuses on achievement of the competencies • Measures achievement according to preset standards • Requires satisfactory performance of each competency
HOW *will learners develop skills, knowledge, and attitudes?* ***(Instruction)***	Not PBI — Moderately PBI — Highly PBI Not PBI: • Teacher delivers all of the instruction • Learners in a PASSIVE role • Few benchmarks and little periodic feedback Highly PBI: • Focuses on learner-centered activities • Learners in an ACTIVE role • Periodic feedback and opportunities for learners to improve performance

Chapter Overview

You were recently at your younger brother's baseball game. He struck out each time he was at bat. Naturally, he came home discouraged and wanted to quit the team. You realized that in order for him to improve his batting skills, he needed to believe in himself, know that he can improve, and be willing to practice. You nudged him into practicing, without his teammates around to watch. First you had him watch videos of good baseball players swinging. You discussed what the players were doing, noticing their stance, placement of elbows, and how far from the plate they stood. Then you went to the backyard and modeled the swing, without using the baseball. Then your brother was ready to practice the swing also without using a ball. In addition, he tried several different types of bats. He made corrections based on what he saw in the video and you literally got behind him and swung to an imaginary ball with him. He was feeling more confident, realizing he was making changes for improvement. From there, you began to pitch ever so slowly to him. This type of practice went on for days. The pitches became faster and the advice was slowing down. He began hitting the ball, eventually swinging with enough force and accuracy that the ball went into the neighbor's yard. At his next game, he still struck out once, but he connected twice!

This scenario is like curriculum, instruction, and assessment. The curriculum "part" of the baseball scenario was develop a plan of action. The plan consisted of many improvement elements in sequential order, using different materials. The instruction "part" of the baseball scenario was the modeling and practicing swinging skills overtime. The practice was differentiated to meet the needs as improvement occurred. The assessment "part" of the baseball scenario was multifaceted. The pre-assessment revealed your brother did not have the skills to hit the fastball. The other assessments varied. Many assessments were done on the spot, correcting and advising for misconceptions and misunderstanding. The final assessment occurred in the next baseball game noting the positive and skill based instruction paid off with two hits!

In this chapter, relationships and interactions between curriculum, instruction, and assessment will be examined. Professional Learning Communities (PLCs), principles of learning, and performance based instruction concepts and their integration into the triad of curriculum, instruction, and assessment will be investigated. Lastly, the Standards of Effective Practice (SEP) and a few state requirements for earning a Minnesota state teacher's license will be analyzed. Decision-makers should reflect upon how these factors enhance the teaching and learning process.

Performance Expectations

DIRECTIONS: *How well do you know the performance expectations? Rate your knowledge of each using Likert scale. You will rate yourself again at the end of the chapter. This is for your information to assess your learning. Visit the online book to record your answers.*

1 = I do not have any knowledge of this concept.
2 = I have minimal knowledge of this concept.
3 = I have some understanding of this concept.
4 = I have a satisfactory understanding of this concept.
5 = I am confident in my understanding of this concept.

Source: Shutterstock.com

This chapter should prepare you to:

Rating	#	Performance Expectations
	1.	Analyze the characteristics of a standards-led educational reform movement.
	2.	Differentiate among curriculum, instruction, and assessment.
	3.	Analyze what "W" question is associated with each element of the triad.
	4.	Explain the preferred sequence of the triad elements for teacher planning.
	5.	If given an education component (e.g., performance expectations, rubrics, etc.) match that component with the appropriate triad element.
	6.	Summarize the six guiding principles for teaching and learning.
	7.	Develop a working definition for a Professional Learning Community and state the two purposes that PLCs tend to serve in a school district.
	8.	Apply the three principles or "big ideas" about PLCs to the teaching and learning process.
	9.	Summarize DuFour's four PLC questions.
	10.	Illustrate the role of and characteristics that support performance-based instruction (PBI) in the teaching and learning process.
	11.	Assess the importance of using PBI to design curriculum, instruction, and assessment.
	12.	Answer the four "W" questions for PBI.
	13.	Develop a working definition for Standards of Effective Practice (SEP).
	14.	Describe the edTPA and the other testing requirements for teacher education.

2.1 Standards-Led Educational Reform

The world of education has changed dramatically since the passage of the No Child Left Behind Act (2001). More than ever in our nation's history, there is a focus on standards, assessment, and accountability. This attention has led administrators and teachers to compare student performance on accepted standards, to examine standardized test scores in great depth, and to develop strategic school improvement plans. Furthermore, parents and community members are paying much more attention to what is happening in our classrooms and asking if our students are being adequately prepared for work, college, and life beyond school.

This new paradigm has been characterized as "standards-led educational reform." Standards-led educational reform emphasizes the output or the results side of the equation, rather than the input side. This emphasis is placed on the end product—greater student achievement or success—rather than on the givens (i.e., money, time, strategies, and texts). Additionally, there is a significant driver—standards (e.g., Common Core State Standards [CCSS], state standards, or district priority standards)—influencing the traditional educational tools of curriculum, instruction, and assessment. Once the standards have been adopted and aligned, school districts need to develop and implement balanced assessment strategies to determine whether or not students have mastered the knowledge, skills, understanding, and dispositions outlined in the standards. Data collected and analyzed from these documents can then be used to complete the school improvement cycle, resulting in enhanced teaching and learning. This process is illustrated in Figure 1.

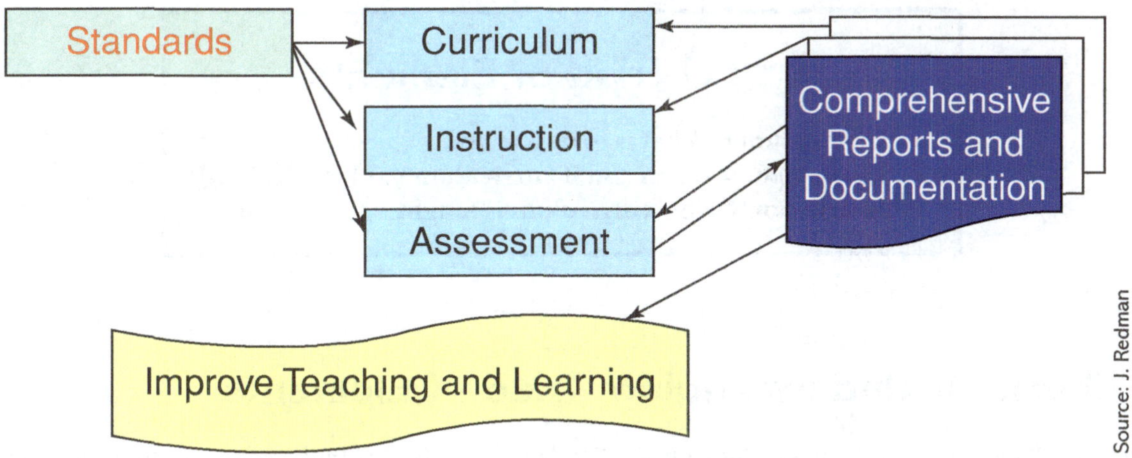

Figure 1: Standards-Led Educational Reform

2.2 Triad of Elements

Curriculum, instruction, and assessment are three essential parts of standards-led education. **Curriculum** identifies what is to be learned, **instruction** defines how it is taught, and **assessment** measures when and if it has been learned. In essence, curriculum addresses the "what," instruction the "how," and assessment the "when" or "how well" questions. These three tools are the same tools that educators have historically used in the schooling process. A graphic organizer illustrating the relationship among the triad of elements is shown in Figure 2. Note the student is the focus (center) of the three elements.

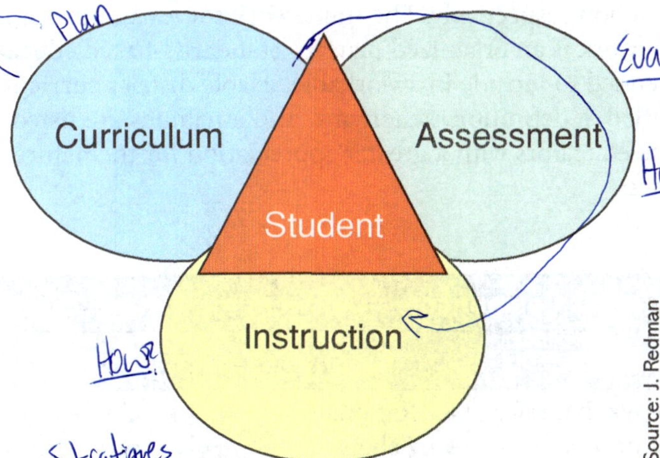

Figure 2: Triad of Elements

When designing each element in the triad, the focus should be on the student. Teachers use curricula when contemplating what to teach to students. They select various pedagogies to determine the how and create formative and summative assessments to measure the when or how well. In the curriculum development cycle, it is recommended that educators first design the curriculum (C), then identify assessment (A) strategies, and finally plan for instruction (I). Throughout this book, many other facets of the educational process (e.g., Professional Learning Community) that support this concept will be discovered. The curriculum and assessment elements are typically fixed by standards and state tests, whereas instruction often becomes a question of academic freedom and/or teaching style preferences while following the curriculum.

Triad of Elements

- **Curriculum = What is to be learned**
- **Assessment = When and if curriculum has been learned**
- **Instruction = How curriculum is taught**

Check for Understanding: Triad of Elements

DIRECTIONS: *Formulate an* ***analogy*** *for the triad of elements. An analogy is a comparison between two things, typically for the purpose of explanation or clarification. Be prepared to share your analogy in class. You will read an example of an analogy comparing curriculum, assessment, and instruction to a game of football. View the online book to read the example.*

2.3 CAI Framework

Curriculum identifies what is to be learned, instruction defines how it is taught, and assessment measures when and if it has been learned. There are several components that are associated with each element of the Triad. As one moves from state to state or district to district, the number of components, as well as what they are called, can vary greatly. Provided in Figures 3, 4 and 5 are the CAI Frameworks for curriculum, assessment, and instruction respectively. The framework serves as a planning resource for curriculum developers. The CAI Framework is an organized plan for standards-based educational reform that outlines what districts are recommended to include in a workable, usable district curriculum. For each of the eleven unique components identified, a definition, synonyms, and attributes are listed. Hopefully, the analysis of this framework will provide educators with a greater appreciation for the nature and complexity of the curriculum development process.

Curricular Components = Answers the "What" Question			
Component	**Definition**	**Synonyms**	**Attributes**
Philosophy Statements	Statements that refer to a delineation of the value system underlying educational planning; rationale upon which actions are based in that discipline	• Rationale • Beliefs/values	• Guide the curriculum development process by establishing curriculum parameters • Determine discipline purposes and priorities • Provide criteria for selecting what and how to teach the content in that subject area *(continued)*

Curricular Components = Answers the "What" Question			
Component	**Definition**	**Synonyms**	**Attributes**
Standards	General expectations of what a student should know and be able to do; referred to as "hybrid outcomes"; standards are often used to establish grade levels or grade band benchmarks	• Common Core State Standards • Content standards • Local district standards • Power standards • Priority standards	• Serve as the basis for curriculum development or auditing an integrated unit • (Unpacking) Identify the "big ideas" worth understanding and the essential questions to be studied • (Unpacking) Identify the knowledge, skills, understanding, and dispositions in a content topic • (Unpacking) Identify the domains and levels of learning to be targeted • (Unpacking) Identify what needs to be assessed and establishes the assessment criteria for evaluation • (Aligning) Determine curricular, assessment, and instructional tools
Enduring Understandings	"Big ideas" that transfer across disciplines and time; enduring understandings summarize the desired insights we want students to realize	• Core concepts • Focusing themes • Underlying assumptions • Essential learnings • Generalizations	• Enable learners to consistently make meaning from their work • Allow learners to transfer or apply their knowledge in new situations • Make sense of facts, skills, and ideas • Provide a conceptual foundation for studying the subject area
Essential Questions	Open-ended and provocative questions designed to guide inquiry and instruction for "uncovering" important ideas and core content; essential questions develop foundational understandings and give meaning, relevance, and definition to a unit of instruction	• Guiding questions • Metacognitive questions	• Provoke deep thought, lively discussion, and a new understanding of the structure of the discipline • Require students to consider alternatives, weigh evidence, support their ideas, and justify their answers • Address the philosophical or conceptual foundations of a discipline • Promote sustained inquiry and raise other important questions • Are framed to provoke and sustain student interest • Engage the student in real-life problem-solving and guide the development of authentic tasks

(continued)

Curricular Components = Answers the "What" Question			
Component	**Definition**	**Synonyms**	**Attributes**
Performance Expectations	The specific expectations of student performance at critical levels of schooling; culminating demonstrations of learning; what students should know, be able to do, and care about	• Outcomes • Core abilities • Competencies • Objectives • Goals • Learning objectives • Learning targets • Benchmarks • Student skills	• Describe the knowledge, performance, or dispositions of a major concept • Begin with an action verb that is observable and measurable • Specify a single performance • Describe an intended outcome, not an instructor activity • Are clear, concise, and precise statements describing the action to be demonstrated • Reflect the various domain and taxonomies of learning
Scope and Sequence	Scope defines the depth and breadth of content coverage; sequence determines the order of curriculum content	• Organization of the curriculum • Vertical and/or horizontal articulation • Curriculum mapping • Scope and sequence charts • Spiral architecture	• Describe the organization of a course of study • Map appropriate content as a vehicle for learning • Revisit content and skills at each grade level, with an expansion in depth and breadth of coverage • Insure a coherent flow across grade levels, avoid unnecessary redundancies, and make sure important knowledge and skills are not falling through the cracks

Figure 3: CAI Framework—Curriculum

Source: J. Redman

Source: Shutterstock.com

Assessment Components = Answers the "When" Question			
Component	**Definition**	**Synonyms**	**Attributes**
Performance Standards (Evidence of Success)	Specifications by which performance is evaluated	• Criteria and conditions • Specifications • Scoring guides • Performance indicators • Rubrics • Checklists • Degree statements	• Identify qualitative or quantitative indicators of success for a product, process, or performance • Inform learners of the specifications for acceptable performance • Provide a precise measuring tool for assessing student growth and achievement • Can be interpreted analytically or holistically
Balanced Assessment Strategies	A collection of various qualitative and quantitative assessment tools and processes used to fulfill multiple evaluation and assessment purposes; a multitiered assessment system that provides meaningful information about student progress, student achievement, and instructional effectiveness	• Formative assessments • Benchmark assessments • Summative assessments • Diagnostic assessments • Self-assessments • Progress monitoring • Portfolios • Observation • Anecdotal records • Criterion-referenced • Norm-referenced • Self-referenced	• Provide a true measure of student performance and growth • Allow the learner to demonstrate his or her knowledge and skills in various ways and varying contexts • Measure student achievement according to clear and appropriate standards and learning targets • Include multiple measures with valid and reliable test items or tasks • Provide quality and accurate assessment data for all educational stakeholders • Promote assessments "of/for/as" learning

Figure 4: CAI Framework—Assessment
Source: J. Redman

Source: Shutterstock.com

Instruction Components = Answers the "How" Question			
Component	**Definition**	**Synonyms**	**Attributes**
Research-Based Strategies	Strategies that are grounded in what is known about how children learn; students learn best when they construct their own knowledge using their own frame of reference; strategies based on research	• Pedagogy • Teaching methods • Evidence-based practices • Instructional strategies	• Are learner centered and inclusive of learning targets • Place learner in an active role and an engaged learning environment • Require learner to build on prior knowledge and construct meaning • Assist the learner in developing transfer and higher order thinking skills • Include opportunities for learner reflection and feedback • Hold the learner responsible for his/her own learning
Differentiation Strategies	Creating a variety of opportunities for meeting the full spectrum of learner abilities, needs, and interests; providing students with different avenues to acquire content, construct knowledge, or make sense of ideas	• Enrichment • Remediation • RtI strategies • Interventions • Accommodations	• Include a variety of strategies to meet the unique and diverse needs of all students • Accommodate various learning styles and multiple intelligences • Consider choice, utility, and flexibility in your options • Address issues of frequency, duration, and intensity • Assess learner abilities, interests, and learning styles • Support funds of knowledge principles and practices
Learning Resources	Learning resources are defined as information, represented and stored in a variety of media and formats that supports student learning	• Equipment and supplies • Teaching materials • Manipulatives • Web sites • Technologies • Textbooks • Trade books	• Are selected for their contribution to meeting the learning targets • Support and enrich the learning experience • Include print materials, video, and software formats including combinations • Are accurate, up to date, and bias free • Compliment 21st century learning strategies • Align with standards and learning targets

Figure 5: CAI Framework—Instruction

Source: J. Redman

Check for Understanding: Triad Examples

DIRECTIONS: Listed online are several examples or components that reflect the triad of elements: curriculum, assessment, and instruction. Define and discuss the components listed below. Ask yourself, which "W question" do they address? This is a ***drag and drop*** *activity. You will compare your answers with a small group in the next class. Visit the online book to complete the activity.*

2.4 Teaching and Learning Principles

The Wisconsin Department of Public Instruction (2016) has also identified six guiding principles for teaching and learning that will complement the CAI Framework. The guiding principles are the underpinnings for effective teaching and learning for every Wisconsin teacher and every Wisconsin student. These tenets are also noteworthy and meaningful for educators from across the United States. The guiding principles emerge from research and provide the touchstone for practices that truly affect the vision of every child a graduate prepared for college and career.

The principles recognize that every student has the right to learn and are built upon three essential elements—high-quality instruction, balanced assessment, and collaboration—and the knowledge that being literate is at the heart of learning in every content area. The six principles of teaching and learning are intended to guide implementation of standards centered on high-quality instruction. They are meant to align with the vision of academic excellence, achievement, and readiness for every student. The six principles are:

- Every student has the right to learn.
- Instruction must be rigorous and relevant.
- Purposeful assessment drives instruction and affects learning.
- Learning is a collaborative responsibility.
- Students bring strengths and experiences to learning.
- Responsive environments engage learners.

Article: Six Principles

Visit the online book to read more information on the six principles from Wisconsin Department of Public Instruction.

Check for Understanding: PLC Characteristics

DIRECTIONS: A ***quick write*** *is a one to five minute assignment and is a great way to ascertain a student's understanding of a particular concept or topic. A quick write provides manageable amounts of timely and useful feedback for a minimal investment of time and energy. Let's apply this formative assessment tool to the concept of PLCs. Answer the following questions in three minutes: What is a PLC? What purpose(s) do PLCs serve? and On what core principles are PLCs based? Be prepared to share your quick write with your "face" partner in class.* ***A face partner*** *is the person who sits directly across from you. Visit the online book to complete the activity.*

2.5 Professional Learning Communities

Many districts will demonstrate their commitment to these teaching and learning guiding principles through their Professional Learning Communities (PLCs). A PLC is a group of educators that meets regularly, shares expertise, and works collaboratively to improve teaching skills and the academic performance of students. PLCs tend to serve two broad purposes (1) improving the skills and knowledge of educators through collaborative study, expertise exchange, and professional dialogue and (2) improving the educational aspirations, achievement, and attainment of students through stronger leadership and teaching (Glossary of Education Reform, 2014).

According to Richard DuFour (2004), a recognized expert on PLCs, the PLC model is a powerful way of working together that profoundly affects the practices of schooling and learning. Initiating and sustaining the PLC concept requires hard work and a change in philosophy. In a PLC school, teachers work together by planning curriculum, writing common assessments, and sharing teaching duties. Teachers often refer to students as "our" students instead of "my" students, reinforcing the collective atmosphere. Teachers work together to identify at-risk students, and teams problem solve to intervene for each student. PLCs often function as a form of action research—as a way to continually question, reevaluate, refine, and improve teaching strategies and knowledge (DuFour, DuFour, Eaker, & Many, 2006). Ultimately, the success or failure of the PLC movement on school improvement will depend on the commitment and persistence of the educators.

The core principles of the PLC movement are based on "three big ideas." PLCs require the school staff to focus on learning rather than teaching, to work collaboratively on matters related to learning, and to hold itself accountable for the kind of results that fuel continual improvement. As the school moves forward with PLC implementation, every professional in the building must engage with colleagues in the ongoing exploration of the crucial questions that drive the work of those within a PLC:

- What do we want each student to learn?
- How will we know when each student has learned it?
- How will we respond when a student experiences difficulty in learning?
- What will we do if they know it? (DuFour, 2004)

PLCs: Three Big Ideas

- **Focus on learning**
- **Work collaboratively**
- **Hold itself acountable**

Check for Understanding: PLC Core Principles

DIRECTIONS: Jigsaw *is an engaging activity where groups divide the reading/researching/learning into parts or "jigsaw pieces." Each group is responsible for understanding their part and then teach/share to the other groups. Just as the name implies, each group has a piece to the jigsaw puzzle. Once all have shared their piece of the PLC puzzle, the puzzle is complete. Visit the online book to read the article.*

2.6 Performance-Based Instruction

The authors of this textbook advocate a philosophy based on the concept of performance-based instruction (PBI). Many of us in our own educational experiences have either asked or been asked age-old questions such as Why do I need to know this? Will this be on the test? How will what I learn today be used for tomorrow?

Today's young people face an enormous challenge in being able to develop the knowledge, skills, understandings, and dispositions they need to succeed in a global, competitive, information-based marketplace that is defined by constantly changing technologies. Willard Daggett summarizes this situation the best when he states, "Present day curricula is essential, but not adequate" (as cited in Redman, 1997).

Far too often students are mere transcribers of the written word rather than active participants engaged in learning process. The end result is that students are "knowledge rich and application poor." It is no longer sufficient for learners only to be able "to know," but rather, they must be able "to do!" A rather simple axiom asks, "How does someone become better at something?" The answer, to quote manufacturers and marketers at Nike, "Just do it!" By doing, the learner is more motivated, more engaged, spends more time on task, and consequently, learning is more meaningful. In Todd Finley's blog in Edutopia (2015), he cited Adam Fletcher's definition of engagement as succinct: "Students are engaged when they are attracted to their work, persist despite challenges and obstacles, and take visible delight in accomplishing their work." The article goes on to say, according to multiple research studies, engaged students:

- Experience improved academic achievement and satisfaction;
- Are more likely to persist through academic struggles;
- Earn higher standardized test scores;
- Have better social skills; and
- Are less likely to drop out of school.

The article states that when the teacher helps students make personal connections to the class, content, and learning, engagement is seven times higher than lively teaching or academic rigor.

Bridging the gap between what is taught and what is needed is the basis for curriculum reform and curriculum improvement at all levels of our educational system. The PBI platform offers great promise to curriculum developers in the area of "doing." As you look at the name itself, you see the word "perform;" perform implies doing, action, and application. Proponents of a PBI philosophy emphasize the importance of writing outcomes that reflect comprehensive performances that reflect behaviors and utilize verbs from higher levels of Bloom's taxonomy (Nickel and Osborn, 2009). In PBI, the outcome question is modified from "what should students be able to know and do" to "what should students be able to do?"

Another basic premise of performance-based learning is that learners are informed of performance expectations and scoring guides in advance of instruction. Expectations are defined in terms of learning outcomes; it is assumed that students participating in any learning experience have a right to know the learning outcomes. Simply stated, if the students do not know where they are going, how can you expect them to get there? The same beliefs and practices also hold true for the assessment process. When performance tasks are assigned, scoring rubrics should also be distributed in advance in a PBI system. Students can then self-assess their work (i.e., score their own papers and projects), before submitting the teacher for final grading.

A summary of the 10 major assumptions that underlie and characteristics that support PBI include:

- Learning should be student-centered and the responsibility of the learner.
- Learning should be active, not passive.
- Learning can be described in terms of performance (i.e., what the learner can do).
- Learning should emphasize the application of knowledge, skills, or attitudes.
- Learning should be stated in observable and measurable performance terms.
- PBI should offer varied learning styles, teaching strategies, and educational environments.
- Achievement is measured using performance standards and/or criteria.
- Learners should be informed of performance expectations, performance criteria (i.e., scoring guides), and grading policies in advance of instruction.
- Learners are provided with benchmarks and periodic feedback.
- The credential is earned by demonstration of the competence (i.e., criterion-referenced assessment).

2.7 Teaching and Learning Cycle

When implementing a PBI philosophy, teachers generally follow a PBI Teaching and Learning Cycle. The cycle is divided into four phases. For the teacher, they are responsible for motivating, teaching, facilitating, and assessing. As the teacher is fulfilling these roles, the students are respectively engaged, learning, practicing, and applying. In each phase, the teacher and student roles are paired. For example, when the student is practicing, the teacher is facilitating. The PBI Teaching and Learning Cycle is shown in Figure 6.

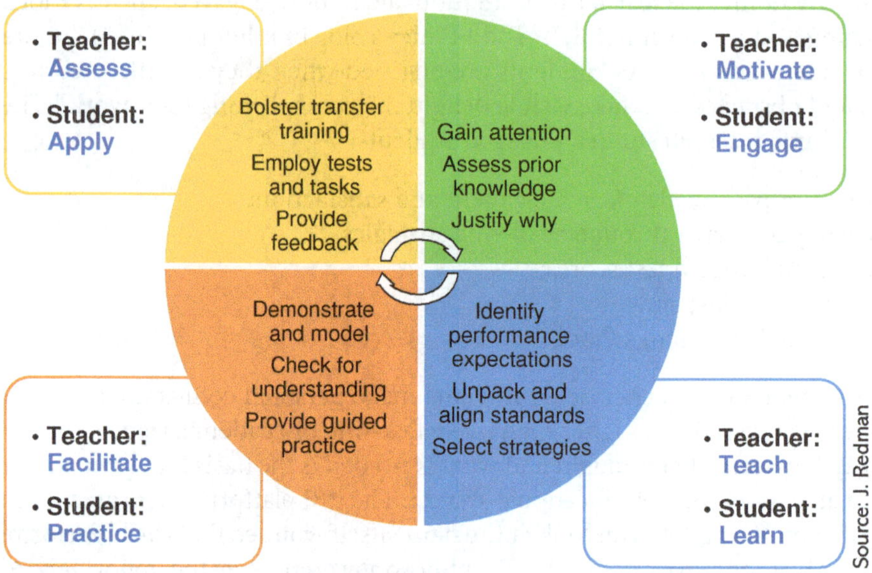

Figure 6: Teaching and Learning Cycle

2.8. Comparing Traditional Instruction and PBI

PBI is a flexible, systematic approach to teaching and learning. PBI connects curriculum, instruction, and assessment. During the PBI instructional design process, four questions are addressed by educators:

- Who is your focus?
- What will students know and do?
- When will we know that students have learned?
- How will students develop knowledge, skills, and dispositions?

PBI Summary

- **Who = Students**
- **What = Multiple types of outcomes**
- **When = Tests, tasks, and rubrics**
- **How = Action learning strategies**

In Figure 7, PBI is compared to traditional instruction.

COMPONENT	TRADITIONAL INSTRUCTION	PERFORMANCE-BASED INSTRUCTION
WHO	• Teachers (Design based on input of teachers)	• Students (Design based on student outcomes and results)
WHAT **Curriculum** (WHAT will students know and do?)	• Textbook based • Focused on what the student should know • Curriculum is centered around chapters and units • Emphasis is on content coverage • Rigor is based on memorizing facts and knowledge	• Based on multiple types and levels of outcomes and targets • Focused on what the learner will do • Emphasis is on application of knowledge, skills, and attitudes • Performance expectations given to the learner in advance of instruction
WHEN **Assessment** (WHEN will we know that students have learned?)	• Based on paper/pencil testing • Formative evaluation often based on quizzes and summative evaluation on exams • Focuses evaluation on knowledge retention of information • Often relies on "seat time" (learners progress when they have logged "enough" time) • Features norm-based grading (comparison to peers) • Allows for averaging of grades (poorer grades can be compensated for by higher grades)	• Based on satisfactory performance of each outcome; students' progress when performance expectations are mastered • Evaluation includes performance tasks and rubrics (given to students in advance of grading) • Focuses on demonstration of the application of knowledge, skills, and attitudes • Measures achievement according to performance criteria or rubrics • Features criterion-referenced grading (comparison to standards) • Holds learners and teachers accountable for achievement of intended outcomes
HOW **Instruction** (HOW will students develop skills, knowledge, and dispositions?)	• Teacher's role is disseminator of information • Places students in a passive role • Includes lots of "sit and get" • Relies very little on student's interests and learning style • Provides few benchmarks and little periodic feedback • Primarily minds-on	• Teacher's role is facilitator of learning • Places students in an active role • Includes many learner-centered activities • Offers differentiated activities for varied learning styles and abilities • Provides benchmarks and periodic feedback with opportunities for learners to improve performance • Both hands-on and minds-on

Figure 7: Instructional Design Comparison Chart
Source: J. Redman

2.9 Standards of Effective Practice

As noted previously, many educational programs sought to improve teaching and learning by increasing performance standards. This trend also brought increased awareness on teacher preparation programs in the 1990s. One of the earliest reform initiatives focused on the preparation, licensing, and ongoing professional development of teachers was the Interstate New Teacher Assessment and Support Consortium (InTASC). Created in 1987, InTASC is a consortium of state education agencies and national educational organizations. The standards were revised in 2011 and are now available on a highly interactive cloud based e-reading platform.

Article: InTASC Standards

Visit the online book for more information on the revised InTASC standards.

InTASC's primary constituencies are state education agencies and national education organizations. The Minnesota Department of Education and the Minnesota Board of Teaching are responsible for teacher licensing, program approval, and professional development and utilize the **Standards of Effective Practice**. Examples of other organizations that utilize the SEP are the National School Board Association (NSBA), National Association of Elementary School Principals (NAESP), and the National Association of Secondary Principals (NASSP). InTASC's (1999) work is guided by one basic premise, "An effective teacher must be able to integrate content knowledge with the specific strengths and needs of students to assure that all students learn and perform at high levels." In other words, InTASC was aimed at strengthening teacher preparation by improving a teacher's ability to integrate content knowledge with pedagogical skills.

Many states have used InTASC's standards to guide the development of their teacher training and teacher preparation programs. In the state of Minnesota, all 31 higher education institutions that prepare teacher candidates have the 10 SEP as a basis for their programs and course work. Within the standards, there are 124 subdivisions, or competencies, that further define the elements of proficient teaching. In essence, the Minnesota SEPs are the InTASC standards.

Article: Standards of Effective Practice

Visit the online book to view the 10 Standards of Effective Practice.

Check for Understanding: Standards of Effective Practice

DIRECTIONS: *What makes a proficient teacher? What measures can be used to guide new teachers as they work to become skillful educators? The Minnesota Standards of Effective Practice (SEP) for Teachers lists 10 standards that guide teachers in professional growth. Read the directions below so you will be ready to work in a small group during class. During this activity, you will examine and discuss the ten SEPs. In class, you will follow the steps below to create a* ***graphic organizer*** *for one of the SEPs:*

1. Form a team of three to four people. It is best if the teacher has the students form groups randomly. As social conditions influence our brain, teachers should orchestrate groupings the majority of time. In the next class, each student will get a picture. "Like" pictures will form a group for the activity.
2. Each team will select a card indicating what standard they have been assigned.
3. In your team, discuss the important ideas, concepts, processes, and teaching behaviors that give meaning to that standard.

4. Create a graphic organizer or graphic representation that represents the intent of the standard as written. Draw the graphic on a sheet of poster paper. Do not indicate which standard you have chosen on your graphic organizer.
5. Hang the poster on the wall. The instructor will assign each poster a letter (e.g., A, B, C)
6. Once all posters have been displayed, as a team, complete a **Gallery Walk** examining each graphic organizer.
7. On a sheet of paper, identify what standard each poster is illustrating.
8. Check your answers, as each team takes a turn sharing their standard and discussing their poster.

2.10 Tests Required for Minnesota Licensure

As part of the accreditation and approval process for their teacher training programs, many organizations and states require the inclusion of performance assessments. Performance assessments are defined as a comprehensive assessment through which candidates demonstrate their proficiencies in subject, professional, and pedagogical knowledge, skills, and professional dispositions, including their abilities to have positive effects on student learning. They provide a critical piece of evidence to determine whether a candidate can perform effectively as a teacher or in another school specialty area (Elliott, 2003). In the state of Minnesota, the Teacher Performance Assessment (edTPA) and Minnesota Teacher Licensing Examination (MTLE) fulfill this requirement. As of July 2016, the National Evaluation Series (NES) replaces the MTLE for basic skills tests, not the pedagogy assessments.

The edTPA was first implemented in the fall semester of 2012 at Winona State University and is designed to engage candidates in demonstrating their understanding of teaching and student learning in authentic ways. According to the research literature (Stanford University, 2012), successful teachers (1) develop knowledge of subject matter, content standards, and subject-specific pedagogy; (2) develop and apply knowledge of varied students' needs; (3) consider research and theory about how students learn; and (4) reflect on and analyze evidence of the effects of instruction on student learning. As part of the edTPA assessment, while student teaching, candidates develop and document lessons demonstrating their skills in planning, instruction, and assessment. Additionally, as they teach their lessons, they are expected to reflect upon the cyclical relationship among planning, instruction, and assessment with a focus on your students' learning needs. Emphasis is also placed upon the academic language inherent in each subject area. Fifteen different rubrics are used to score the student responses.

A second source of evidence is provided from candidate scores on the Minnesota Teacher Licensing Exam (MTLE) and recently the National Evaluation Series (NES). The MTLE tests were developed in alignment with Minnesota regulations and content standards for teachers, including the Minnesota Board of Teaching Rules. MTLE tests are designed to measure a candidate's proficiency levels in basic skills, pedagogy, and a specific content area, based on Minnesota policies for each field. Both the content and pedagogy tests include different subtests and many teacher education candidates take these tests just prior to student teaching. The NES aligns to the common core standards and measures a candidate's proficiency in math, reading, writing, and technology literacy. NES has a nationwide network for teachers and school districts. Candidates must earn a passing score on both the content and pedagogy examinations to earn their Minnesota teaching license.

Minnesota Licensing Tests

- **edTPA = Teacher Performance Assessment**
- **MTLE = Minnesota Teacher Licensing Examination**
- **NES = National Evaluation Series**

Chapter Summary

This chapter calls for all educational stakeholders to become "Teachers as decision makers" and help reinvent schools and schooling for the 21st century. Teachers as decision makers are also thoughtful professionals who embody the growth and learning of their students, understand the curricular, assessment, and instructional components in their schools, and are able to respond to the needs of their students. Teachers as decision makers build bridges; bridges that help us move from where we are to where we need to be. These bridges provide a new path to the future and are necessary for implementing productive change. Teachers as decision makers earn the respect and trust needed for people to follow, even in adverse or risky situations. They take responsibility for the bridges they build and lead by example. By accepting this role, Teachers as decision makers demonstrate the vision and direction enabling them to believe that the outcome will be far greater than the risk. Teachers as decision makers make good schools happen!

A Fable: The Mobius Strip

DIRECTIONS: *Read the Curriculum fable. Think about the connection between the fable and the Triad of Elements. In class with a small group, you will come to consensus on the moral of the fable. Be prepared to share. View the online book to read the article.*

Check for Mastery: Performance Expectations

DIRECTIONS: *You rated yourself on performance expectations at the start of this chapter. Have you now mastered each performance expectation? Rate yourself using the Likert scale online. Compare this to how you rated yourself at the beginning of this chapter. If you do not know an expectation, go back to the text and re-read the information.*

Summary Learning Activity: PBI Perceptions

DIRECTIONS: *PBI is a systematic approach to designing curriculum based on performance expectations, performance standards, and performance tasks. What perceptions of PBI are you bringing to this learning experience? Read each statement carefully about PBI and check those that you currently believe to be true.*

_____ **1.** PBI is a strategic planning tool or platform for designing curriculum, instruction, and assessment.

_____ **2.** PBI emphasizes what, when, and how learners will learn.

_____ **3.** PBI eliminates the teacher from the learning process.

_____ **4.** PBI is based upon the textbook, course content, and seat time.

_____ **5.** PBI relies on performance (demonstration) of the application of skills, knowledge, and dispositions.

_____ **6.** PBI cannot be used to design instruction for the affective domain of learning (i.e., domain of feeling).

_____ **7.** PBI offers little variety in learning styles and teaching strategies.

_____ **8.** PBI encourages learners to be more actively involved in the learning process.

_____ **9.** PBI gives away the right answers for what is on the test.

_____ **10.** PBI holds teachers and learners accountable for the achievement of intended outcomes.

_____ **11.** PBI informs the learners of multiple types and levels of performance expectations in advance of instruction.

_____ **12.** PBI identifies the criteria to be used in assessing achievement in advance of grading.

_____ **13.** PBI focuses on "covering the material" found in a course.

_____ **14.** PBI features norm-referenced grading (i.e., grading on a "curve" or relative to peer achievement).

_____ **15.** PBI allows too many people to get As and lowers standards.

_____ **16.** PBI can be used to assess prerequisite learning, monitor student progress, and provide periodic feedback.

_____ **17.** PBI can only work in a traditional classroom environment.

_____ **18.** PBI requires less preparation and planning time than traditional classroom methods.

Supplemental Learning Exercises

1. Several years ago, Peter Skillman introduced us to an exercise called the Marshmallow Challenge. Its goal is simple: In 18 minutes, teams must build the tallest freestanding structure out of twenty sticks of spaghetti, one yard of tape, one yard of string, and one marshmallow. The marshmallow has to be on top. Though the task seems simple, it's actually pretty hard. At your table, using the materials in your lunch bag, take the Marshmallow Challenge! Review the goals and rules of the Marshmallow Challenge:
   - Build the Tallest Freestanding Structure: The winning team is the one that has the tallest structure measured from the table top surface to the top of the marshmallow. That means the structure cannot be suspended from a higher structure, like a chair, ceiling, or chandelier.
   - The Entire Marshmallow Must be on Top: The entire marshmallow needs to be on the top of the structure. Cutting or eating part of the marshmallow disqualifies the team.
   - Use as Much or as Little of the Kit: The team can use as many or as few of the 20 spaghetti sticks, as much or as little, of the string or tape. The team cannot use the paper bag as part of their structure.
   - Break up the Spaghetti, String or Tape: Teams are free to break the spaghetti, cut up the tape, and string to create new structures.
   - The Challenge Lasts 18 Minutes: Teams cannot hold on to the structure when the time runs out. Those touching or supporting the structure at the end of the exercise will be disqualified.
   - Ensure Everyone Understands the Rules: All team members should follow the rules as given.
2. Interview a teacher who serves as the leader of a PLC. Ask that individual at least five of the questions below:
   - What prompted your school to consider implementing a PLC? Was it the right prompt?
   - What is the primary purpose behind creating and implementing your PLC?
   - What does your PLC look like when it's implemented and operating effectively?
   - What has your school district done in the past that has supported or created barriers for implementing an effective PLC?
   - What operating principles do you employ to conduct effective PLCs? Do you already have a strong, accepted, and universally applied decision-making process?
   - How will you monitor, evaluate, and measure the effectiveness of your PLC?
   - How do you find the necessary time to effectively implement and sustain a PLC?

- How does the PLC impact and influence the comprehensive professional development plan in your school?

3. Work with a small group and determine how you would fill in the blanks for these analogies:
   - Curriculum is to __________ as blue prints are to __________.
   - Instruction is to __________ as __________ are to explorers.
   - Assessment is to __________ as a tape measure is to __________.
   - SEP are to __________ as __________ are to medical doctors.
   - __________ are to questions as __________ are to answers.
   - PBI is to doing as __________ is to __________.
   - DuFour is to __________ as InTASC is to __________.
   - Scope and sequence is to __________ as performance standards are to __________.
   - Differentiation strategies are to __________ as __________ is to assessment components.

Final Test

Directions: *Read each question or statement below. Select the appropriate answer or write the correct answer in the blank provided.*

T F 1. In standards-led education reform, the emphasis is placed on the "input" side of the equation.

_____ 2. What "W" question is answered by instruction?
A. What
B. Who
C. How
D. When

_____ 3. When you think of the term "assessment," what typically comes to mind?
A. Strategies and resources
B. Content and plan
C. Tests and tasks
D. Targets and benchmarks

_____ 4. What is the recommended or ideal order for completing the triad of elements?
A. Curriculum, Instruction, and Assessment
B. Curriculum, Assessment, and Instruction
C. Instruction, Curriculum, and Assessment
D. Assessment, Curriculum, and Instruction

_____ 5. Which of the following is ***not*** a "big idea" associated with PLCs?
A. An emphasis on a learning structure that is based on competition
B. An emphasis on learning, rather than teaching
C. An emphasis on collaboration and teamwork
D. An emphasis on accountability and results

_____ 6. Which of the following is ***not*** one of DuFour's PLC questions concerning student learning?
A. What do we want each student to learn?
B. How will we know when each student has learned it?
C. How will we respond when a student experiences difficulty in learning?
D. How will we shape the learning environment to allow for collaborative work time?

______ 7. All of the following are characteristics of performance-based instruction (PBI) ***except***:
   - A. PBI is a teacher-centered approach to curriculum development.
   - B. PBI increases accountability for mastering knowledge, skills, and attitudes.
   - C. PBI describes learning in terms of observable and measurable instructional targets or expectations.
   - D. PBI features criterion-referenced grading procedures for assessing student achievement.

______ 8. In the PBI Teaching and Learning Cycle, what is the student's role when the teacher is assessing?
   - A. Engaging
   - B. Learning
   - C. Practicing
   - D. Applying

______ 9. Which of the following entities serves as the *primary* basis for the education coursework in Winona State University's teacher preparation program?
   - A. Funds of Knowledge (FoK)
   - B. Standards of Effective Practice (SEP)
   - C. Understanding by Design (UbD)
   - D. Performance-Based Instruction (PBI)

______ 10. Which of the following is a performance-based assessment on which teacher preparation candidates must demonstrate their planning, instruction, and assessment skills?
   - A. edTPA
   - B. MTLE
   - C. SEP
   - D. Praxis

Directions: *Read each scenario below. Write a brief response.*

1. Complete the chart below highlighting PBI features.

Question	PBI Characteristic
Who?	Students
What?	Multiple levels of outcomes
When?	tests tasks rubric
How?	Action learning - engaged

2. Describe the three big ideas concerning PLCs.

Works Cited and Suggested Readings

Aseltine, James, Faryniarz, Judith, & Rigazio-DiGillo, Anthony. (2006). *Supervision for Learning: A Performance-Based Approach to Teacher Development and School Improvement.* Alexandria, VA: Association for Supervision and Curriculum Development (ASCD).

Council of Chief State School Officers (CCSSO). (2013). *InTASC Model Core Teaching Standards and Learning Progressions for Teachers 1.0: A Resource for Ongoing Teacher Development.* Retrieved from: http://www.ccsso.org/resources/programs/interstate_teacher_assessment_consortium_(intasc).html#sthash.4SBe6lY7.dpuf

DuFour, Richard, DuFour, Rebecca, Eaker, Robert, & Many, Thomas. (2006). *Learning by Doing: A Handbook for Professional Learning Communities at Work* (2nd ed.). Bloomington, IN: Solution Tree.

DuFour, Richard. (2004). What is a Professional Learning Community? Schools as Learning Communities, *Educational Week*, *61*(8), Alexandria, VA: Association for Supervision and Curriculum Development (ASCD), 6–11.

Elliott, Emerson (Project Director). (2003). *Assessing Education Candidate Performance: A Look at Changing Practices*. Retrieved from National Council for Accreditation of Teacher Education (NCATE): http://www.ncate.org/portals/0/documents/accreditation/article_assessmentexamples.pdf

Finley, Todd. (2015). *New Study: Engage Kids with 7Xs the Effect*. Retrieved from: www.edutopia.org.

McTighe, Jay and Wiggins, Grant. (2013). *Essential Questions: Opening Doors to Student Understanding*. Alexandria, VA: Association for Supervision and Curriculum Development (ASCD).

Minnesota Teacher Licensure Examinations (MTLE). Retrieved from: https://www.mtle.nesinc.com/.

National Governor's Association and the Council of Chief State School Officers. (2010). *Common Core State Standards*. Washington, DC: Author.

Nickel, Robin & Osborn, Leah. (2009). *WIDS and Performance-Based Learning*. Wisconsin Technical College System Foundation Worldwide Instructional Design System (WIDS).

No Child Left Behind Act of 2001, P.L. 107–110, 20 U.S.C. § 6319 (2002).

The Office of the Revisor of Statutes. *Minnesota Administrative Rules*. Retrieved from: www.revisor.mn.gov.

Professional Learning Community. (2014). In S. Abbott (Ed.), *The Glossary of Education Reform*. Retrieved from: http://edglossary.org/professionallearningcommunity

Redman, Jerry. (1997). Hands-On, Minds-On Curricula: What Teachers Can Do, *Bridging the Gap Newsletter*, Volume (2.4). La Crosse, WI: Western Technical College.

Stanford University. (2012). *Assessment Handbook*. Stanford, CA: edTPA.

Winona State University, College of Education. (2011). *WSU Unit's Conceptual Framework*. Winona, MN: WSU (Approved by TEA 9/1/11 and APA 9/6/11).

Wisconsin Department of Public Instruction. *Guiding Principles for Teaching and Learning*. Retrieved from: http://dpi.wi.gov/standards/guiding-principles.

Chapter 3
Investigating Curricular Concepts and Foundations

> "There is no cost difference between incarceration and an Ivy League education; the main difference is curriculum."
>
> Paul Hawken

Anticipatory Set: Elicitation Poster on Curriculum

DIRECTIONS: *The Elicitation Poster is a tool that educators use to assess prior knowledge. As students develop their posters they become engaged in the new concept, explore other's ideas, and document their previous learning. This activity should make the connection between past and present learning experiences, expose prior conceptions or misconceptions, and organize students' thinking toward the learning expectations. In the next class, small groups will develop an Elicitation Poster for the concept of curriculum. Groups will share posters and questions with the class.*

Nadja Gellermann/Shutterstock.com

Curriculum is operated by content

Chapter Overview

Are you a puzzle person? If you are, or if you know one, these folks love to spend time putting pieces together to form a complete picture. Younger children like puzzles with 50–100 pieces graduating into much more complex puzzles, with 1500+ pieces. Some like 3 dimensional puzzles, and some prefer completing a jigsaw online. No matter what type of jigsaw puzzle you prefer, there are similar components to each, and each with a typical sequence. Most people start by finding the straight edges and completing the border. When that is complete, most categorize the pieces by color or object. From there, contemplation and time take precedent. Patience and reward go hand in hand. It can take a long time to find that "one" piece to make a transition. That demands a small celebration! In hours, sometimes days, the puzzle comes together and a beautiful picture has been created.

Completing a jigsaw puzzle is somewhat like the curricular process in schools. The curriculum process has a specific scope and sequence, as finding borders first does for the puzzle building process. Curriculum developers have criteria for selection, as a puzzle solver decides the type and difficulty of the puzzle. As with curriculum, the more experience a teacher has with the development process, the less difficult it seems. The first time one completes a 500-piece puzzle it seems daunting, but by the 3rd or 4th puzzle, it becomes exciting, especially as the scope and sequence are better understood.

In this chapter, you will develop your own operational or working definition for curriculum after exploring several concepts and sample definitions found in the research literature. This section also introduces several major design concepts associated with the selection and organization of content. Seven methods for presenting content will be illustrated and advantages of each will be discussed. Scope and sequence and their dimensions will be defined and explained to maximize the reader's understanding and eventual application to the curriculum construction process. Finally, Olivia's (1988) 10 axioms for curriculum development will be investigated. As you read and analyze each topic, reflect on your role as teacher as decision maker.

Performance Expectations

DIRECTIONS: *How well do you know the performance expectations? Rate your knowledge of each using Likert scale. You will rate yourself again at the end of the chapter. This is for your information to assess your learning. Visit the online book to record your answers.*

1 = I do not have any knowledge of this concept.

2 = I have minimal knowledge of this concept.

3 = I have some understanding of this concept.

4 = I have a satisfactory understanding of this concept.

5 = I am confident in my understanding of this concept.

Source: Shutterstock.com

This chapter should prepare you to:

Rating	#	Performance Expectations
	1.	Analyze various conceptions and definitions of curriculum.
	2.	Develop a working definition for curriculum.
	3.	Recognize the effects of the hidden curriculum.
	4.	Discuss the role that content plays in the curriculum development process and summarize key criteria that are used by curriculum developers to select content for inclusion in the curriculum.
	5.	Compare and contrast seven methods of presenting content, including illustrations of each.
	6.	Differentiate between scope and sequence.
	7.	Explain the three dimensions of scope: relevance, balance, and integration.
	8.	Explain the two dimensions of sequence: continuity and articulation.
	9.	Cite examples of basic curriculum design concepts, including different types of sequencing.
	10.	Define and give examples of transfer training.
	11.	Analyze the ten curriculum axioms.
	12.	Defend the statement "less is more, different is better."

3.1 Conceptions of Curriculum

In the 1st century before Christ, Roman gladiators had no idea that the oval track upon which their chariots raced would bequeath a word used by all educators in the 21st century. The racetrack, or curriculum, has become one of the key elements found in good schools. The word curriculum comes from the Latin word *currere* which means "to run." With time, the course of the race became the course of study, and in schools the curriculum is the means by which the purpose of education is enacted (Olivia, 1988).

In the field of education, curriculum has a variety of meanings. Traditionally the term curriculum meant a list of courses, but over time, it has come to mean many things to many people. Simply put, a student might view curriculum "as whatever happens to me in school," a teacher might perceive curriculum "as what I am told to teach," or an administrator might view curriculum "as a list of standards to cover." Whatever definition is decided upon, if it is going to be worthwhile, it must be more than a document that is prepared, filed, stored, and ignored. An awareness of the different definitions of curriculum enhances the curriculum developers' ability to plan, implement, evaluate, maintain, and improve curriculum. A sound understanding of curriculum will prepare teachers to better support positive reform efforts while suppressing undesirable trends (Henson, 2001).

According to Rule (1973), there are more than 119 different definitions for curriculum. The field of curriculum began in the United States with Franklin Bobbitt's (1918) small book simply entitled *Curriculum*, and the field quickly became an area of professional study (Wiles and Bondi, 2015). Elliot Eisner (1985) even introduced the paradoxical notion of the "null curriculum—what the schools do not teach." Various modern definitions of curriculum have been offered, ranging from a static document (syllabi or text) to a process or structure for educating (opportunities or plans) to a product (outcomes or performance). More precise definitions of curriculum emphasize (1) guided experiences to which children should be exposed; (2) plans for learning; (3) ends or outcomes of being educated; and (4) systems for achieving educational production

(Tanner and Tanner, 1980). Olivia (1998) concluded his discussion on the definition of curriculum with a series of different curriculum interpretations:

- Curriculum is that which is taught in school.
- Curriculum is a set of subjects.
- Curriculum is content.
- Curriculum is a program of study.
- Curriculum is a set of materials.
- Curriculum is a sequence of courses.
- Curriculum is a set of performance objectives.
- Curriculum is a series of experiences undergone by learners in the school.
- Curriculum is that which is taught both inside and outside of school directed by the school.
- Curriculum is that which an individual learner experiences as a result of schooling.
- Curriculum is everything that goes on within the school, including extracurricular activities, guidance, and interpersonal relationships (pp. 5–6).

3.2 Definitions of Curriculum

What is your operational definition of curriculum? To help you derive your own personal definition, we have sought the assistance of 20 recognized curriculum experts from the research literature. The following list is a collection of their popular definitions for curriculum in chronological order:

- **Dewey** (1902): "Curriculum is a continuous reconstruction, moving from the child's present experience out into that represented by the organized bodies of truth that we call studies . . . the various studies . . . are themselves experience—they are that of the race." (pp. 11–12).
- **Bobbitt** (1918): "Curriculum is the entire range of experiences, both directed and undirected, concerned in unfolding the abilities of the individual" (p. 43).
- **Caswell & Campbell** (1935): "Curriculum is to be composed of all the experiences children have under the guidance of teachers" (p. 66).
- **Tyler** (1957): "Curriculum is all of the experiences that individual learners have in a program of education whose purpose is to achieve broad goals and related specific objectives, which is planned in terms of a framework of theory and research or past or present professional practices" (p. 79).
- **Taba** (1962): "The curriculum is all of the learning of students, which is planned by and directed by the school to attain its educational goals" (p. 11).
- **Gagne** (1967): "Curriculum is a sequence of content units arranged in such a way that the learning of each unit may be accomplished as a single act, provided the capabilities described by specified prior units (in the sequence) have already been mastered by the learner" (p. 23).
- **Johnson** (1967): "Curriculum is a structured series of intended learning outcomes." He further argues that "there is no educational experience until the individual actually interacts with the content in some type of environment" (p. 130).
- **Harnack** (1968): "The curriculum embodies all the teaching-learning experiences guided and directed by the school" (p. 47).
- **Popham & Baker** (1970): "Curriculum is all the planned learning outcomes for which the school is responsible. Curriculum refers to the desired consequences of instruction" (p. 48).
- **Oliver** (1977): "Curriculum is the educational program of the school and divided into four basic elements: (1) program of studies, (2) program of experiences, (3) program of service, and (4) hidden curriculum" (p. 8).

- **Hunkin** (1980): "Curriculum is all the activities necessary for the creation and utilization of a curriculum-instructional plan. It also includes the plan. This plan, the visible curriculum designed for student learnings, possesses the major components of contents, experiences, and environments organized as to assist students in achieving most optimally the goals and objectives designated by the total community, both professional and lay, and students" (pp. 14–15).
- **Tanner & Tanner** (1980): "Curriculum is the planned and guided learning experiences and intended learning outcomes, formulated through the systematic reconstruction of knowledge and experience, under the auspices of the school, for the learner's continuous and willful growth in personal-social competence" (p. 43).
- **Saylor, Alexander, & Lewis** (1981): "Curriculum is a plan for providing sets of learning opportunities to achieve broad goals and related specific objectives for an identifiable population served by a single school center" (p. 8).
- **Hass** (1987): "Curriculum is all of the experiences that individual learners have in a program of education whose purpose is to achieve broad goals and related specific objectives, which is planned in terms of a framework of theory and research or past and present professional practice" (p. 5).
- **Olivia** (1988): "Curriculum is perceived as a plan or program for all the experiences which the learner encounters under the direction of the school" (p. 9).
- **Doll** (1989): "Curriculum is the formal and informal content and process by which learners gain knowledge and understanding, develop skills, and alter attitudes, appreciations, and values under the auspices of that school" (p. 8).
- **Armstrong** (1989): "Curriculum is a master plan for selecting content and organizing learning experiences for the purpose of changing and developing learners' behaviors and insights" (p. 4).
- **Thompson & Greg** (1997): "The curriculum is the primary vehicle for achieving the goals and objectives of its school. Curriculum embraces every planned aspect of a school's educational program" (p. 28).
- **McNeil** (2008): "Curriculum [is] usually thought of as a course of study or plan for what is to be taught in an educational institution" (p. 12).
- **Wiles & Bondi** (2015): "Curriculum is a desired goal or set of values that can be activated through a development process, culminating in experiences for learners. The degree to which those experiences are a true representation of the envisioned goal or goals is a direct function of the effectiveness of the curriculum development efforts" (p. 5).

Check for Understanding: Working Definition of Curriculum

DIRECTIONS: *Review the definitions of curriculum provided in this chapter and reflect on your own use of the term. Write your own* ***operational definition*** *of curriculum. Be prepared to share your definition in the next class. Visit the online book to complete the activity.*

Even if the curriculum is a mutually agreed upon document, various perceptions can still exist depending upon the stakeholder. John Goodlad (1987) identified five such perceptions:

- **Ideal** = A curriculum that schools might implement, if conditions were just right;
- **Formal** = A curriculum expressing intended learnings as set forth by the state and local school boards;
- **Perceived or Instructional** = A curriculum mirroring what teachers say they are trying to do;
- **Observed or Operational** = A curriculum indicating what is really being done—what observers see when present in the classrooms; and
- **Experiential** = A curriculum demonstrating what students are actually experiencing or reacting to.

3.3 The Hidden Curriculum

Implicit in all the definitions of curriculum provided thus far is one commonality; they are all visible and planned. The more obscure, less visible part of the curriculum is referred to as the "hidden curriculum." A hidden curriculum can be defined as the lessons that are taught informally, and usually unintentionally, in a school system. Schubert (1986) states that "the hidden curriculum is that which is taught implicitly, rather than explicitly, by the school experience" (p. 105). It's very nature makes it more covert rather than overt (Henson, 2001). Some would argue that the hidden curriculum is the most important knowledge, skills, and values that student learn in schools today.

The first credited use of the term hidden curriculum was made by Philip W. Jackson (1968) in his book *Life in Classrooms*. The hidden curriculum includes behaviors, perspectives, and attitudes that students pick up while they're at school. Examples of the hidden curriculum might include cocurricular activities, peer relationships, work ethics, basic moral principles, organizational skills, and classroom order and discipline. It is important for curriculum leaders to be aware of the subtle and pervasive influence that elements of the hidden curriculum have on the growth and development of their students.

Article: Hidden Curriculum

Visit the online book to read the article. Note the author gives specific examples of the hidden curriculum in the areas of cultural expectations, cultural values, cultural perspectives, curricular topics, teaching strategies, school structures, and institutional rules.

Video: Hidden Curriculum in Education: Definition & Examples

DIRECTIONS: *While watching this video, write three things about hidden curriculum that are new to you. In the next class, students will be asked to identify the most significant learning or idea they gained from the article with their table mates. This strategy is called* ***Point of Most Significance*** *(POMS).*

3.4 Curriculum Content

At the beginning of the Civil War, British educator Herbert Spencer (1861) posed a profound and enduring question, "What knowledge is of most worth?" Although a question like this is quite simple, it is also very philosophical in nature and its answer can have highly practical implications. As knowledge is the source of the curriculum, so content is the foundation of the curriculum. All curricula are composed of content. Content is what is presented to students and is made available for all to use (Hunkins, 1980).

Selecting and organizing content and activities is a responsibility shared by all teachers and curriculum developers. Hunkins (1980) defines content "as the specialized arrangement(s) of knowledge for purposes of instruction within a structure commonly called curriculum" (p. 215). Hyman (1973) further enhances this definition of content when he states that the content is "the knowledge (i.e., facts, explanations, principles, and definitions), skills and processes (i.e., reading, writing, calculating, dancing, critical thinking, decision making, and communicating) and values (i.e., the beliefs about matters concerned with good and bad, right and wrong, beautiful and ugly)" (p. 4).

Curriculum planning involves making a series of choices. When most curriculum developers, especially secondary teachers, operationalize the curriculum they think in terms of content. Content serves as the vehicle for teaching and learning. For actual use in the classroom, content is often categorized into units, topics, or themes. The oldest curriculum designs, dating back to ancient Greece, are subject matter designs based on content. Subject matter designs are also the best known by both educators and the lay public (Hunkins, 1980).

Although schools have never existed without teaching content, the growing realization that knowledge is increasing at a tremendous rate has forced curriculum developers to reexamine content questions. Curriculum planners and teachers continually struggle with the problem of limiting subject matter. Knowledge, spurred on by emerging technology, is increasing at an exponential rate. It is no longer possible for an individual to encompass even a small portion of the knowledge available; furthermore, computers provide virtually instantaneous access to vast stores of information (Saylor, Alexander, & Lewis, 1981).

Curriculum developers want to select the content that is most effective and efficient in obtaining the purposes and achieving the goals of the educational system. People involved in curriculum construction apply certain criteria as they select the specific elements of content to be included in instructional programs at many different levels of schooling. Some examples of content selection criteria that are often employed include legal constraints, content significance, content utility, motivational appeal, and content complexity (Armstrong, 1989; Zais, 1976).

- **Legal constraints**: Almost every state mandates some content to be included at certain grade levels or in certain courses. Every state has adopted or created state standards and many (especially larger states) regulate textbook adoptions at the district level.
- **Content significance**: Some content is obviously more important than other content and content significance is usually judged in terms of how basic it is to the discipline under study.
- **Content utility**: Content utility is generally restricted to mean useful in the performance of life-long learning.
- **Motivational appeal**: Teachers should select content that appeals to students' interests. Student motivation is a significant factor toward obtaining higher achievement.
- **Content complexity**: Finally, selecting content needs to be developmental appropriate for the population of learners for whom it is intended.

3.5 Presenting Content

Content is selected, organized, and sequenced in the curriculum so that students will gain the knowledge, skills, understandings, and dispositions to become fully functioning adults. One of the key questions that curriculum developers must address is what form or structure will content have in the curriculum? In other words, how will content be presented and in how many formats?

When most educators think of curriculum, they think of content. Content serves as the vehicle in curriculum design. There are seven methods for presenting content in a curriculum. Figure 1 lists the seven methods and gives an example for a science unit on matter.

George Rudy/Shutterstock.com

Methods of Presenting Content

Method 1: Content Outline	
Description:	Listing of Topics and subtopics
Advantages:	• Very familiar—easy to create and easy to understand; • Similar to Table of Contents in a textbook; and • This option is how many teachers operationalize the curriculum development process—in terms of content topics.

Example:

1. Matter
   - A. Definition and examples
   - B. Properties
   - C. States
     1. Solid
     2. Liquid
     3. Gas
   - D. Chemical and physical changes
     1. Temperature
     2. Pressure

Method 2: Outcomes or Expectations	
Description:	Topic + Action
Advantages:	• Identifies what students should know, do, and care about; • Learning is an "active" process—builds in the cognitive process; and • Teachers need to know where they are going before their students can get there.

Example:

1. Define and give an example of matter.
2. List the three general properties of matter.
3. Differentiate among the three states of matter.
4. Compare and contrast chemical and physical changes in matter.

Method 3: Summary or Narrative	
Description:	Topic + Details
Advantages:	• Similar to "Points to Remember" at the end of a Chapter; • Provides supporting details; and • New teachers often use this option to compose their notes and tests.

Example:

1. Matter is defined as anything that has mass and takes up space. Examples of matter include solids, liquids, and gases.
2. Matter has three general properties: mass, space, and inertia.
3. Solids have a definite volume and shape; liquids have a definite volume, but no definite shape; and gases have neither a definite volume nor a definite shape.
4. Matter undergoes chemical and physical changes. Chemical changes result in a new substance being formed, whereas physical changes result in just a different form of the same substance.

Method 4: Essential Questions	
Description:	Topic + Question
Advantages:	• Promotes research and inquiry; • If you can ask it or tell it, always ask it; and • Employs the "W" questions.

Example:

1. What is matter? What is not matter? What properties does matter possess?
2. What states or forms are there of matter? How are they alike? How are they different?
3. What effects do temperature and pressure have on the states of matter?
4. What are the differences between chemical and physical changes? What are some examples?

Method 5: Standards	
Description:	Topic + Evidence
Advantages:	• Current reform efforts require adoption of standards; • Standards provide evidence of student learning; and • Serve as "hybrid" outcomes.

Example:

D. Physical Science: Student will demonstrate an understanding of the physical and chemical properties of matter, the forms and properties of energy, and the ways in which matter and energy interact.

D.4.1 Understand that objects are made of more than one substance, by observing, describing, and measuring the properties of earth materials, including properties of size, weight, shape, color, temperature, and the ability to react with other substances;

D.4.2 Group and/or classify objects and substances based on the properties of earth materials;

D.4.3 Understand that substances can exist in different states—solid, liquid, gas; and

D.4.4 Observe and describe changes in form, temperature, color, speed, and direction of objects and construct explanations for the changes.

Method 6: Tasks	
Description:	Topic + Activities
Advantages:	• Learners are engaged in "hands-on, minds-on" curriculum; • Represents the contextualization of an outcome; and • Similar to "kits" (e.g., science kit).

Example:

Module 1: Exploring the General Properties of Matter
Module 2: Investigating the States of Matter
Module 3: Analyzing the Effects of Temperature and Pressure on Matter
Module 4: Examining Chemical and Physical Changes in Matter

Method 7: Concept Map	
Description:	Topic + Graphic
Advantages:	• Reflects visual learning and illustrates relationships; • Type of graphic organizer; and • Similar to the way the mind works or Piaget's schema.
Example:	

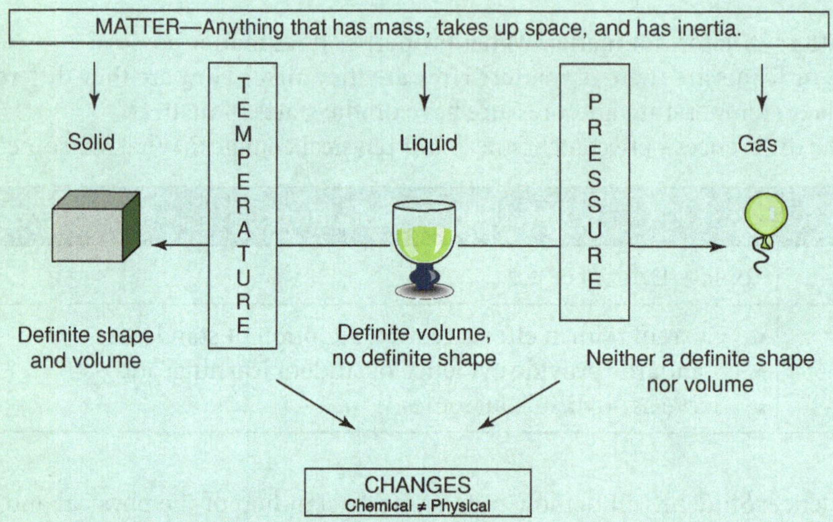

Figure 1: Methods of Presenting Content
Source: J. Redman

Check for Understanding: Presenting Content

DIRECTIONS: *You read seven methods for presenting content.* ***Match*** *each characteristic with the appropriate content method. In the next class, each student will be given a red, yellow, and green card. This strategy is called* ***Traffic Light Cards****. Each student will self-assess their understanding of the methods (green – I understand this very well; yellow – I understand most of it but could use a little help; and red – Help, I don't get it). Visit the online book to complete the activity.*

3.6 Organizing the Curriculum

Content selection and organization deal with the heart of curriculum planning. Determining what knowledge (content) to incorporate into a school's curriculum still leaves one with the challenge of organizing it in ways that will facilitate learning. How educators organize subject matter for curriculum planning depends very much on their view and role of content in the curriculum. When organizing content, one also considers when students will experience it. The selecting and organizing of content requires contemplating several key decisions associated with the concepts of scope and sequence.

The curriculum design and the approach used to implement the curriculum are often determined by the organization of the content. Curriculum design exists along two basic organizational dimensions: horizontal and vertical. **Scope** is horizontal in nature and refers to the breadth and depth of the curriculum.

Relevance, balance, and integration are three dimensions of scope. **Sequence** is vertical in nature and refers to the order of the curriculum. Continuity and articulation are the dimensions of sequencing (Olivia, 1988).

3.7 Scope

Scope is the breadth and depth of the content. The content of any course or grade level—identified as topics, subtopics, learning experiences, activities, or organizing threads—constitutes the scope of the curriculum (Olivia, 1988). In essence, it is the amount of details found in the curriculum. Curriculum developers are always asking how much detail and how much emphasis should be given particular content area be given? How much detail is required at the various levels of schooling? What content should be mandatory for all students? The scope of the curriculum can often be kept in check by carefully selecting appropriate outcomes earlier in the design phase (Doll, 1989).

Scope has three dimensions: relevance, balance, and integration. According to Olivia (1988), everyone agrees that the curriculum should be relevant. No one will stand up and argue for an irrelevant curriculum. The difficulty in determining relevance lies in the multitude of interpretations of the word. Who determines relevance? Is relevance the same in all regions of the country? In different historical contexts? To different groups of students? B. Othanel Smith (1969) offers the best explanation of relevance when he wrote: "The teacher is constantly asked: Why should I learn that?. . .the question of **relevance** boils down to the question of what is most assuredly useful" (pp. 130–131).

Balance refers to the need to assure that no one curricular element is emphasized to the detriment of others (Armstrong, 1989). Curriculum planners and teachers need to assure that there is an equitable coverage of all important content. For example, balance is needed between the learner and subject-centered curriculum, between the arts and the sciences, and between the college prep and vocational subjects. Halverson (1961) espoused of balancing ends and means, as follows: "A balanced curriculum implies structure and order in its scope and sequence (means) leading to achievement of educational objectives (ends)" (p. 4).

Integration is defined as the blending, fusion, or unification of disciplines. Benjamin Bloom (1958) defined an integrated thread as "any idea, problem, method, or device by which two or more separate learning experiences are related" (p. 91). Unlike determination of scope and sequence which must be accomplished, the integration of disciplines is optional (Olivia, 1988). Integration is sometimes seen as the horizontal relationship among various content areas. It is an attempt to correlate content themes, ideas, facts in order to assure students perceiving a unity of knowledge (Hunkins, 1980). Hilda Taba (1962) commented, "It is recognized that learning is more effective when facts and principles from one field can be related to another, especially when applying knowledge" (p. 298). For example, what is learned in science (e.g., Newton's Three Laws of Motion) may be integrated with the field of mathematics (e.g., problem solving) to enhance student learning.

3.8 Sequence

Sequence is concerned with the order of topics over time. Sequence is vertical in nature and is considered the time order in which educational experiences are presented. Sequence answers the question "What learning content is to follow what other?" Whereas scope is referred to as "the what" of curriculum organization, sequence is referred to as "the when" (Olivia, 1988).

The generally accepted view of sequence is that it should depend directly on the nature and structure of subject matter (Doll, 1989). However, if the curriculum planner were to think in terms of how individuals develop and learn, the sequence might be determined by students successfully performing tasks at various stages of development (Hunkins,1980). Several different variations of sequences can be found in school curriculum today, including:

- **Taxonomic** = Movement from simple to complex or study based upon prerequisite learning;
- **Topical** = Movement from parts to whole or whole to parts;

- **Chronological** = Movement from past to present or from present to past;
- **Conceptual** = Movement from concrete to abstract or familiar to less familiar; and
- **Thematic** = Ever-widening circles of understanding or involvement or related to a common idea (Doll, 1989).

Curricular Organization

- **Scope = Horizontal, breadth, and depth**
- **Scope dimensions = Relevance, balance, and integration**
- **Sequence = Vertical and order of the curriculum**
- **Sequence dimensions = Continuity and articulation**

Check for Understanding: Types of Sequence

DIRECTIONS: *Sequence is defined as the order of the curriculum. Review the descriptions and identify what subject areas would most appropriately be taught by each sequence. In the next class, the instructor will say one of the descriptions and one content area. Students will stand if they believe the description and the content area are well suited to each other. This strategy is called* ***Stand Up if You Know****. Visit the online book to complete the activity.*

Sequence has two dimensions: continuity and articulation. Sequence and continuity are usually considered in tandem. **Continuity** describes the continuousness with which the same kinds of experiences are offered over a period of time. Sequence without continuity is possible, but continuity without sequence is not (Henson, 2001). Continuity is the reintroduction of content at progressively more complex levels often seen in a spiral design (Olivia, 1988). Continuity focuses on the relationship between subsequent learning experience and its predecessor (Armstrong, 1989). For example, multiplication is built on the interdependence of what is taught previously. It is almost impossible to understand multiplication if you do not conceptually understand patterns and addition.

Articulation refers to the interrelatedness of various aspects of the curriculum. Albert Oliver (1977) suggests that articulation refers to the relationship between two or more curricular elements that is simultaneous rather than sequential. The term is often used to connect learner experiences had in one discipline with those encountered in another. For example, curriculum organizers might arrange to have a U.S. History course and an American Literature course arranged chronologically, so that students could study the political and social history of the Civil War period at the same time as they studied the literary works of the period. Articulation can also be used to describe the meshing of organizing elements across school levels, such as linking elementary and middle school curricula in reading.

Some curriculum experts view articulation as being both horizontal and vertical in nature. Oliver (1977) used the term articulation synonymously with horizontal articulation or correlation. He also equated the concept of vertical articulation with continuity. For example, teaching four consecutive years of Spanish in a row is vertical articulation (i.e., continuity) and teaching geography and history of the Oregon trail in a 3-hour block of time would be considered horizontal articulation (i.e., correlation).

Sequencing, continuity, and articulation are similar, but different. Sequencing is the order or logical arrangement of content within lessons, units, courses, or grades. Continuity is the planned reintroduction of units of content throughout the grades at ever increasing levels of complexity. Articulation is the planned meshing of units of content across grade levels, so as to assure that the next grade level takes up where the previous grade level left off (Olivia, 1988).

3.9 Transfer of Training

Whatever is taught in the school should in some way possess transfer value. **Transfer training** is the ability to learn some behavior, knowledge, and/or skill in one situation and then apply that behavior, knowledge, and/or skill in a new situation. The transfer of learning or transfer of training refers to the effect that knowledge or skills acquired in one area have on problem solving or knowledge acquisition in other areas. For example, if a student learns about the law of supply and demand when studying world oil supplies and the price of gas at the pump, he or she should also be able to apply the same concept to the effect of drought on grain supplies and the price of cereal at the grocery store.

Olivia (1988) summarizes some current beliefs about transfer:

- Transfer is at the heart of education; it is a—if not the—goal of education.
- The closer the classroom situation is to the out-of-classroom situation, the greater is the transfer.
- Transfer can be increased and improved if teachers consciously teach for transfer.
- Transfer is greater when teachers help pupils derive underlying generalizations and to make applications of those generalizations.
- Generally speaking, when the learner discovers knowledge for himself or herself, transfer is enhanced (p. 514).

3.10 Curriculum Axioms

Peter Olivia (1988) in his book titled *Developing the Curriculum* talks about curriculum principles. Curriculum, as a discipline, possesses an organized set of principles or axioms that govern it. Curriculum axioms may be viewed as whole truths, partial truths, or hypothesis. While all function as operating principles, they are distinguished by their known effectiveness or by their degree of risk. Olivia contends that since many of the principles that practitioners subscribe to have not been fully tested, we might better be served to call them axioms or self-evident truths. The axioms stem not only from disciplines outside of professional education but also from folklore of curriculum, observation, experimental data, and common sense. Listed below are his "10 Axioms for Curriculum Development":

- Curriculum change is inevitable and desirable.
- The curriculum is a product of its time.
- Curriculum changes of earlier periods often coexist with and overlap curriculum changes of later periods.
- Curriculum change results only as people are changed.
- Curriculum development is a cooperative group activity.
- Curriculum development is basically a process of making choices from among alternatives.
- Curriculum development never ends.
- Curriculum development is more effective if it is a comprehensive, not piecemeal process.
- Curriculum development is more effective when it follows a systematic process.
- Curriculum development starts from where the curriculum is.

These axioms need careful consideration from curriculum developers and decision makers.

Chapter Summary

In this chapter, we have examined several curriculum definitions and explored several key concepts for selecting and organizing content. One final thought for curriculum development consideration is "less is more and different is better." With the knowledge explosion, it is virtually impossible to cover all aspects of content within a discipline. Part of the impetus for the development of state standards was to move away from teaching subject matter in a manner that was often described as coverage that "was a mile long and only an inch wide." Most educators today espouse to be constructivists and constructivism involves problem solving. Because constructivism requires more time than direct teaching methods of instruction, students spend more time on fewer activities, which they explore in greater depth. In summary, it is better to focus on the depth of understanding rather than the breadth of content coverage!

A Fable: If You Are Riding a Dead Horse, Get Off

DIRECTIONS: *Read the Curriculum fable. Think about the connection between the fable and the curriculum concepts presented in this chapter. In class with a small group, you will come to consensus on the moral of the fable. Be prepared to share. Visit the online book to read the article.*

Check for Mastery: Performance Expectations

DIRECTIONS: *You rated yourself on performance expectations at the start of this chapter. Have you now mastered each performance expectation? Rate yourself using the Likert scale online. Compare this to how you rated yourself at the beginning of this chapter. If you do not know an expectation, go back to the text and re-read the information.*

Summary Learning Activity: Curriculum Axioms

DIRECTIONS: *An axiom is defined as a self-evident truth. Listed below are 10 axioms for the curriculum development process. Read each axiom and decide if you agree or disagree with the principle. Support your decision by citing appropriate explanations or examples. Be prepared to share in class.*

☐ *Agree* ☐ *Disagree*	1.	Curriculum change is inevitable and desirable. **Support:**
☐ *Agree* ☐ *Disagree*	2.	The curriculum is a product of its time. **Support:**
☐ *Agree* ☐ *Disagree*	3.	Curriculum changes of earlier periods often coexist with and overlap curriculum changes of later periods. **Support:**

☐ *Agree* ☐ *Disagree*	4.	Curriculum change results only as people are changed. **Support:**
☐ *Agree* ☐ *Disagree*	5.	Curriculum development is a cooperative group activity. **Support:**
☐ *Agree* ☐ *Disagree*	6.	Curriculum development is basically a process of making choices from among alternatives. **Support:**
☐ *Agree* ☐ *Disagree*	7.	Curriculum development never ends. **Support:**
☐ *Agree* ☐ *Disagree*	8.	Curriculum development is more effective if it is a comprehensive—not piecemeal—process. **Support:**
☐ *Agree* ☐ *Disagree*	9.	Curriculum development is more effective when it follows a systematic process. **Support:**
☐ *Agree* ☐ *Disagree*	10.	Curriculum development starts from where the curriculum is. **Support:**

Supplemental Learning Exercises

1. One's definition of curriculum is a matter of one's perception. Several definitions that are commonly found in the professional literature were cited in this chapter. Reread each definition carefully and highlight its main idea or ideas. Review the idea(s) in each definition and develop a list of four to six themes commonly used to define the word curriculum.
2. Research indicates that students learn best from applied, integrated, authentic, and contextual curriculum experiences. To the lay person these four "buzz words" may be unfamiliar. Your task is to develop an analogy to explain those words. Write your analogy in the form of a poem. Please note the example provided.

Applied, Integrated, Authentic, and Contextual

Curriculum is like a SHOE

Shutterstock.com

Because both are
uncomfortable when new
but the more they are used
the better it feels.
They need to be laced together.
Both sometimes need an occasional
polish.

3. Content selection and organization deal with the heart of the curriculum. A number of basic terms related to curriculum design comprise part of the professional language of curriculum professionals and decision makers. Among the terms introduced in this chapter were scope, sequence, articulation, continuity, integration, relevance, balance, and transfer. These terms can often be misunderstood and confusing. Devise a scheme, model, illustration, graphic organizer, or some other creative method to define and differentiate among these terms. Share your idea with the rest of your classmates.
4. One of the methods discussed for selecting content was legal constraints. Review the requirements in your state that govern what must be taught in public schools.
   - What specific courses are mentioned?
   - What kinds of content topics are alluded to in the state standards that must be included in those courses?
   - What requirements are there related to how much time must be spent on teaching specific subjects or topics?
   - Do the same requirements apply to every learner?

5. In this chapter you discovered seven different methods for presenting content. Select a content topic in your discipline and illustrate that topic using each of the seven methods for presenting content.

Final Test

DIRECTIONS: *Read each question or statement below. Select the appropriate answer or write the correct answer in the blank provided.*

_____ 1. Curriculum is best defined as:
- A. a means of instruction.
- B. a plan to enact.
- C. an interactive process.
- D. exposure to information.

T F 2. A sound understanding of curriculum will prepare teachers to better support positive reform efforts while suppressing undesirable trends.

_____ 3. All of the following would be examples of the hidden curriculum ***except***:
- A. learning how to get along with your peers through recess activities on the playground.
- B. learning about competition and teamwork by participating in co-curricular activities.
- C. learning about responsibility by completing your homework assignments on time.
- D. learning about a specific procedure by performing a laboratory experiment.

_____ 4. What criterion for selecting content might be described as "how basic is that content to the discipline under study?"
- A. Content significance
- B. Content utility
- C. Content complexity
- D. Content interest

T F 5. Most educators operationalize their curriculum in terms of the content they teach.

_____ 6. What is the best descriptor of presenting content in a narrative/summary format?
- A. Graphic + Topic
- B. Question + Topic
- C. Activity + Topic
- D. Details + Topic

_____ 7. Which of the following is an advantage of the concept mapping method of presenting content?
- A. Illustrates visual concepts and relationships
- B. Provides supporting details
- C. Identifies what students should know and do
- D. Supports research and inquiry practices

_____ 8. What method of presenting content is illustrated by the example to the right?
- A. Essential questions
- B. Outcome
- C. Standards
- D. Tasks

> **1.** Define energy.
> **2.** Compare and contrast different forms of energy.
> **3.** Differentiate between kinetic and potential energy.
> **4.** Solve energy problems.

____ 9. Which methods of presenting content are more student-oriented?
- A. Outline and outcome
- B. Task and outcome
- C. Concept map and task
- D. Outcome and summary

____ 10. What is sacrificed as teachers move across the curriculum continuum from left to right?
- A. Amount of content covered
- B. Student achievement
- C. Teacher autonomy
- D. Student engagement

____ 11. Sequence describes the:
- A. order of the curriculum.
- B. amount of detail in the curriculum.
- C. format of the curriculum.
- D. transferability of the curriculum.

____ 12. Which of the following is ***not*** a dimension of scope?
- A. Continuity
- B. Integration
- C. Balance
- D. Relevance

____ 13. Which of the following descriptions illustrates a taxonomic sequence?
- A. Movement from simple to complex
- B. Movement from past to present
- C. Movement from parts to a whole
- D. Movement from concrete to abstract

____ 14. What term refers to the blending, fusion, or unification of disciplines?
- A. Balance
- B. Articulation
- C. Integration
- D. Continuity

____ 15. Listed to the right are the first seven units in an American History course. What type of sequence is being illustrated by the unit titles?
- A. Topical
- B. Thematic
- C. Chronological
- D. Taxonomic

> **1.** Our Country's Beginnings
> **2.** Developing the English Colonies
> **3.** The New Nation Is Born
> **4.** Expanding the Nation's Frontiers
> **5.** The North and South Conflict
> **6.** The Nation in a New Industrial Age
> **7.** The United States: A New World of Power

DIRECTIONS: *Write a brief response.*

1. What is "transfer training?" Cite an example from your discipline.
2. Defend the statement "less is more and different is better" as it pertains to curriculum development.

Works Cited and Suggested Readings

Armstrong, David. (1989). *Developing and Documenting the Curriculum.* Needham Heights, MA: Allyn and Bacon.

Bobbitt, Franklin. (1918). *The Curriculum.* Boston, MA: Houghton Mifflin.

Bloom, Benjamin S. (1958). Ideas, Problems, and Methods of Inquiry. In Dressel, P. (Ed.), *Integration of Educational Experiences* (57th Yearbook, National Society for the Study of Education, Part 3). Chicago, IL: University of Chicago Press.

Caswell, Hollis & Campbell, Doak. (1935). *Curriculum Development.* New York, NY: American Book Company.

Dewey, John. (1902). *The Child and the Curriculum.* Chicago, IL: University of Chicago Press.

Doll, Ronald C. (1989). *Curriculum Development: Decision Making and Process* (7th ed.). Boston, MA: Allyn and Bacon.

Eisner, Elliot, W. (1985). *The Educational Imagination on the Design and Evaluation of School Programs.* New York, NY: Macmillan.

Gagne, Robert. W. (1967). Curriculum Research and the Promotion of Learning. In R. W. Tyler, R. M. Gagne, & M. Scriven (Eds.), *Perspectives of Curricular Evaluation.* Chicago, IL: Rand McNally.

Goodlad, John (Ed.). (1987). *The Ecology of School Renewal.* National Society for the Study of Education, Eighty-Sixth Yearbook, Part 1. Chicago, IL: University of Chicago Press.

Halverson, Paul, M. (1961). The Meaning of Balance. *Balance in the Curriculum* (1961 Yearbook). Alexandria, VA: Association for Supervision and Curriculum Development (ASCD).

Hass, Glen. (1987). *Curriculum Planning: A New Approach* (5th ed.). Boston, MA: Allyn and Bacon.

Harnack, Robert. (1968). *The Teacher: Decision Maker and Curriculum Planner.* Philadelphia, PA: International Textbook Company.

Henson, Kenneth. (2001). *Curriculum Planning Integrating Multiculturalism, Constructivism, and Educational Reform* (2nd ed.). New York, NY: McGraw-Hill Higher Education.

Hidden Curriculum. (2016). *The glossary of educational reform.* Retrieved from: http://edglossary.org/hidden-curriculum.

Hunkins, Francis P. (1980). *Curriculum Development: Program Improvement.* Columbus, OH: Charles Merrill Publishing Company.

Hyman, Ronald (Ed.). (1973). *Approaches in Curriculum.* Englewood Cliffs, NJ: Prentiss-Hall.

Jackson, Philip W. (1968). *Life in Classrooms.* New York, NY: Holt, Rinehart and Winston.

Johnson, Mauritz, Jr. (1967). Definitions and Models in Curriculum Theory. *Educational Theory, 17*(2), 127–139.

Konieczka, Joanna. (2013). The Hidden Curriculum. *Advanced Research in Scientific Areas,* 249–252. Retrieved from: http://www.arsa-conf.com.

McNeil, John. (2008). *Contemporary Curriculum: In Thought and Action* (7th ed.). New York, NY: John Wiley & Sons, Inc.

Oliver, Albert. (1977). *Curriculum Improvement: A Guide to Problems, Principles, and Process* (2nd ed.). New York, NY: Harper and Row.

Olivia, Peter F. (1988). *Developing the Curriculum* (2nd ed.). Statesboro, GA: Georgia Southern College.

Popham, James, W. & Baker, Eva. (1970). *Systematic Instruction.* Englewood Cliffs, NJ: Prentice-Hall.

Rule, Ian, A.C. (1973). *A Philosophical Inquiry into the Meaning(s) of Curriculum.* Unpublished Doctoral Dissertation. New York University.

Saylor, Galen, Alexander, William, & Lewis, Authur. (1981). *Curriculum Planning for Better Teaching and Learning* (4th ed.). New York, NY: Holt, Rinehart, and Winston.

Schubert, William. (1986). *Curriculum; Perspective, Paradigm, and Possibility.* New York, NY: Macmillan.

Smith, B. Othanel, Stanley, William O., & Shores, J. Harlan. (1969). *Teachers for the Real World.* Washington, D.C.: American Association of Colleges for Teacher Education.

Spencer, Herbert. (1861). *Education: Intellectual, Moral and Physical.* New York, NY: D. Appleton.

Taba, Hilda. (1962). *Curriculum Development: Theory and Practice.* New York, NY: Harcourt Brace Jovanovich.

Tanner, Daniel & Tanner, Laurel. (1980). *Curriculum Development: Theory into Practice* (2nd ed.). New York, NY: Macmillan Company.

Thompson, Sue & Gregg, Larry. (1997). Reculturing Middle Schools for Meaningful Change. *Middle School Journal, 28*(5), 27–31.

Tyler, Ralph W. (1957). *The Curriculum Then and Now.* In Proceedings of the 1956 Invitational Conference on Testing Problems. Princeton, NJ: Educational Testing Service.

Wiles, Jon & Bondi, Joseph C. (2015). *Curriculum Development: A Guide to Practice* (9rd ed.). Boston, MA: Pearson Publishing.

Zais, Robert. (1976). *Curriculum Principles and Foundation.* New York, NY: Thomas Y. Crowell Company.

Rawpixel.com/Shutterstock.com

HQuality/Shutterstock.com

Chapter 4

Exploring the Historical Perspective of Curriculum Development

> "So long as there is education, there has got to be a curriculum."
>
> Ralph Tyler

Anticipatory Set: Pretest

***DIRECTIONS:** One of the functions of an Anticipatory Set exercise is to assess prior knowledge. Pretests serve as great tools for this function. Complete the pretest for this chapter to assess your prior knowledge on the history of the curriculum development. Check the correct answer.*

beeboys/Shutterstock.com

☐ T	☐ F	1.	An examination of the curriculum past can help identify problems or issues that curriculum developers have struggled with before.
☐ T	☐ F	2.	John Dewey is considered the "father of curriculum development."
☐ T	☐ F	3.	John Dewey believed that the goal of curriculum should be the acquisition of subject matter content.
☐ T	☐ F	4.	Franklin Bobbitt is given credit for being the first educator to study the curriculum development process.
☐ T	☐ F	5.	Ralph Tyler's work was greatly influenced by John Dewey's work.
☐ T	☐ F	6.	Ralph Tyler's sources of needs included the philosophy of education and psychology of learning.
☐ T	☐ F	7.	Ralph Tyler believed that learning experiences were the most important part of the curriculum.
☐ T	☐ F	8.	Ralph Tyler's principles were widely welcomed in classrooms and adopted by curriculum developers over the past 50 years.
☐ T	☐ F	9.	Hilda Taba's curriculum model is deductive, whereas Ralph Tyler's curriculum model is inductive.
☐ T	☐ F	10.	The Process of Education was once a syllabus for a curriculum course that Jerome Bruner taught.
☐ T	☐ F	11.	Structure of the disciplines refers to a discipline's basic concepts and methods of inquiry.
☐ T	☐ F	12.	Bruner was not an advocate of conceptual learning and did not believe that students could construct their own knowledge for themselves.
☐ T	☐ F	13.	According to Bruner, the curriculum of a subject is determined most by its underlying principles that give structure to that subject.
☐ T	☐ F	14.	In the spiral curriculum, learning goes from simple to complex and concepts are revisited over time.
☐ T	☐ F	15.	In the spiral curriculum, scope is vertical in nature and sequence is horizontal in nature.
☐ T	☐ F	16.	Curriculum developers who employ a spiral design architecture plan their units with the end in mind.

Chapter Overview

Lost in the woods: Let's time travel back to early 1800. How do you find your way? You would first look at the sun to see if the direction is obvious. If not, find a stick, and look at the stick's shadow to find the directions. Hopefully, there would also be a landmark such as a very large birch tree you may remember. You would then proceed in the correct direction to head back to the camp site.

Lost in the woods: Let's time travel back to early 1900. How do you find your way? You would use your compass. As the compass points to the magnetic north, you would then proceed in the correct direction to head back to the camp site.

Lost in the woods: Let's time travel back to 1950. How do you find your way? You would check your map, a paper representation of the area you are in, with features of roads and trails. You would then proceed in the correct direction to head back to the camp site.

Lost in the woods: Let's time travel back to 2015. How do you find your way? Get out your GPS or ask Siri! Even in the remote woods, you would then proceed in the correct direction to head back to the camp site.

How is the scenario lost in the woods like the historical perspective of curriculum development? Throughout the history of curriculum, the goal has not changed. The goal is always to know where you are headed in order to plan succinctly. Just as the history of being lost, the camper needs to know the final destination. In schools, there have been many curricular models, some sustaining through the years. Just as the compass and maps, curricular concepts have also stood the test of time. While they may get fancier and more modernized, the basic concepts remain intact.

Curriculum developers can profit from an understanding of the history of curriculum planning. Although the history of education dates back to humanity's beginnings, in this chapter, the focus is on key scholars and their works or events that have been critical to the evolution of curriculum development process. Two works, one by Ralph Tyler (1949) and the other by Jerome Bruner (1960), will be discussed in great depth because of their historical and contemporary significance. In this chapter, teachers will be able to reflect on how the historical events cited have had an impact on the curriculum reforms and movements on this generation of educators.

Performance Expectations

DIRECTIONS: *How well do you know the performance expectations? Rate your knowledge of each expectation using this Likert scale. You will rate yourself again at the end of the chapter. This is for your information to assess your own learning. Visit the online book to record your answers.*

1 = I do not have any knowledge of this concept.
2 = I have minimal knowledge of this concept.
3 = I have some understanding of this concept.
4 = I have a satisfactory understanding of this concept.
5 = I am confident in my understanding of this concept.

Masson/Shutterstock.com

This chapter should prepare you to:

Rating	#	Performance Expectations
	1.	Justify the importance of understanding the historical perspective of the curriculum development process.
	2.	Describe early work in curriculum development, especially the contributions of John Dewey and Franklin Bobbitt.
	3.	Explain why Ralph Tyler is considered the "father of curriculum development."
	4.	List Tyler's four questions that guide the Tyler rationale discussed in his book, *Basic Principles of Curriculum and Instruction.*
	5.	Explain what element of the curriculum development process that Tyler believed was the most important.
	6.	Diagram Tyler's Model for curriculum construction.
	7.	Assess the significance of the Tyler rationale and model for curriculum development.
	8.	Outline Taba's Model for curriculum development.
	9.	Compare and contrast Tyler's and Taba's models for curriculum development.
	10.	Summarize Jerome Bruner's contributions to field of curriculum.
	11.	Explain Bruner's concept of "structure of the disciplines." Why is it so important?
	12.	Discuss Bruner's four themes found in his book, *The Process of Education.*
	13.	Interpret the meaning of "There is a difference in degree, not in kind."
	14.	Analyze the principles and benefits associated with the spiral curriculum.
	15.	Apply the concepts of the spiral architecture in your discipline.

4.1 A Historical Perspective

A sense of history is very important for anyone working in the field of curriculum. Without an understanding of history, many contemporary curriculum ideas and practices would seem odd or even illogical. An examination of the curriculum past can help identify problems or issues that curriculum developers may struggle with today. Reviewing the history of curriculum thought and practice can add perspective and develop an understanding of the prominent processes associated with curriculum decision making (McNeil, 1990). The history of curriculum is particularly instructive because of its cyclic nature. A historical perspective also helps curriculum developers focus on the long-term goals of education rather than on the events and programs of the moment.

4.2 Latin Grammar Schools

This history begins only 27 years after the landing of the first English-speaking pilgrims at Plymouth Rock, when they established the first "grammar" school in 1635. The Latin grammar school is the forerunner of our modern day elementary and secondary schools (Armstrong et al., 1997). Early European settlers came to America to escape religious persecution, and they pursued their personal religious beliefs with vigor. Martin Luther had taught that the Bible must be read to ward off the work of the Devil, and so the first known education regulation, the Old Deluder Satan Act (1647), established schools for that purpose (Zais, 1976). The curriculum consisted of reading, writing, arithmetic, Latin and Greek, and classical literature which blended with the religious denominationalism coming from the heritage of the Protestant Reformation.

Among the Puritans were more than a 100 graduates of Oxford and Cambridge universities. Believing in the benefits of a rigorous, high quality education, they were determined to provide equally excellent educational opportunities for their sons. Consequently, the General Court of Massachusetts appropriated approximately $1,000 for a new college. A young minister, who was dying of tuberculosis, willed half of his estate (including 400 books valued at $2,000) to the new college. This gift was given by John Harvard, and that university bears his namesake today (Henson, 2001).

4.3 John Dewey and Progressivism

No discussion on the history of curriculum would be complete without mentioning the contributions of John Dewey (1859–1952), an American philosopher, psychologist, and educational reformer. In his own laboratory school at the University of Chicago, where he chaired the Philosophy and Psychology departments, John Dewey introduced a curriculum that featured manual training and vocational coursework (like sewing and shop work). He believed that the traditional curriculum no longer met the needs of the new society created by the forces of the industrial revolution. Dewey was a champion of progressivism and the progressivist philosophy proclaims "education is life" and "learning by doing" (Olivia, 1988).

Dewey did not believe that the goal of the curriculum should be merely the acquisition of subject matter. He argued that subject matter was interesting only when it served the needs and interest of the learner. Dewey maintained it was time to subordinate subject matter to the learner. According to Dewey (1902),

> "The child is the starting point, the center, and the end. His development, his growth, is the ideal. It alone furnishes he standard . . . Learning is active . . . It is he and not the subject matter which determines both quantity and quality of learning . . . The only significant method is the method of the mind as it reaches out and assimilates. Subject matter is but spiritual food, possible nutritive material. It cannot digest itself; it cannot of its own accord turn into bone, muscle, and blood" (pp. 7–14).

He argued that in order for education to be most effective, content must be presented in a way that allows the student to relate the information to prior experiences, thus deepening the connection with this new knowledge. Contemporary pedagogies, such as hands-on learning, experiential education, and problem-based learning, all incorporate Dewey's beliefs and ideas about learning.

4.4 Franklin Bobbitt

As noted in an earlier chapter, the field of curriculum was born in the United States in 1918 with the publication of Franklin Bobbitt's small book simply entitled *Curriculum* (Saylor, Alexander, & Lewis, 1981). He felt that the curriculum had to adapt to the needs of an individual and to the needs of the new industrial society; people should not be taught what they would never use. Moreover, Franklin Bobbitt (1876–1956) voiced for the first time the importance of studying the curriculum development process. He articulated that it was simply not enough to develop new curricula, but that there was also a need to learn about how new curricula can best be developed (McNeil, 1990). As Bobbitt (1924) himself later said when discussing his experiences as Director of Education in the Philippines, "we needed principles of curriculum making."

Bobbitt created five steps for curriculum making (McNeil, 1990):

1. **Analysis of Human Experience.** The first step is to separate the broad range of human experience into major fields (e.g., social life, vocation, and citizenship).
2. **Job Analysis.** In step two, the major fields are broken down into more specific activities (similar to task analysis, resulting is a list of duties).
3. **Deriving Objectives.** The third step is to derive the objectives of education from statements of the abilities needed to perform the activities (e.g., examples from the language field included to pronounce words properly, to write legibly with ease and speed, and to use grammatically correct language).
4. **Selecting Objectives.** The fourth step is to select from the list of objectives those which are to serve as the basis for planning activities for the students (guidelines such as eliminate this and emphasize this were included).

5. **Planning in Detail.** The last step is to lay out activities, experiences, and opportunities that would be needed to obtain the objectives (details for each activity need to be laid out and the final plans approved by the administration).

Although the expectations for schools have been expanded, elements of Bobbitt's plan can still be found in curriculum development processes that are employed today. The process of curriculum development has remained fairly constant over time. In the 20th century, the structure of curriculum development remained primarily a filling-in activity. Today, through analysis, design, implementation, and evaluation, curriculum developers set goals, plan experiences, select and organize content, and assess outcomes of school programs. These constant processes have contributed to the emergence of a predictable structure in curriculum planning (Wiles & Bondi, 2015).

4.5 Ralph Tyler: Father of Curriculum Development

Ralph Tyler (1902–1994) is known as the father of curriculum development. Ralph W. Tyler graduated with a Ph.D. from the University of Chicago in 1927. Approximately 10 years later, he went on to serve as Director of Research and headed the evaluation staff of the "Eight-Year Study" (1933–1941) at Ohio State. This landmark study involved 30 secondary schools and 300 colleges and universities and addressed the narrowness and rigidity in high school curricula. In 1938, Tyler was lured by Robert Hutchinson to leave Ohio State University to become Chair of the Education Department at the University of Chicago (his alma mater), where he gained real prominence and continued his curriculum work. In 1953, Tyler became the first director of the Center for Advanced Study in the Behavioral Sciences at Stanford University, a position he held until his retirement in 1967. Additionally, the Carnegie Corporation asked Tyler to chair the committee that would eventually develop the National Assessment of Educational Progress (NAEP) in 1969. Tyler probably could not have predicted that over the course of time he would become the most prominent name in curriculum studies in the United States (Pinar, Reynolds, Slattery, & Taubman, 1995; Nowakowski, 1983; Chall, 1976).

Video: Tyler's Syllabus

DIRECTIONS: *This video is about Ralph W. Tyler and his syllabus that became a book. The book outlines his model for curriculum development. For the next class, you will complete a timed pair-share with a classmate about this video. A* ***timed pair-share*** *is a strategy that is a deliberate way to have a guided discussion with a classmate and all voices are heard. Each person gets 30 seconds to 1 minute to share their viewpoint. The next 30 seconds to 1 minute, the other person shares. During this time, the opposite partner is an active listener, without interrupting. When the time is over, the pair can then freely discuss each other's opinions and have a rich discussion. Visit the online book to view the 5-minute video.*

Even though Ralph Tyler published more than 700 articles and sixteen books, he is most remembered for a "little" bestselling book entitled *The Basic Principles of Curriculum and Instruction.* Nearly 90,000 copies have been sold (McNeil, 1990) and the book has since been reprinted in 36 editions (Laanemets and Kalamee-Ruubel, 2013), shaping curriculum and instructional design to this day. The 128-page book was based upon findings gathered from the Eight-Year Study (Ornstein and Hunkins, 1998). While conducting the study, Tyler initially formulated his approach to education research which was grounded in the belief that successful teaching and learning techniques can be determined as a result of scientific study. By applying such methods during the Eight-Year Study, Tyler soon determined that evaluation of student behaviors proved to be a highly appropriate means for determining educational success or failure. In another book, *Appraising and Recording Student Progress,* Tyler wrote:

> "Any device which provides valid evidence regarding the progress of students toward educational objectives is appropriate . . . The selection of evaluation techniques should be made in terms of the appropriateness of that technique for the kind of behavior to be appraised" (Tyler, cited in Pinar et al., 1995, p. 136).

In *Basic Principles of Curriculum and Instruction* (1949), Tyler formalized and documented his thoughts on viewing, analyzing, and interpreting the curriculum and instructional program of an educational institution. Tyler stated his intention was to help the student of education to understand more fully the kinds of problems involved in developing a curriculum and plan of instruction and to acquire some techniques by which these basic problems may be attacked. Tyler also was greatly influenced by the Progressive education movement and the works of its founder, John Dewey (Denham, 2002; McNeil, 1990). Like his mentor, John Dewey, Tyler believed that teachers should encourage children to become actively engaged in discovering what the world is like. He described learning as taking place through the changed behavior of the students; today we would call this a student-centered approach. Reminiscent of Dewey, Tyler (1949) writes: "It is what he does that he learns, not what the teacher does" (p. 63).

4.6 Tyler Rationale

Tyler's book laid out a deceptively simple structure for delivering and evaluating instruction consisting of four parts that became known as the Tyler Rationale. Tyler continued to cultivate his ideas on the rationale, using it in a syllabus for his course on curriculum and instruction and eventually decided to expand and publish the document in 1949. His four-part rationale consists of classical principles focusing on purposes and objectives, instructional strategies and content, organization of learning experiences, and assessment and evaluation that was designed based on four questions. (The questions also serve as the headings for the chapters of his book.) Specifically, the four questions are:

1. What educational purposes should the school seek to attain? (Defining appropriate learning objectives.)
2. How can learning experiences be selected which are likely to be useful in attaining these objectives? (Introducing useful learning experiences.)
3. How can learning experiences be organized for effective instruction? (Organizing experiences to maximize their effect.)
4. How can the effectiveness of learning experiences be evaluated? (Evaluating the process and revising the areas that were not effective.)

The cornerstone element of the rationale was the process for selecting educational objectives. In describing objectives, Tyler referred to them as "goals," "educational objectives," and "educational purposes." In his book, Tyler validates this point:

> "Nevertheless, if an educational program is to be planned and if efforts for continued improvement are to be made, it is very necessary to have some conception of the goals that are being aimed at. These educational objectives become the criteria by which materials are selected, content is outlined, instructional procedures are developed, and tests and examinations are prepared. All aspects of the educational program are really a means to accomplish basic educational purposes. Hence, if we are to study an educational program systematically and intelligently, we must first be sure as to the educational objectives aimed at" (p. 3).

Although Tyler proposed a rather comprehensive framework for curriculum development, the selection of objectives received the greatest attention from his colleagues. The Tyler process for collecting objectives is widely known and practiced in curriculum circles (Olivia, 1988).

4.7 The Tyler Model

Curriculum development is an ongoing, dynamic process whereby the choices of designing a learning experience for students are made and then activated through a series of coordinated activities. Ralph Tyler's curriculum model (shown in Figure 1) is one the best known and most used models for curriculum development today. Please note that Tyler never made use of a diagram in describing his process; Popham and Baker were the first to illustrate the model in graphic form (Olivia,1988). His principles were the accepted approach to curriculum development for almost 30 years and they guide the essential questions of curriculum development today. However, they now are applied to newer ideas and considerations that extend or reinterpret his principles (Howard, 2007). One could almost dare to say that every certified teacher in America has developed curriculum either directly or indirectly using this model or one of the many variations (Thomas, 2014).

Remember Tyler stated that the educational objectives were the most important component of the curriculum development process. He also believed that the structure of the school curriculum had to be responsive to three central factors, or sources, that represent the main elements of an educative experience (1) the nature of the learner (i.e., developmental factors, learner interests and needs, life experiences); (2) the values and aims of society (i.e., democratizing principles, values, and attitudes); and (3) knowledge of subject matter (i.e., what is believed to be worthy and usable knowledge) (Ralph Tyler, 1902–1994). Tyler recommended that curriculum planners identify "general objectives" or goals by collecting data from these three sources.

Check for Understanding: Understanding the Tyler Model

DIRECTIONS: *Tyler is the Father of Curriculum. As you ponder the information about Tyler, think about three concepts. This strategy is called* ***Square-Circle-Call Out****. Write one thing you are "square" with, one thing that is still "circling" in your head, and write one thing that you would "call out" and share with another teacher as you absorbed the information about Tyler, the Father of Curriculum. Visit the online book to complete the activity.*

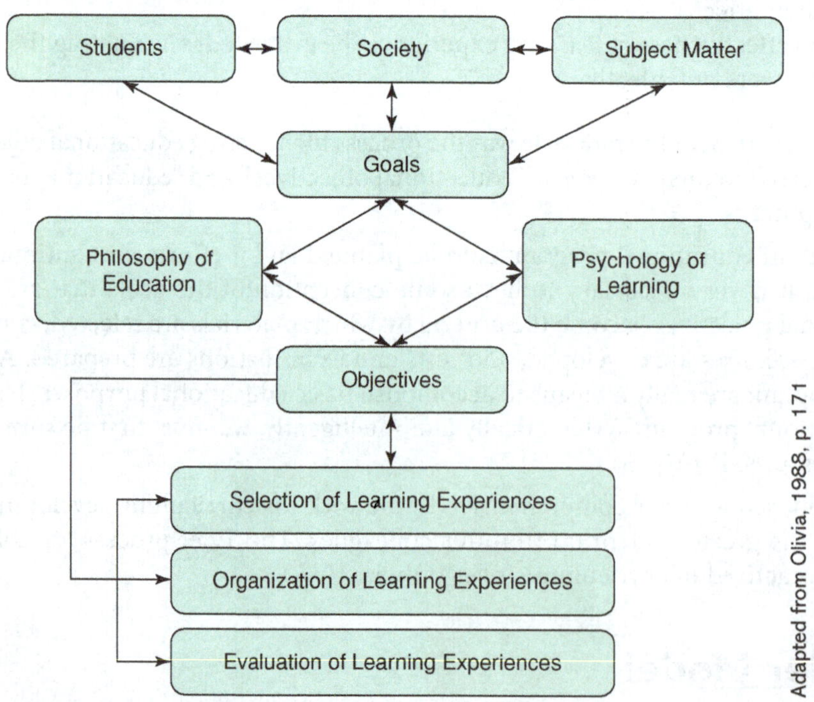

Figure 1: Tyler's Model

Tyler's recommendation that curriculum developers identify goals by gathering data from three sources of needs (i.e., students, society, and subject matter) was heavily influenced by John Dewey. Dewey (1902) had observed earlier that "the fundamental factors in the educational process are (1) the learner, (2) the society, and (3) organized subject matter" (p. 4). These factors set the stage for defining curriculum parameters. By 1945, these three general sources of needs were finding acceptance in most curriculum literature. Hilda Taba (1962), for instance, discussed the three sources of data in curriculum planning as "(1) the study of society, (2) studies of learners, and (3) studies of subject matter content" (p. 58). By the early 1960s, Taba had further refined the study of society to mean cultural demands—a reflection of the changing social milieu of the school.

After identifying the goals, curriculum planners refine these broad educational purposes by filtering them through two screens (1) the philosophy of education for the school and (2) the psychology of learning. Through the screening process, the number of objectives will be reduced, leaving only the ones that are most significant and feasible. The "general objectives" that successfully pass through the screens will become the "specific instructional objectives" that are incorporated into the curriculum (Olivia, 1988). As guide to instructional planning, the objectives that survive must be stated in a form that makes clear the content the learner must use, the situation in which the knowledge is to apply, and the kind of behavior to be exhibited by the learner (McNeil, 1990).

The last three steps of Tyler's model include the selection, organization, and evaluation of learning experiences. Tyler (1949) defines learning experiences as "the interactions between the learner and the extended conditions in the environment to which he (she) can react" (p. 63). He uses the phrase "learning experience" to include a plan for providing learning opportunities that take into account both the previous experience and perceptions the learner brings to the situation (McNeil, 1990). Tyler proposes using the selected objectives as the basis for choosing learning experiences. Once the learning experiences are selected, the activities then are organized sequentially, developed in scope, and interrelated so they focus on the same outcomes. Evaluation, the final step in the model, was to be used to determine whether the objectives were in fact being attained (Doll, 1989).

Ralph Tyler (McNeil, 1990) proposed five general principles for identifying or developing learning experiences (1) appropriate practice (i.e., a means-ends context in which objectives—the ends, determine learning opportunities—the means); (2) satisfaction (i.e., the learning opportunity should be satisfying for students); (3) success (i.e., deciding whether the learning opportunity is within the range of possibilities for the student); (4) multiple approaches (i.e., many different activities can be used to attain the same purpose—utility); and (5) multiple outcomes (i.e., select learning opportunities that are likely to contribute to multiple desirable outcomes—economy).

In *Basic Principles of Curriculum and Instruction*, Tyler (1949) stated his intention to "help the student of education to understand more fully the kinds of problems involved in developing a curriculum and plan of instruction and to acquire some techniques by which these basic problems may be attacked" (p. 1). Tyler's basic principles were widely welcomed in classrooms and curriculum texts across the United States in 1949. Their functionality was well received and teachers generally appreciated the ease with which they could be applied to the daily work of curriculum planning. When the Association for Supervision and Curriculum Development (ASCD) polled six prominent members concerning the worth of the Tylerian model "for current curriculum development," four of the six favored it.

It would be nearly 30 years, in fact, before any significant criticisms were waged against Tyler's work. The most well-known criticism of the rationale makes the argument that the rationale is historically wedded to social efficiency traditions. Some criticisms have centered on conceptions of how objectives should be stated. The argument is that Tyler has provided no real basis for selecting objectives, but rather he has established a confining system of means-ends reasoning with objectives always being the point of beginning (Doll, 1989). Two of the respondents to the ASCD poll criticized the model for failing to address questions of value, specifically questions of moral, political, ethical, or aesthetic nature. In essence, they found the "model too rational and thus insufficiently real" (pp. 4–5). Others have complained that Tyler's rationale is overtly managerial and linear in its position on the school curriculum. Finally, a few critics have characterized it as outdated and theoretical, suitable only to curriculum leaders or administration keen on controlling the school curriculum in ways that are unresponsive to teachers and learners.

Tyler offered no substantive response to these criticisms, believing that criticism of his curriculum development work required some discussion of an alternative model, which none of the critics provided (Ralph Tyler, 1902–1994). However, Tyler did, when asked later, reemphasize the importance of learner participation in the curriculum process (Saylor et al., 1981). After affirming that his 4 questions are still valid, Tyler commented:

> "I would give greater emphasis now to careful consideration of the implications for curriculum development of the active role of the student in the learning experience. I would also give much greater emphasis to a comprehensive examination of the non-school areas of student learning in developing the curriculum" (cited in Molnar & Zahorik, 1977, p. 37).

Tyler concluded, "Where possible and appropriate, the student themselves should participate in the planning and evaluation of the curriculum" (cited in Molnar & Zahorik, 1977, p. 40).

Ralph Tyler set the standard for curriculum development. "The power and impact of the Tyler model cannot be overstated" (Molnar and Zahorik, 1977, p. 3). His rationale still guides the curriculum development process today, especially in educational systems with market economy-based political orientations (Howard, 2007). His approaches are so entrenched in classroom practice that radical critiques of his approaches have left few marked changes in the implementation of curriculum in public schools. For his moderation and his wisdom as well as his impact, Ralph Tyler deserves to be enshrined in whatever hall of fame the field of curriculum may wish to establish (Kliebard, 1970).

4.8 The Taba Model

Hilda Taba (1902–1967) offered a radical departure from Tyler's deductive model for curriculum development. Taba believed that teachers are aware of the student's needs and teachers should be the ones to develop the curriculum and implement it in practice (Laanemets and Kalamee-Ruubel, 2013). She proposed that curriculum decision making start at the teaching level with the planning of specific units of instruction. These units would then create a basis for a general design to be created later (McNeil, 1990). Another name for Taba's model is the grassroots approach or inverted model.

Hilda Taba was born in Estonian and came to America in 1926 to complete her postgraduate studies. She worked and studied with the most prominent educational leaders of the time, such as John Dewey, Benjamin Bloom, and Ralph W. Tyler. She participated in Tyler's Eight-Year Study as the coordinator of the social studies' curriculum and in 1939, after the project staff was transferred to the University of Chicago, she worked as the Director of the Curriculum Laboratory until 1945. In 1962, Taba authored her famous book, *Curriculum Development: Theory and Practice,* which outlined her framework for curriculum development. Her book is still a useful reading material for those making educational policy today (Laanemets and Kalamee-Ruubel, 2013).

Taba's (1962) seven-step model is outlined below:

1. **Diagnosis of Needs;**
2. **Formulation of Objectives;**
3. **Selection of Content;**
4. **Organization of Content;**
5. **Selection of Learning Experiences;**
6. **Organization of Learning Experiences; and**
7. **Determination of What and How to Evaluate** (p. 12).

Taba's inverted approach involves teachers in its development, which gives them a level of commitment and ownership not common to other curriculum models. Additionally, the unit approach links curriculum (planning) to instruction (implementation). By bringing these two entities together, Taba's model ties theory into practice (Henson, 2001).

4.9 Jerome Bruner

Jerome S. Bruner (1915–2016) was one of the best known and most influential psychologists of the 20th century and a key leader in the so-called cognitive revolution. Bruner, who was born blind and after having his sight restored, spent the rest of his life trying to understand how the human mind perceives the world. He earned his Ph.D. at Harvard in 1941, and over the course of his 70-year academic career contributed to many advances in education and the development of the field of cognitive psychology. Bruner died in 2016 at the age of 100 (Shudel, 2016; Smith, 2002).

In the late 1950s, several prominent Americans were calling for a reexamination of schooling in this country, spurred on by the successful launching into space of the Russian Sputnik satellite in 1957. In response, then President Kennedy told an embarrassed nation that America would put the first person on the moon. As part of the reform effort, a special committee under the auspices of the National Academy of Sciences and the National Science Foundation convened in Woods Hole on Cape Cod for 10 days in 1959 to design a better educational system for American youth. Chaired by Bruner, the committee consisted of 35 leaders from government, industry, education, and science. The committee concluded that education should be built around broad theories and concepts, leading to the development of conceptual learning (Henson, 2001). Many curricula that featured hands-on pedagogy, inquiry learning, and problem solving were developed and implemented in the classroom. In 1969, Americans felt a sense of pride and accomplishment when the world saw Neil Armstrong unfurl the American flag on the surface of the moon. President Kennedy's promise was delivered and "our education gap" appeared diminished.

Conceptual learning is an educational method that centers on big-picture ideas and learning how to organize and categorize information. According to Bruner, concepts are created by clustering or organizing facts. All knowledge can be organized by concepts, the building blocks of the structure of knowledge. Bruner (1961) proposes that learners' construct their own knowledge and do this by organizing and categorizing information using a coding system. Bruner believed that the most effective way to develop a coding system is to discover it rather than being told by the teacher. The concept of discovery learning implies that students construct their own knowledge for themselves (also known as a constructivism).

4.10 The Process of Education

Jerome Bruner's book, *The Process of Education* (1960), was an instant classic and had a significant impact on the development of curriculum theory in this country. Bruner authored the 97-page book to provide an account of the major themes and conclusions that emerged from the Woods Hole conference. While the entire book is worth reading (and rereading), the chapter on the importance of structure is particularly significant to curriculum developers. Bruner's book has sold several thousand copies in various editions and has been translated into 21 languages (Harvard University Press Blog, 2013).

Bruner places "structure" at the heart of education. If you give children a sense of the structure of what they are taught, they will learn the responses themselves. The theme of structure as it developed at the Woods Hole conference refers to the importance of presenting the basic structures of the disciplines as the focal points of curricula. **Structure of the disciplines** refers to a discipline's basic concepts and methods of inquiry. Basic structures consist of essential concepts, such as "supply and demand" in economics, "conflict" in history, and "energy" in physics, and the relationships among them. Such concepts, when understood, enable students to understand many of the phenomena in that discipline and similar phenomena that may be encountered elsewhere (Howard, 2007). As Bruner (1960) wrote, "Learning should not only take us somewhere but it should also allow us later to go further more easily . . . The more fundamental or basic is the idea, the greater will be its breadth of applicability to new problems" (pp. 17–18).

In addition, Bruner emphasizes the importance of both structure and meaning in the learning process. In his own words "grasping the structure of a subject is understanding it in a way that permits many other things to be related to it meaningfully. To learn structure, in short, is to learn how things are related" (p. 7). Central to the implementation of a structured discipline approach are four themes that Bruner reflects upon in his book. The four themes are structure, readiness, intuition, and interest and Bruner devotes a chapter to each.

When discussing the first of these themes, Bruner states "the curriculum of a subject should be determined by the most fundamental understanding than can be achieved of the underlying principles that give structure to that subject" (pp. 31–32). Bruner noted several advantages to learning the structure of a discipline. First, it makes a subject more comprehensible. Second, it improves memory since it allows learners to place detail in to a structured pattern. Third, an understanding of fundamental principles and ideas facilitates a "transfer of training" to similar principles. Finally, structure contributes to narrowing the gap between elementary and advanced knowledge.

The second theme that Bruner discusses is readiness. Bruner suggests that many schools have wasted valuable time by postponing the teaching of many important concepts on the ground that they are too difficult. Contrary to this belief, he proclaims "that any subject can be taught effectively in some intellectually honest form to any child at any stage of development" (p. 33). The key to teaching a subject to a child at any particular age is one of representing structure of that subject in terms of the child's way of viewing things. As far as educators are concerned, the lesson to be learned is to match the subject matter to the student's intellectual maturity. For example, some aspects of calculus may be simplified so that they could be understood by an elementary student. There is a difference in degree, not in kind.

The third theme involves the nature of intuition. Intuition refers to the intellectual technique of arriving at plausible, but tentative, formulations without going through the analytic steps. In lay person's terms, Bruner is advocating that teachers facilitate their students to be intuitive thinkers and shrewd guessers. To illustrate this point, here is an example with which many of us can identify. How many times has each one of us written a passage that reflected proper rules of English grammar? And yet if asked that individual to recite what rules they used, they probably could not identify them; they just knew the passage was grammatically correct. In addition, intuition teaches students that they no longer need to fear making a mistake. Instead, errors could be turned into positive learning experiences that promote interest and develop new insights.

The fourth theme relates to the desire to learn and how it may be stimulated. Ideally, interest in the material is the best stimulus for learning. As teachers, there is a need for us to motivate our students, to promote this interest in each of our subject disciplines. Bruner cites such factors as teacher–student rapport, pedagogical variety, the use of concrete examples, real-world problems, hands-on activities, inquiry and discovery techniques, and active participation as tools that the educator can use to help stimulate this interest.

Noted Historians

- **Dewey = Learning by doing**
- **Bobbitt = First to study curriculum development**
- **Tyler = Father of curriculum and deductive model**
- **Taba = Inductive model**
- **Bruner = Structure of the discipline and spiral curriculum**

4.11 The Spiral Curriculum

When you put together all four of Bruner's themes, teachers now have what he advocates as the spiral curriculum. In a spiral curriculum, learning is spread out over time rather than being concentrated in shorter periods. Material is revisited repeatedly over months and across grades. Bruner (1960) proposes:

> "that intellectual activity anywhere is the same, where at the frontier of knowledge or in a third-grade classroom. What a scientist does at his desk or in his laboratory, what a literary critic does in reading a poem, are of the same order as what anybody else does when he is engaged in like activities—if he is to achieve understanding. The difference is in degree, not in kind. The schoolboy learning physics is a physicist, and it is easier for him to learn physics behaving like a physicist than doing something else" (p. 14).

In other words, learning for humans goes from simple to complex, has a sequential nature to it, and that students can be taught to become more logical. The goal of this curriculum is to have students experience the process of doing rather than merely memorizing facts (Howard, 2007).

This notion of revisiting and reexamining fundamental ideas over time is what has become known as a "**spiral curriculum**." As time goes by, students return again and again to the basic concepts, building on them, making them more complex, and understanding them more fully. This concept is also referred to as continuity. A visual of the spiral curriculum for a Language Arts classroom is illustrated in Figure 2. Key features of the spiral curriculum based on Bruner's work are (1) the information is based on the structure of the disciplines or the basic concepts and methods of inquiry in the discipline (i.e., similar to an updraft in the middle of the spiral); (2) the student revisits a topic, theme, or subject several times throughout his/her school career (i.e., revisiting concepts and skills); (3) the complexity of the topic or theme increases with each revisit (i.e., expansion in depth and breadth); (4) expectations and/or yardsticks can be established at each spiral to determine student mastery and learning progress (i.e., grade-level benchmarks are established); (5) the benchmarks can be scoped and sequenced to determine the curriculum's organization (i.e., scope is horizontal and sequence is vertical in nature; and (6) new learning has a relationship with old learning and is put in context with the old information (i.e., transfer training).

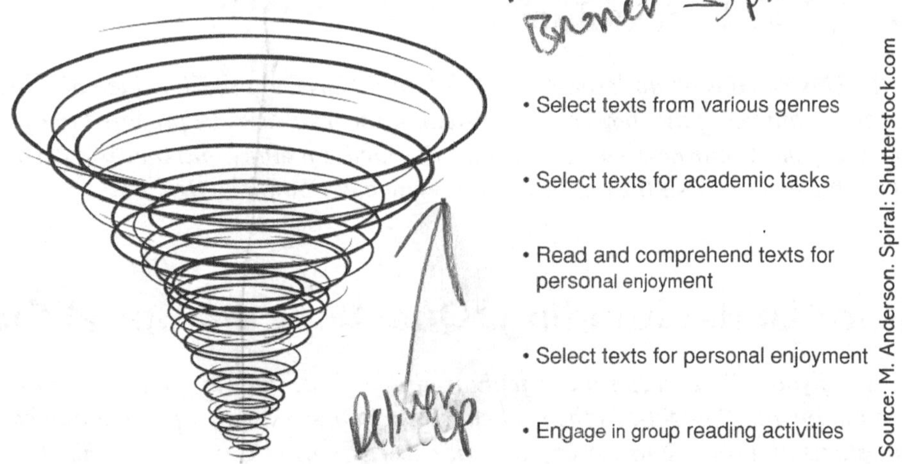

Figure 2: The Spiral Curriculum

Additionally, most curriculum developers would begin designing their curriculum with the "end in mind" in the spiral architecture. This "design-down, deliver-up philosophy" is the same framework that was used to develop state and national standards. Curriculum leaders asked "What should students be able to know and do after twelve grades of schooling?" The answer led to the development of career and college readiness standards (CCRS) that all students should be mastered at the end of their secondary school education. Teachers, on the other hand, deliver these standards from kindergarten up to 12th grade, expanding in breadth and depth the knowledge and skills taught at each successive grade level. The same concept could also be applied by teachers as they design their units of instruction. The planning process begins with the culminating activities ("What should my students be able to do at the end of the unit?), whereas instruction starts on the first day with introductory activities.

The benefits ascribed to the spiral curriculum by its advocates are (1) the information is reinforced and solidified each time the student revisits the subject matter; (2) the spiral curriculum also allows a logical progression from simplistic ideas to complicated ideas; and (3) students are encouraged to apply the early knowledge to later course objectives. Although there is no clear empirical evidence of the overall effects of the spiral curriculum on student learning, "features" of that curriculum have been linked to improved learning outcomes. In addition, the spiral curriculum incorporates many research-based approaches from cognitive science that have been linked, individually, to improved student performance as well (Johnston, 2012).

Characteristics of Spiral Curriculum

- **Design down, deliver up**
- **Based on structure of disciplines**
- **Revisit concepts and skills**
- **Expand in depth and breadth**
- **Establish grade-level benchmarks**
- **Enhance transfer training**

Video: Spiral Curriculum

DIRECTIONS: *This video is about Jerome Bruner's Spiral Curriculum. The video discusses the definition, benefits, and examples of the spiral architecture. For the next class, be prepared to* ***turn and talk*** *to your elbow partner about your new learnings from this video. An* ***elbow partner*** *is a person sitting near you to be able to tap elbows. Visit the online book to view the 5-minute video.*

Check for Understanding: Questions on Spiral Curriculum

DIRECTIONS: *As you reflect on spiral curriculum, think of one question and one comment you have "spiraling" around in your thoughts. In the next class, you will work with a partner and each of you will discuss the questions and comments leading to a rich discussion. This strategy is called* ***One Question, One Comment****. Visit the online book to complete the activity.*

Chapter Summary

Reflect on the history and contributions of Bobbitt, Dewey, Taba, Tyler, & Bruner. Tyler's book, *Basic Principles of Curriculum and Instruction*, and Bruner's book, *Process of Education*, are widely recognized as educational classics. Both authors and their books provide a good beginning, not only because they were among the first books on curriculum to be published, but also because the ideas they contain have been among the most enduring. Indeed, they continue to provide the foundation and concepts for our most current thinking in curriculum development.

A Fable: The Sabor Tooth Curriculum

DIRECTIONS: *Read the Curriculum fable. Think about the connection between the fable and the curriculum concepts presented in this chapter. In class with a small group, you will come to consensus on the moral of the fable. Be prepared to share. View the online book to read the article.*

Check for Mastery: Performance Expectations

DIRECTIONS: *You rated yourself on performance expectations at the start of this chapter. Have you now mastered each performance expectation? Rate yourself using the Likert scale online. Compare this to how you rated yourself at the beginning of this chapter. If you do not know an expectation, go back to the text and re-read the information.*

Summary Learning Activity: Posttest

DIRECTIONS: *Now it is time to retake the pretest. Read each statement and decide if it is true or false. Circle your answer. How does your posttest score compare to your pretest score? Make each false statement true.*

T F **1.** An examination of the curriculum past can help identify problems or issues that curriculum developers have struggled with before.
T F **2.** John Dewey is considered the "father of curriculum development."
T F **3.** John Dewey believed that the goal of curriculum should be the acquisition of subject matter content.
T F **4.** Franklin Bobbitt is given credit for being the first educator to study the curriculum development process.
T F **5.** Ralph Tyler's work was greatly influenced by John Dewey's work.
T F **6.** Ralph Tyler's sources of needs included the philosophy of education and psychology of learning.
T F **7.** Ralph Tyler believed that learning experiences were the most important part of the curriculum.
T F **8.** Ralph Tyler's principles were widely welcomed in classrooms and adopted by curriculum developers over the past 50 years.
T F **9.** Hilda Taba's curriculum model is deductive, whereas Ralph Tyler's curriculum model is inductive.
T F **10.** The Process of Education was once a syllabus for a curriculum course that Jerome Bruner taught.
T F **11.** Structure of the disciplines refers to a discipline's basic concepts and methods of inquiry.
T F **12.** Bruner was not an advocate of conceptual learning and did not believe that students could construct their own knowledge for themselves.
T F **13.** According to Bruner, the curriculum of a subject is determined most by its underlying principles that give structure to that subject.
T F **14.** In the spiral curriculum, learning goes from simple to complex and concepts are revisited over time.
T F **15.** In the spiral curriculum, scope is vertical in nature and sequence is horizontal in nature.
T F **16.** Curriculum developers who employ a spiral design architecture plan their units with the end in mind.

Supplemental Learning Exercises

1. Choose three social developments, events, pressures, or forces in the United States within the last 20 years that have caused changes in the school's curriculum. Cite and briefly describe those changes.
2. In this activity, you will explain Tyler's Model, using your discipline. In 1949, Ralph Tyler offered initial suggestions for developing curriculum and instruction in his book entitled, *Basic Principles of Curriculum and Instruction*. Tyler's four classic tenets of curriculum planning have been modified (see below). Use the information in parentheses below each question to begin your dialogues about your curricular choices.

   Tyler's Four Questions of Instructional Development

   A. What are the purposes of the school? (Think about, justify, and delineate what you are going to teach and how this material is relevant to the common, current purposes of schooling.)
   B. What educational experiences are related to those purposes? (What content, processes, and methods are you going to use to deliver instruction and information that perpetuate the purposes of schools?)
   C. What are the organizational methods that will be used in relation to those purposes? (In the contexts of your educational purposes, how can you best organize your information, presentations, and learning events so that they are most effective?)
   D. How will those purposes be evaluated? (How do you know your learning events, information, and processes were taught successfully—What evidence will you collect?)

3. Choose a topic in your discipline and illustrate that topic using the spiral architecture. In your illustration, please make sure that you address the curriculum design principles that are inherent in a spiral design.

Final Test

DIRECTIONS: *Read each question or statement below. Select the appropriate answer or write the correct answer in the blank provided.*

C 1. Who is considered the "father of curriculum development?"
A. Franklin Bobbitt
B. John Dewey
C. Ralph Tyler
D. Jerome Bruner

A 2. Franklin Bobbitt voiced for the *first* time the importance of:
A. studying the curriculum development process.
B. including vocational education in the curriculum.
C. unpacking and aligning standards in the curriculum.
D. designing learning experiences based on outcomes.

C 3. Which of the following behaviors would John Dewey *most* likely support?
A. Curriculum consisting of reading, writing, and arithmetic
B. Curriculum that focused on the acquisition of subject matter content
C. Curriculum that centered on learning by doing
D. Curriculum that was aligned to state and national standards

____ 4. Which of the following is ***not*** one of the criteria used by Tyler to establish a rationale for curriculum development?
   A. What educational purposes should the school seek to attain?
   B. How can the curriculum best reflect American traditions in education?
   C. What educational experiences can be provided that are likely to attain these purposes?
   D. How can we determine whether these purposes are being attained?

____ 5. According to Ralph Tyler, the *key* to curriculum development is:
   A. conducting a formal needs assessment.
   B. formulating outcomes in all domains.
   C. selecting appropriate learning experiences.
   D. sharing decision-making responsibilities.

____ 6. What are the three sources of information for Tyler's model for curriculum development?
   A. Students, subject matter, and standards
   B. Teachers, students, and society
   C. Students, society, and subject matter
   D. Standards, teachers, and students

____ 7. What step of Tyler's model is associated with the design phase of curriculum development?
   A. Analyzing learning experiences
   B. Organizing learning experiences
   C. Selecting learning experiences
   D. Evaluating learning experiences

____ 8. Which of the following terms *best* describes the nature of Taba's model for curriculum development?
   A. Deductive
   B. Inductive
   C. Exploratory
   D. Social

____ 9. If you were to employ the "design down, deliver up principle" in developing a unit plan, what would you develop *first*?
   A. Introductory activities
   B. Enabling activities
   C. Culminating activities
   D. Enrichment activities

____ 10. In the lessons of the spiral curriculum, as students move to new levels, they encounter:
   A. familiar concepts in more complex forms.
   B. planned repetitions of content.
   C. simplified versions of familiar concepts.
   D. systematic overviews of concepts.

____ 11. Which of the following serves as the *best* illustration of a spiral architecture for implementing the curriculum? Note: C = Concept and P = Practice
   A. C1 P1 C2 P2 C3 P3 C4 P4
   B. C1 P1 C2 C3 C4 P2, 3, 4
   C. C1 C2 C3 C4 P1 P2 P3 P4
   D. P1 C1 P2 C2 P3 C3 P4 C4

___ 12. Jerome Bruner advocates teaching based on the "structure of the discipline." What is meant by the phrase structure of the discipline?
A. The discipline's background and history
B. The discipline's basic concepts and methods of inquiry
C. The discipline's most famous scholars and their ideas
D. The discipline's social influences and values

___ 13. Concerning the concept of readiness, Jerome Bruner would advocate:
A. both a difference in degree and kind.
B. neither a difference in degree or kind.
C. a difference in kind, not in degree.
D. a difference in degree, not in kind.

___ 14. Jerome Bruner cited structure as being one of the *key* factors associated with learning. Which of the following is ***not*** considered a reason why structure is important in the learning process?
A. Structure contributes to the understanding of fundamentals, which in turn, makes a subject more comprehensible.
B. Structure narrows the gap between advanced and elementary knowledge.
C. Structure involves social transmission, and thus, increases student learning of outcomes in the domain of values, attitudes, and interests.
D. Structure provides a pattern for knowledge that contributes to the student's ability to transfer and retain concepts.

___ 15. Which of the following principles is illustrated by a spiral architecture?
A. Unpacking and aligning standards
B. Revisiting concept and skills
C. Identify sources of needs
D. Selecting course content

DIRECTIONS: *Write a brief response.*

1. Discuss two ways the Tyler rationale and model is suitable for current curriculum development. Also discuss two ways the Tyler rationale and model is not suitable for current curriculum development.
2. Illustrate the spiral design and explain three of its key characteristics.

Works Cited and Suggested Readings

Armstrong, David. (1989). *Developing and Documenting the Curriculum.* Needham Heights, MA: Allyn and Bacon.

Armstrong, David, Henson, Kenneth, & Savage, Tom. (1997). *Teaching Today: An Introduction to Education* (5th ed.). Upper Saddle River, NJ: Merrill.

Association for Supervision and Curriculum Development (ASCD). (1980). Is the Tyler Rationale a Suitable Basis for Current Curriculum Development? *ASCD Update.* Alexandria, VA: Author.

Bobbitt, Franklin. (1918). *The Curriculum.* New York, NY: Houghton Mifflin.

Bobbitt, Franklin. (1924). *How to Make a Curriculum.* New York, NY: Houghton Mifflin.

Bruner, J. S. (1961). The Act of Discovery. *Harvard Educational Review, 31,* 21–32.

Bruner, Jerome. (1960). *The Process of Education.* Cambridge, MA: Harvard University Press.

Caswell, Hollis and Campbell, Doak. (1935). *Curriculum Development*. New York, NY: American Book Company.

Chall, Malca. (1976). *Ralph Tyler*. Interview available for Study at The Bancroft Library, University of California at Berkeley and UCLA's Department of Special Collections. (Also in *Kappa Delta Pi*.) Retrieved from: www.wredu.com/~wriles/Tyler.html.

Denham, Thomas J. (2002). *Comparison of Two Curriculum/Instructional Design Models: Ralph W. Tyler and Siena College Accounting Class, ACC205*. Retrieved from: ERIC Database (ED471734), Northeastern Illinois University.

Dewey, John. (1902). *The Child and the Curriculum*. Chicago, IL: University of Chicago Press.

Doll, Ronald C. (1989). *Curriculum Development: Decision Making and Process* (7th ed.). Boston, MA: Allyn and Bacon.

Harvard University Press Blog. (2013). *The Process of Education, 1960*. Retrieved from: harvardpress.typepad.com.

Henson, Kenneth. (2001). *Curriculum Planning Integrating Multiculturalism, Constructivism, and Educational Reform* (2nd ed.). New York, NY: McGraw-Hill Higher Education.

Howard, Judith. (2007). *Curriculum Development*. Elon University, Elon, NC: Center for the Advancement of Teaching and Learning.

Johnston, Howard. (2012). The Spiral Curriculum. *Research into Practice*. Education Partnerships, Inc. Retrieved from: http://www.educationpartnerships.org.

Khataybeh, Abdullah & Ateeg, Najla Abdullah. (2011). How "Writing Academic English" Follows Bruner's Spiral Model in Curriculum Planning. *Journal of Emerging Trends in Educational Research and Policy Studies, 2*(2), 127–138.

Kliebard, Herbert. (1970). The Tyler Rationale. In Arno Bellack and Herbert Kliebard (Eds.), *Curriculum and Evaluation,* (56–67). Berkeley, CA: McCutchan.

Laanemets, Urive & Kalamee-Ruubel, Theatre. (2013). The Taba-Tyler Rationales. *Journal of the American Association for the Advancement of Curriculum Studies, 9*(2), 1–12.

McNeil, John. (1990). *Curriculum: A Comprehensive Introduction*. Glenview, IL: Scott, Foresman/Little, Brown Higher Education.

Nowakowski, Jeri. (1983). On Educational Evaluation: A Conversation with Ralph Tyler. *Educational Leadership, 40*(8), 24–29.

Olivia, Peter F. (1988). *Developing the Curriculum* (2nd ed.). Statesboro, GA: Georgia Southern College.

Ornstein, Allan C. and Hunkins, Francis P. (1998). *Curriculum Foundations Principles and Issues*. Needham Heights, MA: Allyn and Bacon.

Pinar, William, Reynolds, William, Slattery, Patrick, & Taubman, Peter (Eds.). (1995). *Understanding Curriculum*. New York, NY: Peter Lang.

Ralph W. Tyler (1902–1994). *Contribution to Testing and Curriculum Development, Advisory Role - School, Educational, University, and Education - StateUniversity.com* Retrieved from: http://education.stateuniversity.com/pages/2517/Tyler-Ralph -W-1902-1994.html#ixzz41JAie99G

Saylor, Galen, Alexander, William, & Lewis, Arthur. (1981). *Curriculum Planning for Better Teaching and Learning* (4th ed.). New York, NY: Holt, Rinehart, and Winston.

Schudel, Matt. (2016). Jerome Bruner Obituary. *The Washington Post*. Retrieved from: https://www.washingtonpost.com/.../jerome...bruner.../033e5870-2...

Smith, Mark. (2002). Jerome S. Bruner and the Process of Education. *Encyclopedia of Informal Education*. Retrieved from: http://infed.org/mobi/jerome-bruner-and-the-process-of-education/.

Taba, Hilda. (1962). *Curriculum Development: Theory and Practice.* New York, NY: Harcourt, Brace & World, Inc.

Thomas, Darrin. (2014). Curriculum Development: *The Tyler Model.* Retrieved from: https://educationalresearchtechniques.com.

Tyler, Ralph. (1977). Desirable Content for a Curriculum Development Syllabus Today. In Alex Molnar and John Zahorik (Eds.), *Curriculum Theory.* Washington DC: Association for Supervision and Curriculum Development.

Tyler, Ralph W. (1949). *Basic Principles of Curriculum and Instruction.* Chicago, IL: University of Chicago Press.

Wiles, Jon & Bondi, Joseph C. (2015). *Curriculum Development: A Guide to Practice* (9th ed.). Boston, MA: Pearson Publishing.

Zais, Robert. (1976). *Curriculum Principles and Foundation.* New York, NY: Thomas Y. Crowell Company.

Svetlana Lukienko/Shutterstock.com

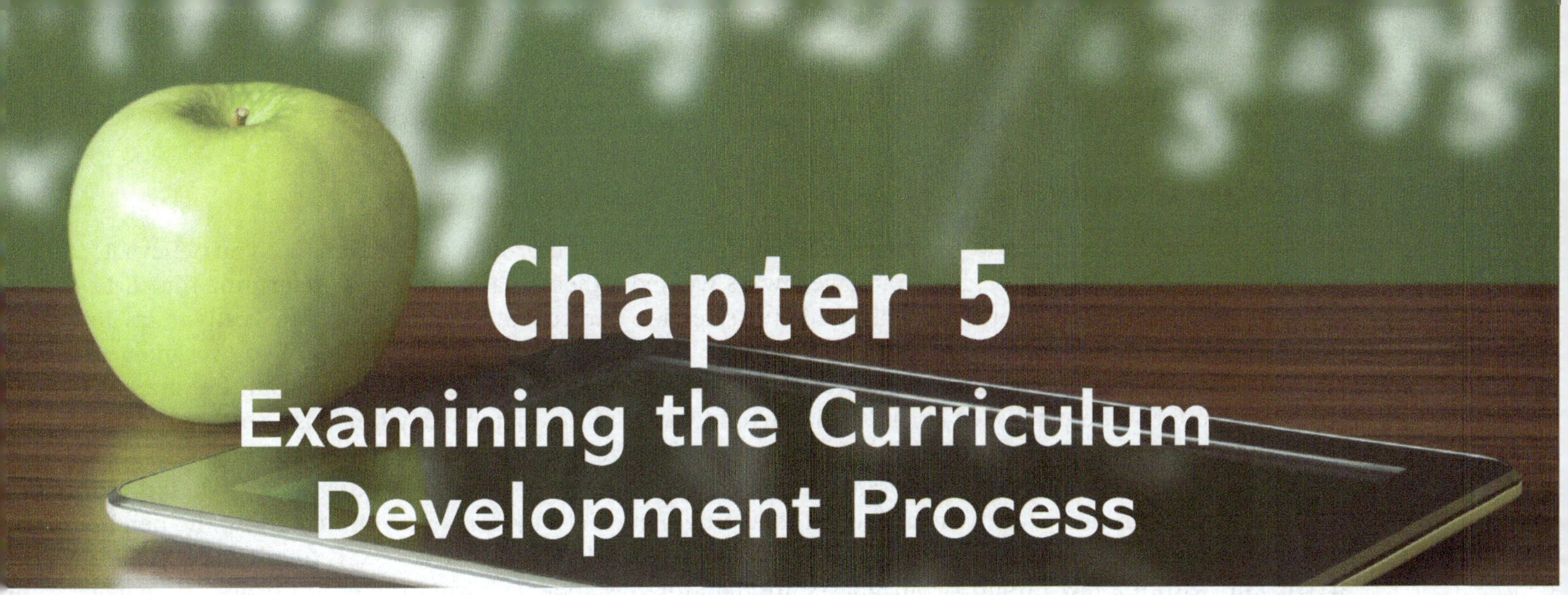

Chapter 5
Examining the Curriculum Development Process

> "You can and should shape your own future, because if you don't someone else surely will."
>
> Joel Barker

Anticipatory Set: Pre-Assessment KWL Chart

DIRECTIONS: *Effective curriculum planning and decision making process is key to the success of educational programs. What is your own personal knowledge and understanding of the curriculum development process? Use the KWL chart to write what you already know and what you want to know about the curriculum development process. You will fill out the last column at the end of the chapter.*

CURRICULUM DEVELOPMENT PROCESS		
WHAT DO YOU ALREADY KNOW?	WHAT DO YOU WANT TO KNOW?	WHAT DID YOU LEARN?

Chapter Overview

Your parents have offered to pay for your 21st birthday party and provided a budget. Can you believe it? How exciting! The planning begins! You have always wanted a theme party. That will determine the party props and expenses. From there, you will decide the selection and cost of food. Now, you are ready to invite guests based on the budget. As hard as it is, you whittle the number to the point you do not go over budget. You are ready to send the invitations. Now the "behind the scenes" work begins. You buy all the supplies, order the food, make a playlist of music, decide what to wear at the theme party (an '80s event) and go to Goodwill to get your outfit. As the day approaches, you finalize the food amount based on the guests that can attend, you start preparing to decorate the party area with disco balls and flashing lights, you test the speakers so you can easily hear Olivia Newton John sing, Let's Get Physical, and you make sure the neighbors know you are having a loud party and need parking. Whew! The day arrives—it is finally here! Guests arrive, and within a few minutes your guests are dancing 80s style, laughing the entire time. The party whips by in a flash. The next day you wake up with a smile on your face as you know it was a great birthday celebration.

Planning a 21st birthday party with an 80s theme is similar to examining the curriculum development process. Yes, it is! As a curriculum decision maker, you have four phases or cycles to complete to ensure all K-12 students have a viable curriculum as the party planner has the same phases. The first phase is analysis. You have to analyze the needs of the students, subjects, society and standards, just as the party planner has to decide what the needs are for the party. The next phase is design. The curriculum and the party both need to be designed based on the analysis of needs. From there the phase of implementation is next. The party happens and so does the instruction. This is the work coming to fruition! The final phase, evaluation, also happens in the classroom, school district, and the party. There are countless ways to evaluate students' learning and the curriculum. Exams, formative assessment, standardized tests, and curricular maps are just a few ways to evaluate for improvement. The party evaluation is to debrief on how much fun the guests had, how much food was consumed, and if the birthday party went without any glitches. Parties and curricular planning do have similarities!

In this chapter, you will examine the curriculum development process. Curriculum development is defined as the planned and systematic process for improving teaching and learning in our schools. Most school districts have their own process for making curriculum decisions that contribute to positive improvements in their educational system. However, each school district often follows a similar cycle that often involves four cyclic stages: analysis, design, implementation, and evaluation: In this chapter you will further investigate the components and decisions that educators tackle during curriculum planning and development.

Performance Expectations

DIRECTIONS: *How well do you know the performance expectations? Rate your knowledge of each expectation using this Likert scale. You will rate yourself again at the end of the chapter. This is for your information to assess your own learning. Visit the online book to record your answers.*

1 = I do not have any knowledge of this concept.
2 = I have minimal knowledge of this concept.
3 = I have some understanding of this concept.
4 = I have a satisfactory understanding of this concept.
5 = I am confident in my understanding of this concept.

This chapter should prepare you to:

Rating	#	Performance Expectations
	1.	Outline the four cyclic phases of the curriculum development process.
	2.	Analyze the key decisions associated with the analysis phase.
	3.	Explain the needs assessment process.
	4.	Describe the four sources of needs and two screens of analysis.
	5.	Analyze the key decisions associated with the design phase.
	6.	Summarize the essential components or parts that should be included in a prototypical curriculum.
	7.	Analyze the key decisions associated with the implementation phase.
	8.	Justify why the implementation phase gives curriculum developers the greatest challenge.
	9.	Analyze the key decisions associated with the evaluation phase.
	10.	Discuss the five technical properties of an effective curricular program.
	11.	Explain the concept of referencing.
	12.	Investigate the planning considerations associated with curriculum construction.
	13.	Interpret Marzano's research on curriculum and its effects on student achievement.
	14.	Design a model to illustrate the curriculum development cycle.

Video: Curriculum Development

DIRECTIONS: *As you view the YouTube video, think about why the author made a satirical video. What seems realistic and what does not? In the next class, tablemates will come to consensus on a* ***One Sentence Summary*** *for what is realistic and a one sentence summary what is not realistic. Each table will share their two sentences in class.*

Article: Defining the Effective Curriculum

DIRECTIONS: *The article "Where We Stand," will give the reader a comprehensive, yet brief, overview on the effective components of curriculum. While you read this article, "****do jots.****" To "do jots" have four to six post-it notes ready. When you read a compelling component, have a question, a disagreement, or need more information, jot on a post-it note. Bring your jots to class. Jots will make your understanding deeper for a rich conversation with a classmate. View the online book to read the article.*

5.1 Curriculum Development

If curriculum is perceived as a plan for providing sets of learning opportunities under the direction of the school, the process for developing that plan is known as curriculum development. Curriculum development is a comprehensive term, which includes analysis, design, implementation, and evaluation. Since curriculum development implies change and betterment, curriculum improvement is often synonymous with the term curriculum development (Olivia, 1988).

Curriculum development at the local school district level should be an ongoing and dynamic process. The process should yield a workable, usable, student-centered product. An effective curriculum increases students' understanding about their world and prepares them to live in the 21st century. It enlarges their experiences, sharpens their awareness, enhances creativity, teaches problem solving, and reinforces critical thinking. Good curriculum, like good schools, helps the student become a knowledgeable citizen, an informed consumer, a productive worker, an inspired leader, and a life-long learner.

The curriculum development process should result in a teacher-friendly document (template) that serves as a blueprint for teaching and learning. It should also be recognized, however, that many curriculum developers, especially novice teachers, do not follow a specific model or process. Educators often plunge right in the process by preparing lesson plans or instructional materials without necessarily going through any systematic process. Others simply state, "Tell me what to do, and I will get it done!" These issues would result in a chaotic and non-beneficial curriculum product.

5.2 Four Cyclic Stages

In its simplest form, curriculum development is a cycle of activities. The process often involves four cyclic stages: analysis, design, implementation, and evaluation.

- **Analysis** = The process of identifying needs, clarifying values, and searching for a purpose.
- **Design** = The process in which the purpose is translated into a plan for constructing or revising the curriculum.
- **Implementation** = The process during which the plan is activated through instruction using various pedagogies and resources.
- **Evaluation** = The process of collecting information for monitoring progress and validating achievements (Wiles & Bondi, 1986).

A Cyclic Process

- **Analysis = Identifying needs**
- **Design = Plan development**
- **Implementation = Instruction**
- **Evaluation = Monitoring progress**

Many curiculum developers use a similar procedure, often named the ADDIE model. ADDIE is an acronym for Analysis, Design, Develop, Implement, and Evaluate. Morrison et al. (2011), in his book *Designing Effective Curriculum*, states that there is no actual ADDIE model; rather the terms are simply associated with effective instructional processes. The ADDIE process has five stages, the cyclical process has four stages. However, the design and develop stages in ADDIE are the same as the design stage in the cyclical process.

Ralph Tyler (1949), the father of curriculum development, in his classic book entitled *Basic Principles of Curriculum and Instruction* outlined his four questions that support these cyclic steps which are still in use today:

- What educational purposes should the school seek to attain? (Analysis)
- What educational experiences can be provided that are likely to attain these purposes? (Implementation)
- How can the educational experiences be effectively organized? (Design)
- How can we determine whether these purposes are being effectively attained? (Evaluation)

5.3 Analysis: Sources of Needs

During the analysis phase, curriculum developers compare "what is" to "what should be" in order to identify programmatic needs. This process often is referred to as **needs assessment**, self-study, or some other data collection process. Gaps that are identified in the process are often the primary focus of the design phase.

Data are usually collected from the four "S" sources: students, society, subject, and standards. Effective curriculum planning requires that data be collected, analyzed, and interpreted from all four sources and used for curriculum decision making. Historically, an effective curriculum was based on data from only three major sources (i.e., Tyler's Model) (1) the nature of learners to be educated; (2) the society which provides and operates the institution; and (3) the accumulated knowledge available and feasible for educating learners (Saylor, Alexander, & Lewis, 1981). The passage of the No Child Left Behind Act in 2001 added standards to the mix; the legislation required all states to adopt, adapt, or create their own standards. These four sources of needs help the curriculum developer to determine the educational outcomes.

The first source of data is **student needs and interests**. Generally speaking, a curriculum is planned for an identified group of learners. Curriculum developers investigate demographic and participation data, growth and developmental characteristics, personal traits, individual interests, and learning style preferences. For example, ask any curriculum director "What effect does a changing demographic have on the curriculum?" Additionally, insights and generalizations about infants, children, youth, and adults can readily be observed in any school district's curriculum. Curriculum planners always need to be cognizant of the fact and acknowledge that learners *learn* in different ways and that teachers have different styles of *teaching*.

Society, culture, and our American system of values, unclear as they appear at times, have always had a profound effect on efforts to improve curriculum (Doll, 1989). John Dewey believed that each generation brings on a new culture (Henson, 2001). If this is true, then society's needs should permeate the curriculum. **Societal data**, the second source of needs, aid curriculum developers in identifying and understanding the role of family, peers, and community on educational programs. The needs that arise from these influences can appear in many forms. For example, when you live in a mobile society the population of a nation is on the move and many new faces appear in the classroom. During all but the earliest years of life the peer group is an important source of pressure, influence, and support. What effects have the deterioration of the nuclear family or increased poverty had on our schools? As societal issues and challenges emerge (e.g., substance abuse, AIDS, sexual promiscuity, and illegal immigration), curriculum developers are often assigned the task of educating our youth through the school system and its curricula.

Societal data also include the wishes and desires of the community and school stakeholders. When analyzing the needs for curriculum development, it is vital to include the perspectives of school board members, teachers, support staff, administrators, and students (student council representatives as an example). Community members also play an important role in sharing perspectives. Community members may include the retired population, adults without children in schools, organizations within the community such as Rotary, Kwiannis, and town councils, and staff from the local businesses. For a curriculum to be viable, all stakeholders' voices need to be heard. The data can be gathered through online surveys, focus groups, attendance at meetings, and mailings.

Example: Parental Feedback on Math Curriculum

Visit the online book to read an example of parental feedback on math curriculum from the Waterloo, Iowa School District.

The third source of needs is **subject matter**. A subject-centered design has dominated the curricula in American schools throughout their existence (Henson, 2001). Most of what is taught in schools today is knowledge that is organized into subjects. Many secondary teachers are trained as subject matter experts and when they think of operationalizing the curriculum they think in terms of content. Most elementary teachers are trained as generalists in several content areas, with a focus on the development of the whole child. Identifying suitable subject matter and placing it in the curriculum has been complicated by a monumental explosion of knowledge (Doll, 1989). With the amount of knowledge growing exponentially rather than linearly, the question for curriculum planners becomes "What knowledge should be taught?" Examples of this third source of need that can be found in many school districts are the STEAM (i.e., Science, Technology, Engineering, Art, and Mathematics) programs which illustrate the evolving advances in science and technology. Additionally, when analyzing subject matter needs, testing data and multiyear assessment trends are closely examined.

Standards are evidence-based, hybrid outcomes that serve as our fourth set of needs. Standards are defined as benchmarks or patterns of evidence to judge a student's performance. Many states and organizations created standards to ensure that all students graduate from high school with the skills and knowledge necessary to succeed in college, career, and life, regardless of where they live. Standards typically focus on developing the critical-thinking, problem solving, and analytical skills students will need to be successful. Federal legislation requires that all states must adopt, adapt, or create their own standards that focus on Math and English Language Arts. Many states have adopted the Common Core standards. Today, curriculum developers are always unpacking, aligning, or embedding some set of standards into their curriculum and assessment activities.

Check for Understanding: Sources of Needs

DIRECTIONS: *Goals are based upon the sources of needs. Examine the goals and determine what* ***primary source*** *they reflect. In the next class, students will participate in a* ***Choral Response****. For each goal, students will say their answer in unison. Visit the online book to complete the activity.*

5.4 Analysis: Screens

In Tyler's deductive model, once the array of data has been collected, broad goals and tentative objectives are determined. To eliminate unimportant and contradictory objectives, Tyler (1949) recommends that they are funneled through two screens (1) **philosophy of education** and (2) **psychology of learning**. Tyler talks about the educational and social philosophies to which the school is committed and urges curriculum developers to omit any general objectives that are not in keeping with the faculty's agreed-upon philosophy. Effective application of the psychology screen, which assumes some degree of training in educational psychology, enables curriculum workers to distinguish between objectives that are feasible from those that are not and gives us an idea on the appropriate age and length of time required to obtain each objective. Results from the screening process part of analysis lead to the development of precise instructional objectives during the design phase.

The analysis stage concludes with the development of a **philosophy statement**. Defined literally, philosophy means "love of wisdom" (Zais, 1976). Philosophy statements are collections of thoughts and ideas about the overall intentions of the program. They help guide the curriculum development process by establishing curricular parameters and determining discipline purposes and priorities. Philosophies provide criteria for selecting what and how to teach the content in that subject area. The role of the learner and the teacher should be discussed, thus revealing your school's philosophy for teaching your subject area. Elements typically covered in a philosophy statement include definition and components of the discipline, rationale for studying that subject area, expected student outcomes, references to aligned standards, beliefs and core values, and current discipline trends and issues.

Example: Philosophy Statement

Visit the online book to read an example of the philosophy of curriculum from Broken Arrow Public School District in Broken Arrow, OK.

Analysis

- **Needs assessment process**
- **Four sources of needs**
- **Two screens or filters**
- **Philosophy statement**

5.5 Design

During the design phase, the purpose is translated in an action plan for changing the curriculum. Design is a way of organizing the structure of the curriculum that permits all the elements "to hang together" and function appropriately (Doll, 1989). Five key decisions occur during this phase (1) presentation of the content; (2) unpacking and alignment of standards; (3) identification of outcomes or performance expectations; (4) determination of the organization (i.e., scope and sequence); and (5) establishment of platform and the documentation of essential elements. The answers to questions associated with each step will help curriculum developers construct the school district's curriculum template.

When most teachers think of curriculum or, more importantly, when they operationalize the curriculum, they think in terms of content. Questions involving content are the first set of design decisions to be made. **Content** should serve as the "vehicle" for developing the knowledge, skills, understandings, and dispositions (KSUDs) contained in the essential learning outcomes. Research would indicate that there are seven possible options for presenting content, ranging from outlines to outcomes to concept maps (see Chapter 2). When choosing what content to teach, Armstrong (1989) recommends faculty should address questions such as:

- What content is to be selected?
- How is content to be selected?
- How is content to be organized?
- How is content to be sequenced?
- How is content to be prioritized?
- How is content to be transmitted?
- How is content acquisition to be evaluated?
- How are curriculum content decisions to be reflected in written form? (p. 8).

The second set of design decisions involves **unpacking and aligning standards.** Generally speaking, standards are very verbose, complex in nature, and contain many components. During the "unpacking" phase, curriculum developers investigate each standard, trying to simplify its components and understand its student expectations. Each standard's knowledge, skills, understandings, and dispositions (KSUDs) components are the products of the unpacking process. The last step in the unpacking process is to develop a learning target for each standard or combined set of standards. Learning targets are outcomes or performance expectations.

Next, a school district determines where they are on the alignment continuum and how they are going to document the process. Most school districts prefer an outcome-driven (i.e., identify what students should know and be able to do—outcomes—and then matching appropriate standards) versus a standards-driven approach (i.e., teaching standard one—identifying corresponding outcomes—on day one, then the same process for standard two on day two). Either approach will "look the same" on the final template, but the outcome approach is more realistic in terms of operationalizing the curriculum. Additionally, some school districts will "chunk" similar standards together according to recognized learning progressions, the structure of the discipline, and prerequisite skills or behaviors.

Some school districts also choose to develop power or priority standards. Power standards are defined as the body of knowledge all students need to acquire in a content area. They are the "essential learnings" that endure and prepare students for their future. In essence, power standards are the most important concepts and skills to know and do in a discipline. Because knowledge is doubling every twelve months, soon to be every twelve hours (Schilling, 2013), district's "power" standards become critical. An additional benefit for districts to develop these standards is the ownership and local control of these decisions.

Example: Power Standards

Visit the online book to peruse the power standards from the Redson School District. Note that the English Language Arts standards have been prioritized and categorized for ease of teacher usage for this district. Power standards should both drive and guide the curriculum, instruction, and assessment in a subject area.

The third set of design decisions center around the development of **outcomes** or **performance expectations**. Performance expectations are defined as "what students should know, do, and care about." These learning targets provide an organizing framework for planning and implementing a learning experience. For districts that employ spiral design architecture (i.e., design targets with the end in mind), they serve as the culminating demonstrations of learning. Synonyms for outcomes and performance expectations are instructional aims, goals, learning objectives, core abilities, competencies, learning targets, benchmarks, strands, student skills, and essential learning outcomes. Most curriculum experts recommend that at least three types or levels of outcomes should be included in a local curriculum document. Outcomes or performance expectations determine the what (what content you will teach), drive the how (your selection of teaching and learning strategies), and dictate the when (what you will measure to test or assess achievement).

Scope defines the depth and breadth of content coverage. **Sequence** determines the order of curriculum content. Collectively, these elements describe the organization (the fourth set of decisions) of unit, a course, and a discipline of study. Often curriculum is said to be "a mile wide and an inch deep" referring to a scope and sequence that represents only a surface level content coverage of many topics, rather than carving out key ideas and emphasizing conceptual understanding of them. Many school districts today employ "spiral architecture" in which they design with the end in mind and include planned repetitions of content at successive levels, each time at an increased level of complexity (also called the principle of continuity).

The last set of decisions in the design phase refers to what **essential components** or parts are contained in the template, how are they arranged, and what will the final format look like. In their *Guide to Curriculum Planning* (1987), the Wisconsin Department of Public instruction offered recommendations for the elements that should be typically found in curriculum guides for any discipline:

- A philosophy or rationale for the educational program;
- Goals and objectives for each learning level;
- Sequences of learning, both within and between grade levels;
- Instructional strategies for meeting goals and objectives;
- Instructional activities designed to meet the needs of students with varying abilities and needs;
- A variety of methods for evaluating progress toward learning objectives (p. 4); and
- Alignment of academic standards.

Sometimes a particular platform, such as Performance-Based Instruction (PBI) or an Understanding by Design (UBD) might serve as the critical driving or organizing element on the curriculum template. A variety of templates may be used, ranging from curriculum or parent guides to a compilation of daily lesson plans or units of study, to pacing calendars, to course syllabi or course outcome summaries. Many school districts turn their paper and pencil template into an electronic format by purchasing software from a company such as Eclipse, Xam, Link for Learning, WIDS, Tutor, or Build Your Own Curriculum (BYOC). Additionally, curricular mapping software is an electronic means to generate ideas and to review curriculum practice (Jacobs, 2010).

Design

- **Presenting content**
- **Unpacking and aligning standards**
- **Outcomes and expectations**
- **Organization (scope and sequence)**
- **Essential components (platform)**

5.6 Implementation

The implementation phase is synonymous with instruction. For those school districts in a five- or seven-year cycle, this phase takes the longest time and offers the greatest challenge to curriculum leaders. No matter how great a curriculum looks on paper there is no guarantee it will be implemented in its intended format. Curriculum developers realize that teachers hold a "pocket veto on any curriculum plan developed." Therefore an effective strategy for curriculum change needs to address a double agenda (1) to change ideas about curriculum and (2) to change human dynamics (Saylor, Alexander, & Lewis, 1981). That is why school district faculty **ownership** in the curriculum development process at every phase is so important.

The purpose of all curriculum planning is to provide opportunities for students to achieve higher success and benefit from participation in selected learning activities. For teachers, selecting the most appropriate **instructional strategies** and teaching methods is a key decision. In many cases, the curriculum plan may suggest or even specify that certain teaching strategies or learning activities be selected. Instructional strategies can also be derived from a number of sources including learning outcomes, student learning styles, teacher preferences, research, PLCs, professional development, personal learning networks, and subject matter content. Additionally, the activation of the curriculum design often calls for the selection of textbooks and/or trade books, application of resources, planning of professional development opportunities, and the discussion/consideration of basic "time, distance, and rate" questions (Wiles & Bondi, 1986). Time, distance, and rate questions ask: How much time should we spend on this topic or unit? How much detail should we cover? What is the depth and breadth of our content coverage? How much time on task is needed? What is our pacing schedule?

The implementation of the curriculum also requires **resources**. Resources are educational materials that provide curriculum, instructional, and assessment experiences for P-12 students. Often they are teaching and learning materials that are concrete, tangible vehicles for supporting and enhancing student mastery and achievement. Resources range from textbooks and trade books to lab equipment and manipulatives to computers and other technology tools. Resources enrich teaching in every subject, engage students in multidimensional learning, and build students' abilities to apply their knowledge.

Another aspect of implementation is differentiated instruction. **Differentiation** is a way in which a teacher anticipates and responds to a variety of student needs in the classroom. This framework or philosophy for effective teaching involves providing different students with different avenues to learning (often in the same classroom). This may include acquiring content, processing, constructing, or making sense of ideas. It also includes developing a variety of teaching materials and assessment measures so that all students within a classroom can learn effectively, regardless of differences in ability. Students vary in culture, socioeconomic status, language, gender, motivation, ability/disability, personal interests, and more, and teachers need to be aware of these varieties as they are planning their curriculum, instruction, and assessments. To meet students' needs, teachers differentiate by modifying the content (what is being taught), the process (how it is being taught), the product (how students demonstrate their learning), or the learning environment (physical locations, contexts, and cultures in which students learn). According to Tomlinson (2010), in a differentiated classroom the teacher proactively plans and carries out varied approaches to content, process, and product in anticipation of and response to student differences in affect, readiness, interest, and learning profile.

Effective instructional models (1) are effective in bringing about the achievement of specific outcomes of instruction; (2) provide opportunities for students to become active participants in the learning process; (3) take students through a step-by-step procedure or sequential set of steps; and (4) reflect the effective schools research on thinking and learning (Gunter, Estes, & Schwab, 1990, p. 67). Later in this series of books, instructional processes and teaching models are examined in far more depth.

Implementation

- **Ownership challenge**
- **Pedgagy and teaching strategies**
- **Resources**
- **Differentiation**

5.7 Evaluation

The evaluation of curriculum development efforts includes four lenses: (1) student success and/or achievement measures; (2) program effectiveness criteria; (3) teacher effectiveness; and (4) technical qualities of the curriculum document. Curriculum analysis, design, and implementation involved a series of choices, and curriculum evaluation is used to judge the appropriateness of those choices. Evaluation is the final step in the curriculum development process, and results from this phase often lead to curricular improvements in the next cycle.

Evaluation of student success and/or achievement should be based on the protocols and practices identified in a District **Assessment Plan**. This comprehensive, multitiered, and balanced system should provide meaningful data and information about student progress, student performance, and instructional effectiveness. In most cases, these assessments are based on standards and many districts have adopted standards-based report cards. Data should be used to evaluate student learning in the district, in the building, in a program, in classrooms, over time, and according to the **standards**.

In addition to evaluating student success and/or achievement, the functioning of the curriculum effectiveness as a whole must also be evaluated. Program effectiveness models such as Daniel Stufflebeam's CIPP (context, input, process, and product) Model (1971) are often used for this purpose. Context evaluation is the most basic kind of evaluation and its purpose is to provide a rationale for determining objectives. The purpose of input evaluation is to provide information for determining how to utilize resources to achieve project objectives. Process evaluation provides for periodic feedback while the curriculum is being implemented to detect program defects. The primary purpose of the final stage, product evaluation, is to measure and interpret achievement at the end of the curriculum cycle.

A solid curriculum evaluation system is also usually tied to teacher effectiveness evaluation. While a curriculum evaluation system and a teacher effectiveness system are separate entities, it is important to note that effective teachers follow the curriculum and implement strategies for student success.

The fourth lens involves the technical qualities of the curriculum document itself. The contrast between schools with and without an effective curriculum suggests the major characteristics of an effective curriculum. Association for Supervision and Curriculum Development (1998) outlines the five characteristics or technical qualities of an effective curriculum in its Curriculum Handbook:

- **Meaning** = Goals focusing on fundamental knowledge and skills;
- **Coherence** = Opportunities to learn and relearn fundamental knowledge and skills;
- **Articulation** = Learning at different levels is appropriately sequence and related;
- **Alignment** = Connects curriculum, instruction, and assessment; and
- **High Standards** = Promotion of high standards of learning for all students.

An effective curriculum is meaningful, coherent, articulated, aligned, and promotes high standards for all students.

Additionally, all the pieces of the puzzle or the decisions made during the development process should fit together. Certain elements that appeared to be needs during the analysis stage should be addressed a certain way during the design phase. Certain evaluation strategies "match up" much better with certain pedagogies. Higher student gains can be anticipated for greater alignment or better matches among the four cyclic stages. This evaluation procedure is called **referencing**.

Evaluation

- **Four lenses (assessment plan)**
- **Standards based**
- **Technical qualities**
- **Referencing**

Check for Understanding: Curriculum Phases

DIRECTIONS: *Without looking back at the text, you will be asked to answer 3 sets of questions (1) What are 3 things you now know? (2) What are 2 questions you have? and (3) What is 1 take away? These questions refer to the four phases of curriculum development. This strategy is called **3-2-1 Formative Check**. Be prepared to share your answers with a partner in the next class. Visit the online book to complete the activity*

As the four cyclical phases are abstract and confusing if one has not experienced the process, an analogy to building a house may be beneficial.

Analogy: House Building

Visit the online book to view a table that compares building a house to "building" a complete curricular cycle.

5.8 Teamwork and Professional Development

At the school district level, a curriculum director would use his/her knowledge of the curriculum development process (from its cyclic steps, design decisions, and contemporary construction models) to work with several teacher teams to design a workable, usable curriculum. Some of those teams might include:

- **Curriculum Leadership Team** = Develop template and product and process recommendations.
- **K-12 Content/Grade-Level Team** = Create philosophy and power standards and benchmarks.

- **K-12 Teachers** = Complete templates for units taught and align standards. All teachers are intimately involved in the Implementation Phase.
- **Horizontal and Vertical Teams or Discipline Team** = Analyze scope and sequence to identify strengths, weaknesses, gaps, and overlaps.

The completed work of each team ensures the district will have an end product that guarantees a rigorous, relevant, and usable curriculum.

Heidi Hayes Jacobs (2010), launches a powerful case for transforming schools through the curriculum process to become learning organizations that match the times we live in. She suggests these key areas to be included in the curricular process: content and assessment, program structures, technology, media literacy, globalization, sustainability, and habits of mind.

Video: Curriculum Planning in Today's World

DIRECTIONS: *View the 20-minute YouTube video prior to class. Be prepared to complete a* ***Three Minute Pause*** *in the next class. The Three Minute Pause provides a chance for students to stop, reflect on the concepts and ideas in the video, make connections to prior knowledge and seek clarification. Some questions to ponder in the 3 minutes are (1) I changed my attitude about. . . . (2) I became more aware of . . . (3) I was surprised about . . . (4) I felt . . . (5) I related to . . . and (6) I empathized with . . . Visit the online book to view the video.*

One interesting fact that is worthy of commenting on is how districts choose "to get the work done." Traditionally, school districts were on some sort of cycle (e.g., five years) and when it was your year (e.g., mathematics), your workload increased significantly. This approach reinforced the concept that curriculum development was an activity (rather than an ongoing, dynamic process)—the attitude was get it done quickly—and the end result was a "notebook that sat on a shelf somewhere." The very structure, organization, and timing of this practice prevented many districts from achieving their goal of developing a workable, usable curriculum.

A much better process might be "to bring everyone along together!" During this approach, the curriculum development process is broken down into the triad of elements—curriculum, instruction, and assessment. The phases remain the same. Each year, all faculty members in the district work on a particular element—and only complete the components associated with that element. This approach provides for joint planning, allows everyone to come along together, supports just-in-time training if needed on any topic (e.g., how to write essential questions), and breaks a huge task down to more meaningful and manageable subtasks that faculty often favor.

Chapter Summary

Curriculum planning is a complex task that involves transforming the effective schools research into action (i.e., theory into practice). Robert Marzano (2003), in his *What Works in Schools: Translating Research into Action*, has identified a **"guaranteed and viable curriculum"** as the number one school factor that correlates with higher student achievement. He further concludes that although this school-level factor has the most impact on student achievement, it probably is the hardest to implement, especially within the context of the current standards movement. Schools must identify essential (versus supplemental) content and ensure that the essential content is scoped and sequenced appropriately and can be adequately addressed in the instructional time available. Multiple levels of performance expectations must be developed and aligned to appropriate standards. Applied, integrated, and contextual learning experiences need to be selected, and balanced assessment strategies, including performance tasks and rubrics, need to be implemented. Then, and only then, will a workable, usable, and teacher-friendly curriculum lead to greater student success!

Post-Assessment KWL Chart

DIRECTIONS: *Effective curriculum planning and decision making process is key to the success of educational programs. What is your own personal knowledge and understanding of the curriculum development process? You already completed What You Know and What You Want to Know. Now is the opportunity to complete What Did You Learn? Visit the online book to record your final answers.*

CURRICULUM DEVELOPMENT PROCESS		
WHAT DO YOU ALREADY KNOW?	WHAT DO YOU WANT TO KNOW?	WHAT DID YOU LEARN?

A Fable: Animal School

DIRECTIONS: *Read the Curriculum fable. Think about the connection between the fable and the curriculum concepts presented in this chapter. In class with a small group, you will come to consensus on the moral of the fable. Be prepared to share. View the online book to read the article.*

Check for Mastery: Performance Expectations

DIRECTIONS: *You rated yourself on performance expectations at the start of this chapter. Have you now mastered each performance expectation? Rate yourself using the Likert scale online. Compare this to how you rated yourself at the beginning of this chapter. If you do not know an expectation, go back to the text and re-read the information.*

Source: Thinkstock/Getty

Summary Learning Activity: The Curriculum Development Process

DIRECTIONS: *The curriculum development process contains four phases: analysis, design, implementation, and evaluation. Match each of the following statements with the appropriate phase of the curriculum development process. Choose from:*

A = Analysis, *D = Design,* *I = Implementation,* *E = Evaluation.*

_____ **1. Definition**: The process in which the purpose is translated into a plan for constructing or revising the curriculum.

_____ **2. Definition**: The process during which the plan is activated through instruction using various pedagogies and resources.

_____ **3. Definition**: The process of identifying needs, clarifying values, and searching for a purpose.

_____ **4. Definition**: The process of collecting information for monitoring progress and validating achievements.

_____ **5. Characteristics**: Utilizes sources of needs such as student, society, subject, and standards.

_____ **6. Characteristics**: Content in the three domains of learning serves as the vehicle.

_____ **7. Characteristics**: Most challenging stage for curriculum developers because of lack of ownership, time, resources, etc.

_____ **8. Characteristics**: Criteria serve as benchmarks for monitoring student progress.

_____ **9. Strategies**: Utilizes the needs assessment process to identify curricular gaps.

_____ **10. Strategies**: Utilizes multiple intelligences and differentiation strategies to meet individual student needs and interests.

_____ **11. Strategies**: Utilizes criterion-referenced rubrics to assess student mastery.

_____ **12. Strategies**: Utilizes the question "What should the student know and be able to do?" to develop multilevel, performance-based expectations.

_____ **13. Products**: Scope and sequence charts are developed.

_____ **14. Products**: School philosophy or mission/vision statements are developed.

_____ **15. Products**: Performance tasks and measures are developed and utilized to determine student achievement.

_____ **16. Products**: Applied, integrated, and authentic teaching/learning techniques are developed and implemented.

Supplemental Learning Exercises

1. Interview someone who is responsible for curriculum development in a school district. You might wish to ask them questions concerning the four stages of curriculum development process, including the following:
   - What is their process?
   - What components are found on their template?
   - Do they use any curriculum development software?
   - How do you make decisions about what content to include?
   - How have they shifted to 21st-century learning?
   - What role do standards play in the curriculum construction process?

- How do you evaluate the effectiveness of your curriculum?
- What kind of constraints place limitations on your curriculum?

2. A PLC of upper (grades four and five) elementary teachers is concerned about learning progress and student achievement in mathematics. Scores on the state test have declined, especially in the area of mathematical processes and statistics and probability. The district just implemented a new math program last year and purchased new math texts, manipulatives, and supplemental resources for program implementation. As the PLC discussed the fourth and fifth grade data, their attention was drawn to the characteristics and needs of children these age groups. Common cognitive characteristics of fourth graders include: being industrious and curious; beginning to see "bigger world," including social issues; still very concrete in their thinking; can draw information from printed material (they've moved from "learning to read" to "reading to learn"); and are easily overwhelmed. Common cognitive characteristics of fifth graders include: being good at memorizing facts; increasingly able to think abstractly; good at solving problems; enjoy rules and logic; enjoy collecting, classifying, and organizing; take pride in schoolwork and able to concentrate for longer periods of time (Wood, 2007). Given the information provided, what inferences can you make about the program? What additional information would you need to know? What curricular changes and/or improvements would you recommend?
3. Develop a philosophy statement for your discipline. A philosophy statement provides a clear, concise account of your teaching approach, methods, and expertise. Each statement should be unique and have meaning for the reader. Your philosophy should reflect your personal values and the needs of your students, society, standards, and your subject area of expertise. It should NOT be a summary of the experiences on your resume, nor is it an article on pedagogy. A Teaching Philosophy Statement should answer fundamental questions such as (1) definition and components of your discipline, (2) rationale for studying that subject area, (3) expected student outcomes, (4) references to aligned standards, (5) beliefs and core values about teaching and learning, (6) how we will use assessments to improve the program and student learning, and (7) current discipline trends and issues. Often a well-written philosophy statement will serve as a valuable tool for establishing curriculum parameters, determining instructional priorities, and providing criteria for selecting what and how to teach.
4. Working within your PLC, create a model to demonstrate your understanding of the curriculum development process. A model is defined as a graphic representation to aid in the comprehension of an abstract idea or to understand a complex process. Your model should represent key concepts and explain the four cyclic stages. You might want to include in your design some of the terms that are listed below. Additionally, you may want to enhance your model with an analogy, metaphor, poem, song, skit, role play, etc. Be prepared to present your model to your class colleagues.

For great examples of models to demonstrate the curriculum development process, visit the online book. These projects were done by Winona State University students. Enjoy!

Source: Thinkstock/Getty

Final Test

DIRECTIONS: *Read each question or statement below. Select the appropriate answer or write the correct answer in the blank provided.*

____ 1. What is the accepted order of the four steps involved in curriculum planning or development?
- A. Analysis, Design, Implementation, and Evaluation
- B. Design, Analysis, Implementation, and Evaluation
- C. Analysis, Design, Evaluation, and Implementation
- D. Design, Analysis, Evaluation, and Implementation

____ 2. Which description is the _most_ appropriate for the design phase?
- A. The process of clarifying values and searching for a purpose.
- B. The process of monitoring progress and validating achievement.
- C. The process in which the purpose is translated into a plan.
- D. The process during which the plan is activated through instruction.

____ 3. Which descriptor is the _most_ appropriate for students, society, subject, and standards?
- A. Screens or filters
- B. Sources of needs
- C. Goal and objective areas
- D. Differentiation strategies

T F 4. As part of the analysis phase, unimportant and contradictory outcomes are often eliminated by two sets of screens, the philosophy of education and the psychology of learning.

____ 5. Analysis is to needs assessment as implementation is to:
- A. pedagogy.
- B. standards.
- C. sequence.
- D. competencies.

____ 6. A key decision in the design stage of curriculum development involves:
- A. conducting a needs assessment.
- B. determining curricular outcomes.
- C. selecting a textbook.
- D. developing performance tasks and rubrics.

____ 7. Sequence describes the:
- A. order of the curriculum.
- B. amount of detail in the curriculum.
- C. format of the curriculum.
- D. transferability of the curriculum.

T F 8. Priority or power standards are the most important concepts and skills to know and to do in a discipline.

____ 9. The organization of a course is determined by the:
- A. priority standards identified.
- B. learning activities chosen.
- C. taxonomic levels of the performance expectations.
- D. scope and sequence of the content.

____ 10. What is the product that results from the implementation stage of curriculum development?
- A. Scope and sequence charts
- B. Discipline philosophy statements
- C. Action learning teaching strategies
- D. Performance tasks and rubrics

T F 11. Of the four cyclic stages curriculum development, evaluation presents the greatest challenge to curriculum developers.

____ 12. The concept of referencing is <u>best</u> described as:
- A. aligning curricular components in order to maintain the internal rigor of the curriculum.
- B. establishing meaningful curriculum goals for the 21st century.
- C. designing the opportunities to learn and relearn fundamental knowledge and skills at each level.
- D. articulating between what is taught and what is learned in the classroom.

____ 13. The curriculum design or approach of a course you teach is <u>*primarily*</u> determined by the:
- A. outcomes you select.
- B. scope and sequence of the content you choose.
- C. standards you embed.
- D. needs analysis data you collect.

____ 14. What is the preferred process for curriculum development and alignment that is advocated today?
- A. Have all teachers complete the entire template on an annual basis
- B. Have all teachers within a discipline complete the entire template on a five-year cycle
- C. Have all teachers complete the template by curricular phases on a three to four-year cycle
- D. Have all teachers complete the template by curricular components on a three-year cycle

____ 15. According to Marzano, the <u>*most*</u> significant school-level factor associated with higher student achievement is/are:
- A. a safe and orderly environment.
- B. a guaranteed viable curriculum.
- C. effective formative assessments.
- D. parent and community involvement.

DIRECTIONS: *Read each scenario below. Write a brief response.*

1. Name the four stages of the curriculum development process. Choose one of the stages, describe that phase, and discuss why you think it is the most relevant and useful of the four.
2. You are a member of the curriculum leadership team. The team was assigned the responsibility to design the curriculum template that will be used by all k-12 teachers. What essential components would be included on your template? Explain your choices.

Works Cited and Suggested Readings

Armstrong, David. (1989). *Developing and Documenting the Curriculum*. Needham Heights, MA: Allyn and Bacon.

Association for Supervision and Curriculum Development. (1998). *Curriculum Handbook*. Alexandria, VA: Author.

Doll, Ronald C. (1989). *Curriculum Development: Decision Making and Process* (6th ed.). Boston, MA: Allyn and Bacon.

Glatthorn, Allan, Carr, Judy, & Harris, Douglas. (2001). *Curricular Handbook: Planning and Organizing for Curriculum Renewal*. Alexandria, VA: ASCD. Retrieved from: http://www.ascd.org/publications/curriculum-handbook/398.aspx.

Grover, Herbert J. (1985). *A Guide to Curriculum Planning: Purpose and Procedures*. Madison, WI: Wisconsin Department of Public Instruction (WDPI).

Gunter, Mary Alice, Estes, Thomas, & Schwab, Jan Hasbrouck. (1990). *Instruction: A Models Approach*. Needham Heights, MA: Allyn and Bacon.

Henson, Kenneth. (2001). *Curriculum Planning: Integrating Multiculturalism, Constructivism, and Educational Reform*. New York, NY: McGraw-Hill Higher Education.

Jacobs, Heidi Hayes, (Ed.). (2010). *Curriculum 21: Essential Education for a Changing World*. Alexandria, VA: Association for Supervision and Curriculum Development (ASCD).

Jacobs, Heidi Hayes & Johnson, Ann. (2009). *The Curriculum Mapping Planner: Templates, Tools, and Resources for Effective Professional Development*. Alexandria, VA: Association for Supervision and Curriculum Development (ASCD).

Marzano, Robert J. (2003). *What Works in Schools: Translating Research into Action*. Alexandria, VA: Association for Supervision and Curriculum Development (ASCD).

Morrison, Gary, Ross, Steven, Kalman, Howard, & Kemp, Jerrold. (2011). *Designing Effective Instruction*. John Wiley and Sons, Inc.

No Child Left Behind Act of 2001, P.L. 107–110, 20 U.S.C. § 6319 (2002).

Olivia, Peter F. (1988). *Developing the Curriculum* (2nd ed.). *Statesboro, GA:* Georgia Southern College.

Reavis, George. (1953). The Animal School. *The Educational Forum* (*17*)2.

Saylor, Galen J., Alexander, William M., & Lewis, Arthur J. (1981). *Curriculum Planning for Better Teaching and Leaning* (4th ed.). New York, NY: Holt, Rinehart and Winston.

Schilling, David. (2013). *Knowledge Doubling Every 12 Months, Soon to be Every 12 Hours*. Retrieved from: http://www.industrytap.com.

Stong, James. (2007). Qualities of Effective Teachers. Alexandria, VA: Association for Supervision and Curriculum Development (ASCD).

Stufflebeam, Daniel L. (1971). *Educational Evaluation and Decision Making*. Itasca, IL: F.E. Peacock.

Tomlinson, Carol Ann. (2010). Leading and Managing A Differentiated Classroom. Alexandria, VA: Association for Supervision and Curriculum Development (ASCD).

Tyler, Ralph W. (1949). *Basic Principles of Curriculum and Instruction*. Chicago, IL: Chicago University Press.

Wiles, Jon & Bondi, Joseph C. (1986). *Supervision: A Guide To Practice* (2nd ed.). Columbus, OH: Charles E. Merrill.

Wood, Chip. (2007). *Yardsticks: Children in the Classroom Ages 4–14*. Turners Falls: MA. Northeast Foundation For Children.

Zais, Robert. (1976). *Curriculum: Principles and Foundations*. New York, NY: Thomas Y. Crowell Co.

Chapter 6
Developing Performance Expectations and Unpacking Standards

"If you don't know where you are going,
you'll end up someplace else."

Yogi Berra

Anticipatory Set: What Teachers Say

DIRECTIONS: *What do you know about standards? You will answer each question about standards with a yes/no. To respond, your instructor will have you text your answers to www.PollEverywhere.com and the respondents' answers will appear on the SmartBoard. Your instructor will give you specific directions for taking the poll.*

	About Standards	Yes	No
1.	I feel very well prepared to align state standards to my curriculum.		
2.	I am very well prepared to unpack state standards.		
3.	I am very well prepared to design a unit of instruction based on state standards.		
4.	The standards are a critical component of the educational reform movement.		
5.	The academic standards have reduced the time spent on teaching the fine arts and vocational education classes education classes (e.g. art, music, industrial arts).		
6.	The academic standards adopted by my state are set at an appropriate level.		
7.	Standards have led teachers to design curriculum to teach to the test.		
8.	Students will learn more because of a state's adoption of standards.		
9.	There are plenty of curricular resources available to help teach the state standards.		
10.	There is not enough class time available to teach what the state standards require.		

Chapter Overview

You are close to graduating. Congratulations! One of the many graduations requirements is to write a resume and make sure it is in tip-top shape. The first thing you must do is to establish a career objective. For example, an objective could be to gain employment as a middle school math teacher in an urban area, focusing on best practices and building relationships. To achieve that career goal, you need to brainstorm several things in your past to help you prepare for your career. Brainstorming may include several questions you might ask (1) How have I demonstrated mastery of the state licensing requirements? (2) What relevant small and large group instruction have I had? (3) What performances or teaching experiences do I have to show? (4) What volunteer experiences have I had that will enhance my background? (5) What extra-curricular organizations or activities have I participated in? and (6) How do I make my resume stand out? This is the start of building a resume. Along with the above questions, you need to make sure you include any criteria that is required for the job application, you need to weave your educational philosophy into the document, and you need to highlight what you have "done" versus what you "know." This is a large task, yet a very necessary one. Keep in mind, you will have help from your classmates, your professors, and even an expert at the university.

Creating a resume is good practice for developing performance expectations and unpacking/aligning standards. There are many similarities. Developing performance expectations and unpacking standards need to identify knowledge, skills, understandings, and dispositions just as a resume needs to unpack the coursework, teaching opportunities, volunteer activities and extra-curricular organizations you have experienced. Both are built with criteria and selecting priorities. Teaching and learning priorities are essential especially when developing curriculum, instruction and assessment. Priorities for a resume also need to be taken into consideration so the most important information is clear to the reader. Educational philosophy is also important for both; schools need a consensus in which to build an action plan, and a resume needs to implicitly draw the reader to the philosophy and thoughts of the writer. The task may be large, but no teacher ever does this alone. Like the resume writer, the teachers work collaboratively to unpack standards and develop performance expectations.

Anyone having a passing acquaintance with curriculum documents is probably aware that, whatever else they contain, there are always sections on outcomes and standards. In order to successfully unpack and align standards and develop well-written outcomes, you need to have a basic understanding of these two concepts. In this chapter, a series of questions on each topic will be answered. For outcomes: What are their components? Why are outcomes important? What sources are used to develop them? What do you label them? How many different types or forms should be included in a curriculum? What are the characteristics of a well-written outcome? How do you write them correctly? Do they reflect the different domains and levels of learning? For standards: What are standards? What is the purpose of standards? Why do we have standards? How were the standards developed? How do you unpack and align standards? What learning progressions are evident within the standards? The development of outcomes and unpacking and alignment of standards are of utmost importance in developing a workable, usable curriculum. This chapter is a "skills-based" chapter. After understanding outcomes and standards, teachers will develop the skill to write outcomes effectively and to unpack and align standards correctly.

Performance Expectations

DIRECTIONS: *How well do you know the performance expectations? Rate your knowledge of each expectation using this Likert scale. You will rate yourself again at the end of the chapter. This is for your information to assess your own learning. Visit the online book to record your answers.*

1 = I do not have any knowledge of this concept.

2 = I have minimal knowledge of this concept.

3 = I have some understanding of this concept.

4 = I have a satisfactory understanding of this concept.

5 = I am confident in my understanding of this concept.

This chapter should prepare you to:

Rating	#	Performance Expectations
	1.	Develop a working definition for the term outcome or performance expectation.
	2.	Assess the significance of action verbs in an outcome.
	3.	Defend or reject the statement that teachers who use performance expectations are more successful in generating student learning than those who do not.
	4.	Identify sources that can be used to develop performance expectations.
	5.	Use the outcome hierarchy to differentiate among various synonyms for outcomes.
	6.	Describe how many levels of outcomes are recommended to be included in a curriculum document.
	7.	Analyze the four characteristics of a well-written performance expectation or outcome.
	8.	Critique performance expectation statements for technical errors.
	9.	Discriminate among the three domains and their respective levels of learning, including examples of each.
	10.	For each taxonomy, discriminate between the "knowing" and "doing" segments.
	11.	Compare and contrast the "old" and "new" Bloom's taxonomies.
	12.	Write a well-developed, error-free performance expectation at various taxonomic levels.
	13.	Trace the history of the standards movement and discuss the internal and external forces that contributed to the advent of the standards movement.
	14.	List the criteria that were used to develop the CCSS and NGSS.
	15.	State the definition and explain the philosophy of standards.
	16.	Differentiate between standards-based (standards-led) and standards-referenced.
	17.	Explain the four steps to "unpacking" and "aligning" a standard and then use those four steps to unpack and align a given standard.
	18.	Explain the concepts of power (priority) standards and learning progressions. What three criteria does Reeves recommend for identifying power standards?.
	19.	Analyze the relationship between the standards and the spiral curriculum.
	20.	Outline three ways to increase the complexity of standards as you progress through the grade levels.

6.1 The Role of Outcomes

Curriculum development should be an ongoing and dynamic process. The process often involves four cyclic stages: analysis, design, implementation, and evaluation. A key component of this cyclic process involves the development of performance expectations, learning outcomes, or instructional targets. These terms—expectations, outcomes, targets—and others synonyms such as aims, goals, competencies, objectives, benchmarks, and/or student's skills are frequently confused and often times used interchangeably. Unfortunately, no universal agreement as to the precise meaning of these words exists among curriculum developers

(Zais, 1976). Throughout the discourse in this chapter, special attention has been given to clarify synonyms for the word outcome; hopefully, this will match what is encountered in local districts.

Performance expectations or outcomes are defined as "**what students should know, do, and care about.**" They describe the major skills, understandings, attitudes, or abilities needed to perform a task effectively and efficiently. For districts that employ a spiral design architecture (i.e., design targets with the end in mind), outcomes serve as the culminating demonstrations of learning. Whether we use the word like "ends" or "purposes," curriculum developers understand the reference that is being made to some terminal point toward which we are moving or working. In curriculum work, it is quite common for developers to identify an end—something like drawing a conclusion from a science experiment or writing a coherent, well-organized paragraph—and then prescribe the means or learning activities that will most effectively move the student toward acquiring that skill.

For curriculum development purposes, performance expectations should be stated in terms of types of learning outcomes expected. According to Ronald Doll (1989), the majority of persons in the curriculum field now say that objectives should be stated behaviorally—that is, according to the behavior to be expected. Outcomes that are performance based state what the learner will do, under what conditions, and at what level of performance if the given outcome is regarded to having been achieved. James Popham (1969) said it this way: "A properly stated behavioral objective must describe without ambiguity the nature of learner behavior or product to be measured" (pp. 34, 37).

The outcome equation is **outcome = verb + content**. The verb refers to the learning behavior and the product is the content. The "verb" is particularly important in any type of outcome. Verbs define the performance expectations, indicate observable and measurable performances, and often signify the type of assessment required. They also clarify both the domain and taxonomic levels of learning required by the student. A workable, usable curriculum clearly states what learners will be able to know, do, and care about as the result of a learning experience. In performance-based instruction (PBI), the emphasis shifts from "knowing" to "doing."

Performance expectations provide an organizing framework for planning and implementing a learning experience. In essence, performance expectations determine the "what," drive the "how," and dictate the "when." Ralph Tyler, the father of curriculum development, believed that objectives were the most important part of the curriculum. Popham (1971) in support of outcomes wrote, "There are at least three realms in which measurable objectives have considerable potential dividends: in curriculum (what goals are selected); in instruction (how to accomplish those goals); and in evaluation (determining whether objectives of the instructional sequence have been realized)" (p. 76).

Regardless of what label is used, performance expectations or outcomes provide a framework for learners to organize their plans for successfully completing a course and, more importantly, break learning down into manageable and meaningful segments. Performance expectations may be compared to a blueprint when building a house. A blueprint sets the specifications and standards of the house and shows the buyer what the finished product will look. Outcomes also force the teacher to be more precise about what is to be accomplished and, more notably, enable the teacher to communicate with students on what they must achieve (Olivia, 1988). The learner with performance expectations knows what is expected of him/her before the course begins. There should be no surprises throughout the year. Teachers who develop and use performance expectations or outcomes in their classrooms have a more manageable curriculum, better instruction and assessment, and more efficient learning results (Popham, 1987).

6.2 Selection of Outcomes

The world of education has changed dramatically since the passage of the No Child Left Behind Act (2001). More than ever in our nation's history, there is a focus on content and performance standards. This attention has led administrators and teachers to compare student performance on accepted standards, to examine standardized test scores in great depth, and to develop strategic school improvement plans. As a general rule, the selection of outcomes should be based on sound principles and theories of learning.

The standards also call for moving away from "knowing" to more "understanding and doing." Furthermore, parents and community members are paying much more attention to what is happening in our classrooms and asking if our students are being adequately prepared for college and life beyond school. As educators, we must be able to espouse that our students are:

- Learning challenging content at high levels of understanding;
- Developing essential skills and competencies, particularly in communication;
- Evolving in their capacity to think critically, solve problems creatively, and integrate new learning into prior knowledge; and
- Develop strong inter- and intrapersonal skills that support their connections to family, community, and the world of work (Aseltine, Faryniarz, & Rigazio-DiGillo, 2006, p. 2).

In Tyler's Model, students, society, and subject matter serve as the three sources of needs for developing broad goals. Today, we have added the fourth "S" in the form of standards. Clark & Starr (1986) further expand and clarify these sources when they suggest nine elements to consider when selecting or developing outcomes:

- The nature and structure of the subject;
- The needs of the students;
- The readiness of the students;
- The interests, attitudes, and other characteristics of the students;
- The larger educational goals and general aims of education;
- (The teacher's) philosophy, inclinations, and capabilities;
- Community expectations;
- The feasibility of the objective (i.e., facilities, equipment, and time available etc.); and
- Other elements in the curriculum (p. 142).

Although many sources of needs and/or external forces can affect the selection or development of course and unit outcomes, many curriculum developers rely on three significant factors. The first factor is standards. Every state has adopted, adapted, or created its own sets of standards due to requirements found in federal legislation. Later in this chapter you will learn how to unpack and align standards to your performance expectations. The second factor is curriculum resources, such as curriculum guides or textbooks that help many teachers determine course outcomes. Most textbooks, especially the Teacher's Manual, list the objectives for each chapter or unit of study. The final factor is to rely on your own knowledge, experience, and training. Ask colleagues to share their unit outcomes or learning plans with you.

6.3 Outcome Terminology

The educational literature uses an abundance of terms, rather freely and often interchangeably, to signify the expectations of education. Whereas these terms may be used synonymously in common language, it is helpful to make distinctions among the terms for curriculum development purposes. In this book, the term performance expectations and/or outcomes are used extensively. These two terms are synonymous and can be substituted for each other. They also serve as general descriptors for more specific types of expectations such as aims, competencies, learning targets, goals, and/or objectives (to just name a few).

Curriculum developers recommend that at least a three or four step hierarchy of outcomes should be included in the curriculum. This vertical hierarchy is based on differing types of outcomes, centered on varying levels of planning. Figure 1 illustrates an example of this hierarchy that is often associated with standards-led educational reform.

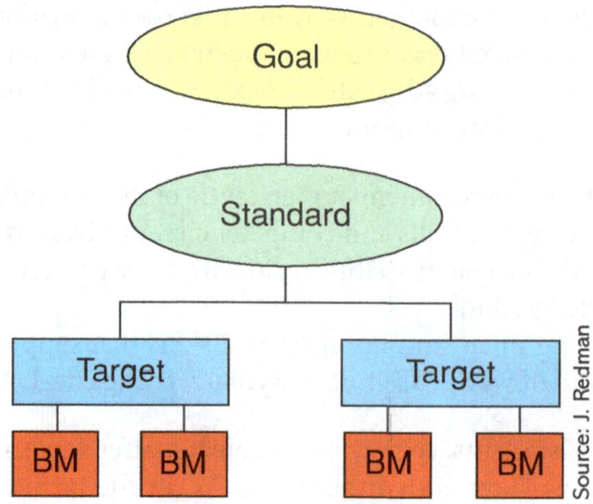

Note: BM = Benchmark

Figure 1: Outcome Hierarchy

The most general type of educational outcomes are curriculum aims. Aims are statements that describe expected life or school district outcomes (Zais, 1976). Sometimes also referred to as core abilities or mission/vision statements, curricular aims serve as statements of ideals or aspirations that express the views of educators, administrators, students, and lay citizens. Because of their global nature, aims should be few in number and clearly stated (Hunkins, 1980). An aim does not often relate directly to the classroom, but it does provide both shape and direction to more specific actions designed to achieve some future product or behavior. One statement of aims that has been extremely influential in shaping the curriculum in American schools is the "Cardinal Principles of Secondary Education." The Commission on the Reorganization of Secondary Education (1918) utilized the organizational principles of important life activities to identify curriculum aims in seven major areas (1) health; (2) command of fundamental processes; (3) worthy home membership; (4) vocational education; (5) civic education; (6) worthy use of leisure; and (7) ethical character (pp. 11–16).

Goals refer to school or discipline outcomes. A curriculum goal is a purpose or end stated in general terms without the criteria of achievement (Zais, 1976). If you were to ask a group of fifth grade teachers to identify the 10 most important things that a student will learn in mathematics, those 10 things might be referred to as goals. Some districts may refer to their goals as power or priority standards. By definition, goals differ from aims in that goals are attainable even though they may go unattained. It may take weeks, months, or even years to achieve all of your goals. Because goals are group oriented, the successful attainment of goals does not require every student to succeed (Henson, 2001).

Competencies and learning targets often refer to unit outcomes. These primary types of intended outcomes are derived from the goals and result from unpacking the knowledge, skills, understandings, and dispositions (KSUDs) found in the standards. For curriculum that is designed using a backward framework (e.g., Understanding by Design) or spiral architecture, these types of outcomes emphasize "doing" or performance of higher order thinking and feeling processes. The general outcome question of "What should students know and be able to do?" becomes "What should student be able to do?" Examples of competencies or learning targets might be developing a model of the cell, writing a persuasive speech, or comparing and contrasting the three branches of government. Both competencies and learning targets are written in observable and measurable language.

Objectives are the most specific type of outcomes and usually refer to what is expected of each student daily. Learning objectives or behavioral objectives are defined as the most immediate specific outcomes of classroom instruction on a daily lesson basis. Objectives are like roadmaps in that they chart the course for each day (Henson, 2001). Synonyms for objectives include student skills, benchmarks, and student expectations. Objectives can be developed for all types of content, ranging from memorizing definitions to problem solving to reflecting on a particular topic. Good teachers inform their students of what the lesson's objectives are for the day. Student achievement of the primary learning targets is dependent on the students learning the supporting outcomes.

As stated previously, some of these terms found in the hierarchy are used interchangeably. What is called a goal in one district may be called a learning target in another district. At what point in the hierarchy does an aim become a goal, or a goal become a competency, and/or a competency become an objective, maybe impossible to specify. In some cases, the fuzziness will make the classification dubious or ambiguous. Most educators would, however, agree that the distance between an objective and a goal is great, but that the distance between an objective and an aim is enormous. The overall goal of the hierarchy is to help developers organize the curriculum into a logical coherent structure or framework. Figure 2 traces the changes in terminology with different educational eras.

Outcome Terminology			
Hierarchy Level	**Traditional**	**Performance Based**	**Standards Led**
Life or district outcomes	Aims	Core abilities	Mission/Vision statement
School or discipline outcomes	Strands	Goals	Power or priority standards
Unit outcomes	Goals	Competencies	Learning targets
Daily learning plan	Objectives	Learning objectives	Benchmark

Figure 2: Outcome Terminology Used in Different Eras

Here is another important word about the hidden curriculum. When a curriculum evaluation indicates that teachers have been successful in attaining a goal or achieving an expectation, the curriculum is judged to be effective. These are the intended outcomes. Unknown to us, however, might be the unintended outcomes or hidden curriculum. Some people say that these are the most important outcomes. How much of that success or achievement, either directly or indirectly, is related to the unintended outcomes? One way to signify the importance of the hidden curriculum is try to make these "unintentional" outcomes more "intentional." A concept or value like good work habits could very easily be documented in the curriculum at some level of the hierarchy.

6.4 Characteristics of a Well-Written Outcome

Performance expectations that are the most useful in the classroom adhere to four characteristics of a well-written outcome:

- **Is student oriented;**
- **Defines a learning outcome;**
- **Describes an observable and measurable performance; and**
- **Is clear, concise, and precise.**

These four criteria are used to evaluate outcomes for their effectiveness at all levels of the hierarchy. Sometimes a fifth criterion, "is at the application (doing) level," may be added for unit level outcomes.

A Well-Written Outcome

- **Is student oriented**
- **Defines a learning outcome**
- **Describes an observable and measurable performance**
- **Is clear, concise, and precise**

A performance expectation that is student oriented places the emphasis on what the student is expected to do, not on what the teacher will do. Most curriculum developers believe that the curriculum should be student focused or student oriented. For this to be valid, outcomes need to be written in terms of the student.

The second criterion defines a learning outcome, meaning that the outcome states what the student should know, do, and care about. In other words, it is the learning *outcome* that is important, not the *activities* that lead to the outcome. For example, watching a video clip or studying a set of story problems are activities, not outcomes or expectations. For these activities to become outcomes, the teacher needs to identify what the student will get out of watching the clip or studying the problems.

In the third criterion, curriculum developers need to make sure that they utilize verbs that are observable and measurable. Commonly used verbs such as "to know," "to learn," and "to understand" are not observable and measurable. A partial list of similar types of "taboo verbs" that should be avoided in outcome statements is included in Figure 3. The litmus test for determining if a verb is observable and measureable is to ask "How do I know if the students can _____ (insert verb)?" For example, using the verb "to understand" and the concept of the law of supply and demand, the question becomes "*How do I know if the student understands the law of supply and demand*?" If the answer to the question asked employs the same verb you inserted, chances are that the chosen verb is observable and measurable. If the verb selected is replaced by another verb when the question is answered, then the verb is probably not acceptable and should be replaced by the verb you used to answer the question. In our example, you would not answer the question by stating "*by understanding the law of supply and demand*," but instead might state by "*explaining the law of supply and demand*." Thus to satisfy the third criterion of observable and measurable verbs (rather than vague verbs), this outcome should read "The student will be able to explain (not understand) the law of supply and demand."

Taboo Verbs		
Vague and Unobservable Verbs for the Cognitive Domain		
To know	To believe	To familiarize
To understand	To appreciate	To realize
To comprehend	To think	To learn
To remember	To gain insight	To grasp the significance
To enjoy	To value	To like

Figure 3: Taboo Verbs to Be Avoided

The last characteristic of a well-written performance expectation is that it is clear, concise, and precise. This criterion implies that there is not only a clearly defined verb and accompanying object but also only one possible meaning for each outcome statement. Clear refers to both the behavior (verb is not what was intended taxonomically) and the content (object is not well defined). Concise refers to economy of phrasing (does the outcome contain excess verbiage or unnecessary words). Precise refers to the fact that a single specific performance is identified (if multiple performances are implied, write the outcome using the highest performance level that is desired—the lower levels are assumed to be demonstrated by the performance at the higher level). Four common examples of performance expectations not being clear, concise, or precise are described below:

- **Taxonomy misrepresentation** = A lower level verb is used when a higher level action is intended;
- **Product clarity** = Specified content is too broad or too specific;
- **Economy of phrasing** = Excess wording is used and the specific action that is intended is not evident; and
- **Multiple performances** = Multiple actions or verbs are identified—should use the highest level verb as lower levels are implied.

If used, the fifth criterion is at the application level or above and is only applied to unit outcomes such as learning targets and competencies. This criterion evolved from a performance-based instruction (PBI) philosophy. In PBI, as we transition from knowing to doing, the outcome question changes from "what should students know and be able to do" to "what should students be able to do?" Thus, at the unit level, we are looking for performance or the demonstration of higher order thinking and feeling processes. This criterion asks the question, "Does the learning target or competency imply performance?"

Check for Understanding: Am I a Well-Written Outcome?

DIRECTIONS: *Listed online are 10 performance expectations. Are they correctly written? If they are poorly written, what error(s) do you see in each expectation? In the next class, we will discuss ideas on how to fix the ones that are poorly written. You will work with your "**face partner**." Your face partner is the person sitting directly across from you, the person you are facing. Visit the online book to complete the activity.*

6.5 Writing Good Outcomes

Performance expectations can communicate to learners what is expected of them—but only if they are shared with learners in an accessible manner. In 1962, Robert Mager, in his book entitled *Preparing Instructional Objectives,* pioneered a new programed approach to instructional design which involved establishing objectives for instruction. This approach made such an impact on educators that subsequent editions of the book were viewed as the "how to" manual for preparing instruction because of its clearly outlined steps on how to develop objectives. It so revolutionized instructional methods in schools that a bill was passed in California (the Stull Act, 1972) that required teachers to describe what they wanted their students to achieve (i.e., behavioral outcomes) by writing these as objectives (Taylor, 2005).

Robert Mager (1962) recommended that three components be included in an instructional objective:

- The **performance** expected of the student;
- The **conditions** under which the performance is to be demonstrated; and
- The **criteria** for master or acceptable performance.

A sample objective in this format might read: After completing a laboratory experiment, the student will be able to explain each of the six steps of the scientific method to the satisfaction of the teacher. In this case, "after completing the laboratory experiment" is the condition; the behavior is stated as "to explain the six steps of the scientific method"; and acceptable performance is "to the satisfaction of the teacher."

Another approach that is used to write objectives is called the ABCD Method (Krypsin & Feldhusen, 1974; Heinich, Molenda, Russell, & Smaldino, 2001): In this method, A = Audience, B = Behavior; C = Conditions; and D = Degree. A described group of subjects (audience) performing an observable and measurable activity (behavior) with certain specified limits (conditions) to a predetermined acceptable level (degree).

The following questions, descriptions, and examples are cited to aid your understanding of the ABCD Method:

- Audience = Who is to exhibit the performance? Audience describes the learners for whom the objective is written (e.g., the student and fifth graders).
- Behavior = What observable and measurable performance is the learner to exhibit? The behavior is the selected verb that describes what the audience will be able to do (e.g., describe, explain, synthesize, and argue).
- Condition = What conditions are provided for the learner at the time of evaluation? The condition describes the circumstances under which the audience will perform the behavior (e.g., with or without resources, after watching a video, and given a ruler).
- Degree = What constitutes a minimum acceptable response? Degree components explain the standard(s) for acceptable performance of the behavior (e.g., attributes of acceptable performance, to the satisfaction of the teacher, with no more than three errors, and a specified number.).

Although both the Mager approach and the ABCD Method are still used today, the authors of this book prefer to write performance expectations using the outcome equation. The outcome equation simply calls for verb plus content. Note the examples in Figure 4 for a science unit on cells:

After completing the Unit on Cells, the student will be able to:

- Explain Hooke's cell theory.
- Label the organelles in a cell diagram.
- Match each organelle with its function.
- Compare and contrast mitosis and meiosis.
- Differentiate among three types of cell transport.
- Create a model that illustrates the cell.

Figure 4: Sample Outcomes

Performance expectations are the intended outcomes of the learning experiences. They describe what you want learners to be able to know, do, and care about and they must be stated in observable, measurable terms. There are just a few simple rules for writing effective performance expectations. Good, instructionally sound outcomes should:

- Describe the performance of a major skill.
- Begin with an action verb.
- Must be measurable and observable.
- Are clear, concise, and precise statements describing the action.
- Specify a single performance/outcome, not a combination.
- Describe an intended outcome, not the learning process.

6.6 Domains and Taxonomic Levels of Learning

The verb component in each outcome determines the domain of learning that is being emphasized. Most curriculum developers recognize three domains of learning (1) **Cognitive = domain of knowing**; (2) **Affective = domain of feeling**; and (3) **Psychomotor = domain of doing**. The three domains, see Figure 5, are not completely independent of one another, nor does attaining success in one domain, guarantee accomplishment in another. At one time curriculum development was focused exclusively on the cognitive domain as it was believed that if students were successful in the cognitive aspects of schooling, the other domains would take care of themselves (Hunkins, 1980). Although not completely balanced today, as cognitive domain expectations still dominate, curriculum leaders include many more affective and psychomotor outcomes in their curriculums.

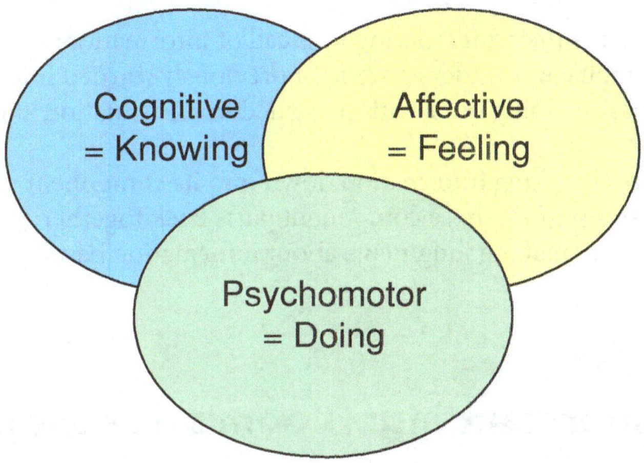

Source: J. Redman

Figure 5: The Three Domains of Learning

The Domains

- Cognitive = Domain of knowing
- Affective = Domain of feeling
- Psychomotor = Domain of doing

Check for Understanding: Domains of Learning

DIRECTIONS: *Examine the performance statements online and determine the domain of learning they represent. In the next class, you will write C if a Cognitive Domain statement; A if Affective; and P if Psychomotor. To help yourself, ask: What is the primary focus or primary intent? You will work with a partner. To get into pairs, each student will receive an* ***"opposite" card****. Students will find their matching card, and hence their partner. Cards will have pictures of night/day, before/after, and cold/hot. Visit the online book to complete the activity.*

Taxonomy is defined as the science of classification. Each domain consists of a hierarchy of taxonomic levels reflecting a range of student behaviors from simple to complex. As performance expectations are developed, knowledge of each domain and its levels are useful in providing students with opportunities to engage in a variety of behaviors to accommodate their diverse interests, needs, and abilities (Kindsvatter et al., 1992). Each domain also has its taxonomic levels divided into "knowing" and "doing" sections. According to most curriculum developers, performance expectations must be written at the "application level," at a minimum, in order to be performance based.

The cognitive domain deals with all types of knowledge—facts, concepts, generalizations, principles, theories, and laws. Cognitive outcomes refer to the intellectual dimensions of an individual's learning. Benjamin Bloom (1956) defined the cognitive domain as including objectives that "deal with the recall and recognition of knowledge and the development of intellectual abilities and skills" (p. 7). **Bloom's taxonomy** contains six levels:

- **Knowledge** = Emphasizes the remembering or recall of information;
- **Comprehension** = Emphasizes understanding of previously learned information;
- **Application** = Emphasizes using information learned in one situation and applying that information in another;
- **Analysis** = Emphasizes breaking information down into its component parts;
- **Synthesis** = Emphasizes putting those component parts back together; and
- **Evaluation** = Emphasizes making judgments about information based on criteria.

Check for Understanding: Bloom's Taxonomy

DIRECTIONS: *For the next class, read online each of the performance statements and categorize them using Bloom's taxonomy. Write the appropriate letter(s) in the blank. Select from: K = Knowledge; C = Comprehensive; Ap = Application; An = Analysis; S = Synthesis; and E = Evaluation. In the next class, there will be six posters on the wall, labeled with the above taxonomies. Students will form six groups; each group will be responsible for one taxonomy. The students will list the performance words on the poster and then share with the class. This type of activity is adapted from a learning activity called "Graffiti" (Rutherford, 2002). Visit the online book to complete the activity.*

Figure 6 depicts what learners do in each level of Bloom's taxonomy.

Cognitive Domain Taxonomy	
Taxonomic Level	**Do Learners . . .**
Knowledge	Recall information?
Comprehension	Grasp the meaning of content?
Application	Do it/use?
Analysis	Break it down into parts?
Synthesis	Create something new?
Evaluation	Judge quality/effectiveness?

Figure 6: Bloom's Taxonomy for the Cognitive Domain

Figure 7 contains a list of verbs that are associated with each level of Bloom's taxonomy.

Level 1—**Knowledge**: Recalling, remembering, and recognizing

Outcomes at the knowledge level include the ability to:

define	state	describe	record
identify	recall	match	recognize
select	memorize	label	name
cite	count	indicate	list

Level II—**Comprehension**: Understanding, explaining, summarizing

Outcomes at the comprehension level include the ability to:

translate	transform	illustrate	extrapolate
restate	interpret	rearrange	paraphrase
explain	express	estimate	summarize
give examples	generalize	comment	convert
trace	discuss	extend	report

Level III—**Application**: Using ideas, applying concepts, and solving problems

Outcomes at the application level include the ability to:

apply	compute	choose	organize
use	transfer	operate	practice
dramatize	solve	demonstrate	discover
complete	change	calculate	perform
modify	structure	show	improve upon

Level IV—**Analysis**: Reasoning or breaking into component parts

Outcomes at the analysis level include the ability to:

discriminate	put into lists	analyze	diagnose
diagram	categorize	contrast	compare
subdivide	differentiate	classify	experiment
separate	distinguish	infer	deduce

Level V—**Synthesis**: Creating or putting components back together

Outcomes at the synthesis level include the ability to:

write	produce	create	originate
design	modify	develop	formulate
construct	compose	plan	manipulate
role play	revise	generate	integrate
prepare	outline	assemble	sequence

Level VI—**Evaluation**: Making a judgment or evaluating based on criteria

Outcomes at the evaluation level include the ability to:

judge	evaluate	appraise	critique
weigh	rate	conclude	criticize
rank	defend	justify	support
assess	validate	verify	measure
check	test	persuade	recommend

Figure 7: Cognitive Domain Verb List

The affective domain includes those outcomes that deal with attitudes, values, feelings, appreciations, and interests. Krathwohl, Bloom, & Masia (1964) defined the affective domain as including objectives that "emphasized a feeling tone, an emotion, or a degree of acceptance or rejection" (p. 7). Affective outcomes include such expectations as voluntarily reading a book, developing an appreciation for a sculpture, checking your work, and following safety rules in the science classroom. Of the three domains, affective level outcomes are the most difficult to assess. The five categories of the affective domain, from lowest to highest, are as follows:

- **Receiving** = Emphasizes awareness to new information or experiences;
- **Responding** = Emphasizes reacting to phenomena, communication, or a request by someone or some external force;
- **Valuing** = Emphasizes attaching worth or value to something out of one's own accord;
- **Organizing** = Emphasizes bringing different values together to build a value system; and
- **Characterizing** = Emphasizes putting component parts back together;

Figure 8 depicts what learners do in each of Krathwohl's taxonomies.

Affective Domain Taxonomy	
Taxonomic Level	**Do Learners . . .**
Receiving	Show awareness?
Responding	Change behavior because asked?
Valuing	Attach personal worth or value internally?
Organizing	Relate values to those that already exist?
Characterizing (or Internalizing)	Respond consistently, make part of character?

Figure 8: Krathwohl's Taxonomy for the Affective Domain

Figure 9 contains a list of verbs that are associated with each level of Krathwohl's taxonomy.

Level 1—**Receiving**: Attending and becoming aware of a stimulus

Some words or phrases used to indicate receiving are:

to accept	to acknowledge	to be aware
to view	to show awareness	to show interest
to tolerate	to show alertness	to perceive
to notice	to pay attention	to hear

Level II—**Responding**: Doing something about the phenomenon because of some external force

Some words and phrases used to indicate responding are:

follow	care for	accept responsibility
obey	agree to	communicate
respond	comply	contribute
assist	conform	cooperate
consent	visit	will do

Level III—**Valuing**: Developing attitudes; action perpetuated by intrinsic motivation

Some words and phrases used to indicate valuing are:

adopt	commit	initiate
desire	volunteer	assume responsibility
answer freely	express	participate willingly
seek	exhibit loyalty	use resources to
value	be willing to	show concern

Level IV—**Organizing**: Arranging values systematically or establishing a values system

Some words and phrases used to indicate organizing are:

adapt	group	conceptualize
adjust	arrange	rank
disclose	classify	reveal
prefer	choose	select

Level V—**Characterizing**: Internalizing a set of values so the response becomes automatic

Some words or phrases used to indicate characterizing are:

serve	devote	influence
advocate	exemplify	justify behavior
defend	exhibit	show continual desire to
display	expose	show consistent devotion to
support	maintain	act upon

Figure 9: Affective Domain Verb List

The psychomotor domain involves the development of motor and manipulative skills. Sometimes referred to as the perceptual-motor skills, psychomotor learning deals with a student's physical responses, including bodily movements and muscular coordination. This domain has always been relevant to subjects such as physical education, art, music, drama, business, industrial arts, family and consumer sciences, and other vocational education courses.

Several different taxonomies, each with their own set of strengths and weaknesses, have been developed over time. Elizabeth Simpson's (1972) psychomotor taxonomy included seven levels: Perception, Set, Guided Response, Mechanism, Complex Overt Response, Adaptation, and Origination. Another taxonomy was developed by Anita Harrow (1972) that focused on observable behaviors ranging from simple to complex: reflex movement, basic fundamental movement, perceptual abilities, physical abilities, skilled movements, and non-discursive communication. Savage and Armstrong (1987) suggested a simplified framework that included four levels: Awareness, Individual Components, Integration, and Free Practice. The taxonomy used in this book is an eclectic approach that draws upon several of the ideas found in the other taxonomies:

- **Observing** = Emphasizes sensing cues and attending to the mental aspects of a physical event;
- **Imitating** = Emphasizes attempting to copy a physical behavior;
- **Practicing** = Emphasizes trying a physical event over and over again; and
- **Adapting** = Emphasizes fine-tuning and performing the activity on several occasions with no supervision or support.

Figure 10 depicts what learners do in each eclectic taxonomy.

Psychomotor Domain Taxonomy	
Taxonomic Level	**Do Learners . . .**
Observing	Watch others to detect cues to act?
Imitating	Mimic the action?
Practicing	Do it or perform it over and over again?
Adapting	Make minor adjustments in order to perfect the performance?

Figure 10: An Eclectic Taxonomy for the Psychomotor Domain

Shutterstock.com

Figure 11 contains a list of verbs that are associated with each level of the eclectic psychomotor taxonomy.

Level I—**Observing**: Recognizing and detecting sensory cues

Some words that describe behaviors at the perception level are:

detect	observe	sense
feel	perceive	smell
hear	recognize	taste
listen	see	view
watch	touch	read

Level II—**Imitating**: Mimicking the action or becoming ready to act

Some words and phrases that describe behavior at the imitation level are:

copy	manipulate with guidance	achieve a posture
duplicate	operate under supervision	place hands, arm, etc.
imitate	assume a body stance	position the body
repeat	try the activity	establish a body position

Level III—**Practicing**: Performing the activity and increasing efficiency

Some words or phrases that describe behavior at the practice level are:

conduct	improve efficiency	complete with confidence
produce	make	show dexterity
demonstrate	practice	execute
pace	increase speed	perform

Level IV—**Adaptating**: Performing automatically or applying to a new situation

Some words and phrases that describe behavior at the adaptation level are:

apply	advance with assurance	control
direct	maintain efficiency	guide
excel	perform automatically	manage
master	organize	perfect
proceed	correctly install	adjust

Figure 11: Psychomotor Domain Verb List

6.7 A Revised Bloom's Taxonomy

As stated earlier, Benjamin Bloom's original taxonomy provided a carefully developed definition for each of the six major levels of learning in the cognitive domain. The categories were knowledge, comprehension, application, analysis, synthesis, and evaluation. These categories were ordered from simple to complex and concrete to abstract. Furthermore, it was assumed that the taxonomy represented a cumulative hierarchy, where each simpler category was a prerequisite to mastery of the next more complex level (Krathwohl, 2002).

The Anderson and Krathwohl (2001) revision of the original taxonomy maintained the six levels, but renamed three of the categories. The knowledge category was renamed remember, the comprehension category was renamed understand, and the synthesis category was renamed creating. Reviews felt that each category of the original taxonomy not only implied a knowledge dimension, but a cognitive processes dimension as well. The cognitive processes dimension of the framework implies thinking or action, and, as such, should employ verb like terms or gerunds for labels. They also felt that creating was the highest level of learning in the cognitive domain. Part of this rationale may be traced to the influence of the standards and the use of backward design models. Figure 12 summarizes the traditional and revised Bloom's taxonomies.

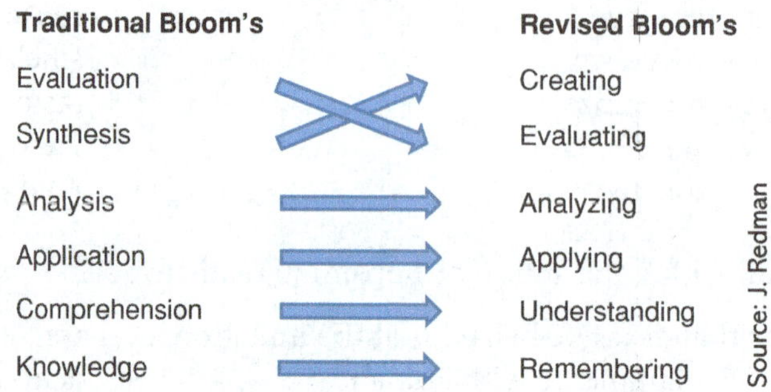

Figure 12: A Comparison of the Old and New Bloom's Taxonomies

Bloom's Digital Taxonomies

For information on an adaptation of Bloom's taxonomy, digital version, visit the online book. This link will provide the reader with what types of technologies/apps fall into which taxonomy. For example, Wordle is in the remembering taxonomy, a Google search is understanding, and Prezi is in creating.

6.8 History of The Standards Movement

Educational reform over the past decade has been characterized as "standards-led educational reform." The reauthorization of the Elementary and Secondary Education Act (ESEA), entitled Every Student Succeeds Act (ESSA), is again based upon a foundation of standards, assessment, and accountability. Standards-led educational reform emphasizes the results side, rather than the input side, of the equation. End products and results (i.e., greater student achievement or success) are mandated and no longer can customary "givens" (i.e., money, time, strategies, and texts) be used as excuses. Additionally, there is a new driver—Common Core State Standards in English and Mathematics and Next Generation Standards in Science—influencing the traditional educational tools of curriculum, instruction, and assessment. Many educational experts agree that unpacking and aligning the new standards will be as much about "how" as it is about "what."

The vision for standards-based education began with the publication of *A Nation at Risk* in 1983. This publication is considered to be a landmark event in educational history. Dissatisfied with the performance of American students on standardized tests, the then Secretary of Education, Terrel Bell initiated the National Commission on Excellence in Education. The report essentially said American schools were failing and this touched off a wave of reform. Almost thirty-five years later, the *A Nation at Risk* agenda, right or wrong, is still at the heart of the reform movement which called for the establishment and implementation at the state and local levels of some form of nationally approved, uniform, and world class academic standards (Henson, 2001).

Many forces contributed to the perceived need for standards, including declining standardized test scores, poor international comparisons, employer dissatisfaction, lack of curriculum relevance, lack of capacity, changing societal/student demographics, and philosophical beliefs of politicians, educators, and the public.

Standards were created and chosen on what a student needs to be literate and to be competitive in the job market. Standards were to have high expectations; outline what students need to know, understand, and be able to do; ensure that excellence and equity are valued; and place an emphasis on effective teaching and instruction.

The standards initiative is a "sea change" in education for teaching and learning. By 1994, a reauthorization of ESEA under President Clinton entitled The Improving America's Schools Act (IASA) was passed into law to ensure all states had rigorous standards for all subject areas and grade levels. IASA required all states to (1) adopt, adapt, or create their own standards and (2) create assessments and accountability plans to measure student progress. This momentum carried forward with No Child Left Behind (NCLB) in 2001 under President Bush. NCLB required states to make annual progress toward all students demonstrating proficiency of the state standards by 2014 as measured by standardized testing. Public disapproval was high as no state reached the goal. Common Core standards, a national curriculum, were the only waiver approved during the NCLB era. In 2015, under President Obama, ESSA replaced the NCLB. The key highlights of ESSA according to Educator Advocates, ASCD (2015):

- Shifting key decisions about accountability, evaluations, and school improvement to the state and school districts;
- Ensuring personalized and embedded educator supports;
- Allowing states to limit the amount of time testing and decide on how much weight to give tests;
- Requiring state accountability to include academic and other indicators such as engagement, safety, and climate; and
- Requiring states to show how they are improving conditions for learning.

In 2010, the Common Core State Standards were released to the states. Resulting from a voluntary joint initiative on behalf of the National Governor's Association (NGA) and the Council of Chief State School Officers (CCSSO), the intent of the Common Core Standards will help ensure that students are receiving a high quality education consistently, from school to school and state to state. Teams of educators and administrators from three primary organizations developed CCSS: Achieve, ACT (American College Testing), and the College Board. Common Core State Standards were reviewed by organizations such as NEA (National Education Association), AFT (American Federation of Teachers), International Reading Association (now called International Literacy Association), NCTE (National Council of Teachers of English), and NCTM (National Council of Teachers of Math).

Common Core Information

For more information on the Common Core Standards, visit the online book.

Additionally, through a collaborative, state-led process, new K-12 science standards, called the Next Generation Science Standards (NGSS), have also been developed. These standards are rich in content and practice and are arranged in a coherent manner across disciplines and grades to provide all students an internationally benchmarked science education.

The CCSS in English Language Arts and Mathematics represent a set of expectations for student knowledge and skills that will result in high school graduates who are prepared for success in college and careers. A particular standard was included in the final document only when the best available evidence indicated that its mastery was essential for college and career readiness in a 21st century, global competitive society. The Common Core is intended to provide clearer standards that will help students and parents understand what is expected of them and allow for more self-directed learning by students. Additionally, Common Core expectations will be consistent for all kids and not dependent on a student's residence. Students will be able to transition between states much more easily due to their portability. Moreover, the Common Core will provide the opportunity for instructors to tailor curriculum and teaching methods and will assure what is taught is aligned with new assessments and future accountability measures.

Criteria used to develop the Common Core are listed below:

- Fewer, clearer, higher, and different;
- Aligned with college and work expectations;
- Include rigorous content and application of knowledge through higher order skills;
- Build upon strengths and lessons of current state standards;
- Informed by top performing countries, so that all students are prepared to succeed in our global economy and society;
- Evidence and/or research based; and
- Realistic and practical for the classroom.

The CCSS were designed using spiral architecture. As students' progress through the grade levels, content and skills are revisited and expanding upon in the depth and breadth of coverage.

In 1994, every state was to have a set of standards. By 2009, the shift went from each state to the nation, having a set of common standards. As of August 2015, 42 states, the Department of Defense Education Activity, Washington, DC, Guam, the Northern Mariana Islands, and the U.S. Virgin Islands have formally adopted the CCSS in ELA/Literacy and Mathematics. As many as 46 states had adopted the CCSS in the past (www.commoncorestandards.org). Adoption means that the Common Core State Standards will serve as the policy document on which curriculum, instruction, and assessment in the state are based. Figure 13 depicts a timeline that led to the standards movement from 1965 to present.

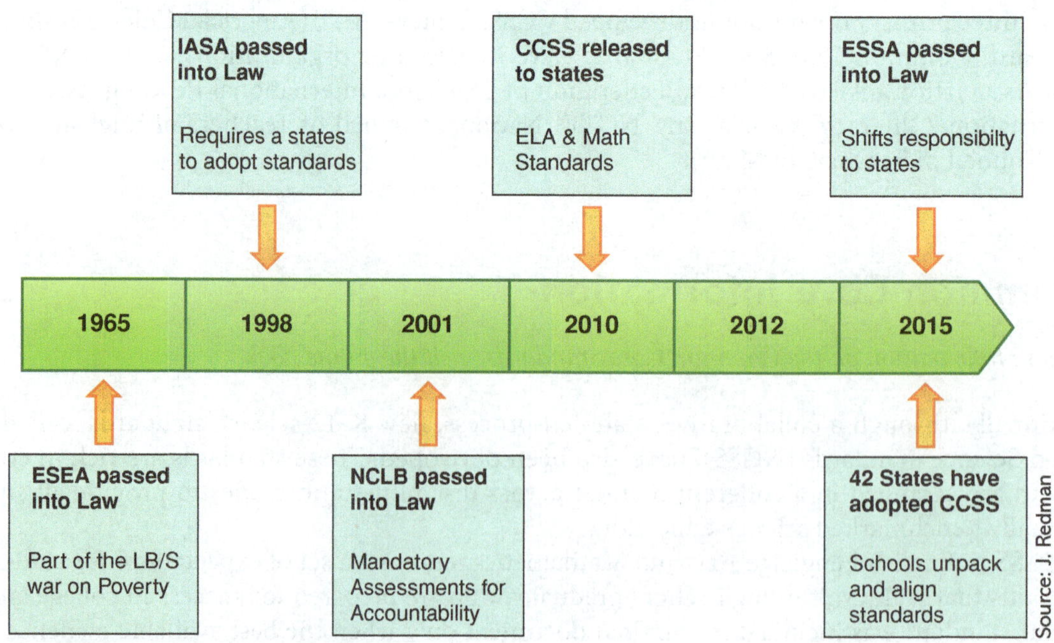

Figure 13: Standards Timeline

There is, however, a national philosophical debate about the Common Core. The "pro" Common Core debate centers on the continuity of standards for all students in all states, so every student has access to the same standards. The "con" Common Core debate centers on the desire for local control to decide which specific standards are taught. The vast majority of people, though, agree that standards are necessary in today's educational world.

6.9 Definition and Philosophy of Standards

According to Guskey and Jung (2013), standards are statements that describe what educators want students to learn and be able to do as a result of their experiences in school. Standards serve as patterns of evidence to judge a student's performance. The standards philosophy states that all students can learn and achieve at high levels. Here is an example of a Minnesota fourth grade number and operation math standard: Demonstrate mastery of multiplication and division basic facts; multiply multi-digit numbers; solve real-world and mathematical problems using arithmetic (http://education.state.mn.us/MDE/EdExc/StanCurri/K-12AcademicStandards/Math/index.html).

Standards may be viewed as "hybrid outcomes." They are very similar to outcomes in that they identify the expectations that students should know and be able to do. They also are performance statements that exhibit many of the characteristics of a well-written outcome. The insertion of the word hybrid refers to the heavy density and complex nature of the standards. Each standard is chalk full of information and expectations, unlike outcomes, which we hope are rather simple, clear, concise, and precise. It is due to this hybrid nature that forces curriculum developers to unpack and align standards.

Why set standards? School districts establish standards (1) to encourage the community in dialogue with educators about the schools, (2) to make external and explicit our "understood" or "assumed" ideas of good education, (3) to identify clear, visible goals for teaching and learning, and (4) to help make educational opportunities equitable and to hold all accountable. Furthermore, it is the law of the land.

6.10 Unpacking and Aligning Standards

School districts need to align their curriculum so that it is **standards-led**, not **standards-referenced.** According to Linda Darling Hammond (2013), "Standards are nothing but words on a piece of paper until they are translated into expectations and actions guiding what students and teachers actually do on behalf of learning." The first step in aligning standards is unpacking the knowledge, skills, understandings, and dispositions (KSUDs) found within their dense structure.

Think about your last vacation. You thought about what you needed—clothes, toiletries, books to read, and, of course, your technology needs. You packed up your duffle bag and headed out. When your trip was over and you walked in the door, no doubt you had to unpack that duffle bag. When you unpacked, you returned some of your items to their place in your home. The charger went back in the outlet; the sandals went back in the closet. Some items were placed in the laundry basket, and others, not worn, went back to the drawer. Unpacking standards, in its simplest form, is similar to unpacking a bag. All the standards are packaged in a clear and sequenced format (the duffle bag). However, until teachers take out each standard, examine them, and get to understand them, they will not be able to use them effectively. They need to unpack the "duffle bag" to know about each packed item, the standards.

Most school districts have teams of teachers unpack the standards. Often this is accomplished by grade level and/or department teams. **Unpacking** may also be called "breaking apart" the standards. It is a timely process, yet when done well, the teacher's job becomes much more consistent and each teacher can then plan lessons to suit the needs of his/her students. **Aligning** refers to matching KSUDs to curriculum, instruction, and assessment components. There are four key steps to unpacking and aligning standards:

1. Select standard and review related standards;
2. Underline content demand (usually noun phrases) and highlight the cognitive process demands (verbs or verb-like phrases);
3. Identify key KSUDs. KSUDs stand for:
   - **K**nowledge: What does the student need to know? What are the basic concepts?
   - **S**kills: What skills does the student need in relation to the knowing? What will the student do?
   - **U**nderstanding: What will the student understand as a result of this standard? Can the student explain, summarize, and/or interpret the information?
   - **D**ispositions: What character or mindsets does the student need? What habits of the mind are called for?
4. Align the KSUDs with the triad of elements. Develop curricular, instructional, or assessment components for each significant KSUDs.

Figure 14 visually depicts the KSUDs for a standard. Please note that some alignment processes also ask the curriculum leaders to determine the cognitive rigor of the standard. The concept of cognitive rigor is particularly important for assessment, especially state-mandated testing. As such, the authors of this text have chosen wait and will have that discussion in the assessment chapters of the book.

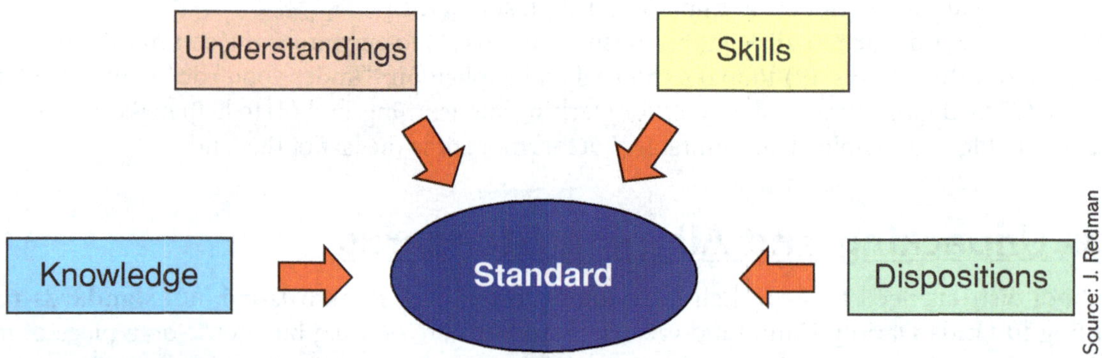

Figure 14: KSUDs for a Standard

Unpacking and aligning is often done visually. A typical way to unpack and align is shown in Figure 15 using an ELA example:

Unpacking and Aligning Standards		
Step 1	**Unpacking** Select standard and review related standards.	*Find:* **CCSS ELA.W.7.8** Gather relevant information from multiple print and digital sources, using search terms effectively; assess the credibility and accuracy of each source; and quote or paraphrase the data and conclusions of others while avoiding plagiarism and following a standard format for citation. *Related standards:* CCSS ELA.W.6.8; CCSS ELA.W.8.8 CCSS ELA.W.7.7 CCSS ELA.W.7.9
Step 2	**Unpacking** Underline content demand (usually noun phrases) and highlight or bold the cognitive process demands (verbs or verb-like phrases).	**Gather** relevant information from multiple print and digital sources, **using** search terms effectively; **assess** the credibility and accuracy of each source; and **quote** or **paraphrase** the data and conclusions of others while **avoiding** plagiarism and **following** a standard format for citation.
Step 3	**Unpacking** Identify key KSUDs.	*Knowledge:* Identifying appropriate sources; Defining plagiarism; Identifying parts to include in a citation *Skills:* Gathering data from print and electronic sources; Learning how to cite a source; Using search terms; Drawing conclusions based on data *Understandings:* Knowing what makes a source credible; Understanding the characteristics of credible and accurate source; Avoiding plagiarism *Dispositions:* Recognizing the importance of citing sources appropriately; Valuing Wikipedia as a source
Step 4	**Aligning** Align the KSUDs with the triad of elements found on your school's template. *(Note: Option that is illustrated is underlined.)*	*Curriculum Options:* Outcomes, Content (Enduring understandings), Scope & sequence, Spiral design *Example:* Cite a source using APA style; Develop a set of search terms for a topic *Instruction Options:* Teaching strategy; Resources; Differentiation; Practice activity *Example:* Small group activity by PLC --Given the topic on your card, identify five credible sources you could use to research that topic. *Assessment Options:* Checks for understanding, Test item; Task; Rubric; Homework assignment *Example:* T F Wikipedia is generally considered to be a very appropriate and credible source for research.

Figure 15: Unpacking and Aligning Standards

Check for Understanding: Anatomy of a Standard

DIRECTIONS: *Standards represent a set of expectations for student knowledge and skills that will result in high school graduates who are prepared for success in college and careers. Educational reform over the last decade has been characterized as "standards-led reform." Unpacking and aligning standards are key processes in this movement. Select one of the ELA Common Core State Standards online or find and use one that is in your content area. In the next class, you and a partner will use the steps outlined in Figure 15,* ***unpack*** *and* ***align*** *the standard. Visit the online book to complete the activity.*

6.11 Power Standards and Learning Progressions

In his book *Power Standards,* Larry Ainsworth (2003) stated, "So many standards, so little time! How can educators at every grade level and in every content area effectively teach and assess all the standards within the given instructional time each year (p. 1)?" Standards do have the promise and potential to help focus and bolster your curriculum, instruction, and assessment. The challenge still remains, however, that there are many standards and very little time to cover them all. Many school districts have met this challenge by developing **priority** or **power standards**. Power standards separate the standards that are "absolutely essential" from those that are "nice-to-know." Reeves (2002) offers three criteria to help with this selection process:

- **Endurance** = Will this standard provide students with knowledge and skills that will be of value beyond a single test date?
- **Leverage** = Will this standard provide knowledge and skills that will be of value in multiple disciplines?
- **Readiness** = Will this standard provide students with essential knowledge and skills necessary for success in the next grade level or level of instruction?

Standards are woven into clear and developmentally aligned learning progressions that chart a course from kindergarten to twelfth grade. The term **learning progression** refers to the purposeful sequencing of teaching and learning expectations across multiple stages, ages, and grade levels. Learning progressions descriptors help to "unpack" how learning might unfold for most students over time, moving from novice to expert performance (Hess, 2008). These progressions offer a framework for thinking about, studying, and understanding a content topic. Learning progressions often can be used to predict how students best learn content knowledge, skills, and conceptual understanding over time within a specific discipline of study. A sample set of learning progressions for fractions is depicted in Figure 16.

Learning Progression Example
• Gr. 3. Develop an understanding of fractions as numbers. • Gr. 4. Extend understanding of fraction equivalence and ordering. • Gr. 4. Build fractions from unit fractions by applying and extending previous understandings of operations on whole numbers. • Gr. 4. Understand decimal notation for fractions and compare decimal fractions. • Gr. 5. Use equivalent fractions as a strategy to add and subtract fractions. • Gr. 5. Apply and extend previous understandings of multiplication and division to multiply and divide fractions. • Gr. 6. Apply and extend previous understandings of multiplication and division to divide fractions by fractions.

Figure 16: Learning Progression Example for Fractions

Learning progressions also have much in common with the spiral curriculum. As previously stated, the standards were developed using a backward design or design-down, deliver-up approach. The College and Career Readiness Standards (CCRS) are at the top of the spiral and serve as the anchor standards. Goal achievement of those anchor standards should be one of our top public educational priorities. The updraft in the spiral (what Brunner called the structure of the disciplines) is very similar to the learning progressions in each discipline. At each successive grade level, the content and skills are revisited and expanded in depth and breadth. Finally, many school districts unpack and align the standards to their curriculum, instruction, and assessment documents, materials, and resources. During this process, learning targets and benchmarks are often developed as part of the curriculum development process.

Standards are hybrid outcomes and as a type of outcome follow the outcome equation of verb + content. Educators discover this fact in the unpacking process when asked to underline the content and highlighted the verbs. This fact, coupled with the spiral architecture design, is how educators increase the complexity and determine the learning progressions within a subject area. How do you increase the complexity of a standard at each successive grade level? Three options exist:

- Increase the level of learning (i.e., the taxonomic level of the verb);
- Expand the depth and breadth of content coverage; and
- Enhance the connections, interplay, and integration of concepts within the standards.

Chapter Summary

Curriculum evaluation in this country is based exclusively on determining the degree to which the stated curriculum purposes have been achieved. Every school improvement effort espouses increased student achievement as its foundation. The standards establish specific K-12 grade-by-grade standards (and in some cases grade spans in high school) in specific disciplines with a steady progression of development leading to college and career readiness by the end of high school. Through their PLCs, teams of teachers address, "What should students know?"; "How do I know that they know?"; and "What do I do if they do not know?" Participants will unpack the standards, investigate the KSUDs inherent in the standards, and build a common language for K-12 literacy in all disciplines. In turn, the KSUDs will guide the selection or facilitate the development of life, school district, discipline, unit, and daily outcomes. School leaders need to accentuate learning rather than teaching, to work collaboratively on matters related to learning, and to hold themselves accountable for the kind of results that fuel increased student learning and achievement. Teachers need to be good decision makers!

A Fable: The Sea Horse

DIRECTIONS: *Read the Curriculum fable. Think about the connection between the fable and the curriculum concepts presented in this chapter. In class with a small group, you will come to consensus on the moral of the fable. Be prepared to share. View the online book to read the article.*

Check for Mastery: Performance Expectations

DIRECTIONS: *You rated yourself on performance expectations at the start of this chapter. Have you now mastered each performance expectation? Rate yourself using the Likert scale online. Compare this to how you rated yourself at the beginning of this chapter. If you do not know an expectation, go back to the text and re-read the information.*

Summary Learning Activity: Analyzing Performance Expectations

DIRECTIONS: *Examine the following list of performance expectations or outcome statements. First, check the box that most appropriately describes the taxonomic level of that outcome. Second, some of the performance expectations are effective and some are weak. Decide which are well written and effective and which are weak and lack the characteristics of a good performance expectation. Indicate which outcome statements are well written by writing "OK" on the blank. For each outcome statement that you decide is weak, note in the margin which characteristic(s) it does not meet. Then rewrite the performance expectation so that it is correct.*

______	
☐ Low-level outcome ☐ High-level outcome	1. Read, interpret, and construct bar graphs.
______ ☐ Low-level outcome ☐ High-level outcome	2. Study a diagram on the structure of the atom.
______ ☐ Low-level outcome ☐ High-level outcome	3. Help the students appreciate classical music.
______ ☐ Low-level outcome ☐ High-level outcome	4. Trace the flow of blood through the heart.
______ ☐ Low-level outcome ☐ High-level outcome	5. Follow safety rules in the industrial technology laboratory.
______ ☐ Low-level outcome ☐ High-level outcome	6. Describe how a bill becomes a law.
______ ☐ Low-level outcome ☐ High-level outcome	7. Write a research paper using multiple sources on a chosen history topic.
______ ☐ Low-level outcome ☐ High-level outcome	8. Understand the connection between matter and energy.
______ ☐ Low-level outcome ☐ High-level outcome	9. Develop the ability to solve story problems.
______ ☐ Low-level outcome ☐ High-level outcome	10. Learn the rules for capitalization.
______ ☐ Low-level outcome ☐ High-level outcome	11. Identify the differences among igneous, metamorphic, and sedimentary rocks.

______ ☐ Low-level outcome ☐ High-level outcome	12.	Compare and contrast the executive, legislative, and judicial branches of government.
______ ☐ Low-level outcome ☐ High-level outcome	13.	Use a topographic map to gather information about Minnesota.
______ ☐ Low-level outcome ☐ High-level outcome	14.	Identify, give examples, and apply statistical skills to real-life problems.
______ ☐ Low-level outcome ☐ High-level outcome	15.	Assess the impact of alternative energy sources on the environment.
______ ☐ Low-level outcome ☐ High-level outcome	16.	Explain the light and dark reactions of photosynthesis.
______ ☐ Low-level outcome ☐ High-level outcome	17.	View a video clip on the Civil War.
______ ☐ Low-level outcome ☐ High-level outcome	18.	Use appropriate dictionary skills.
______ ☐ Low-level outcome ☐ High-level outcome	19.	Describe an analysis of short story elements.
______ ☐ Low-level outcome ☐ High-level outcome	20.	Apply the concepts of scope and sequence in ordering your course performance expectations.

Supplemental Learning Exercises

1. One of the signature assessments for "good" teaching is the ability to develop a unit of instruction. Performance expectations or outcomes determine the what, drive the how, and dictate the when of that unit. Select a topic from your discipline and develop eight performance expectations, using the outcome equation format for your topic. For the cognitive domain, write one expectation for each of the levels of Bloom's taxonomy and label them as such. Then add two more, one reflecting the affective domain and one representing the psychomotor domain. Check to make sure your outcomes reflect the characteristics of a well-written performance expectation.
2. For the same unit of study identified in option 1, select a standard that would also be aligned to that topic. Once the standard has been selected, demonstrate the unpacking and alignment process outlined below:

   There are four key steps to unpacking and aligning standard:

   - Select standard and review related standards.
   - Underline content demand (usually noun phrases) and highlight the cognitive process demands (verbs or verb-like phrases).

- Identify at least one key KSUDs in each area.
- Align the KSUDs with the triad of elements. Develop one example for each curricular, instructional, or assessment components.

3. It has been estimated that since 1983 there have been over 500 local, state, and national conferences and commissions that have issued reports pertaining to the quality and quantity of American education. Reform efforts have focused on standards, assessments, and accountability. In small groups, discuss the following questions and record your summary comments.
   A. Defining the Problem: What are some of the "indicators of risk" or "types of data" that support the need for standards-led educational reform? What internal or external forces or groups of people are advocating change?
   B. Positive Results and Challenges: In your opinion, what positive educational results have occurred as a result of the standards movement? What challenges do educators face in implementing standards-led reform? What lessons are we learning?
   C. Standards-Referenced versus Standards-Led: The federal law governing education requires all states to have standards. Schools have adopted and implemented standards to varying degrees. What is the difference between being "standards-referenced" and "standards-led" district?
   D. Unpacking and Alignment: As part of the implementation process, school districts need to unpack and align standards. How do you define the term "unpacking?" How do you define the term "aligning?" Are the two terms synonymous?
   E. Sea Change: Some experts have said, "The CCSS or NGSS initiative is a sea change" in education for teaching and learning. Do you agree or disagree? What does this mean? What are the implications?
   F. Effective School Reform: What do you think are some of the attributes for an effective school reform movement? What do you think are the characteristics of a successful standards-led curricular, instructional, and assessment program?

4. In this activity you will practice linking standards to student work. For each of the standards, identify a student task that would enable students to learn that standard. An example is provided below.

> *Standard*: Use maps and scale drawings to represent real objects or places.
> *Student Work*: Construct a scale model of a house.

- Apply in writing the rules of grammar, punctuation, and spelling.
- Gather information from a variety of sources and then organize, summarize, and analyze the information.
- Perform operations with numbers including decimals, ratios, percents, and fractions.
- Understand how and why rotation and revolution of Earth affect day, seasons, and weather.
- Understand best procedures for statistical data collection, organization, and display.
- Make observation of the local environment using senses and instruments.
- Understand systems of the human body.
- Understand characteristics of parallel and perpendicular lines.

Final Test

DIRECTIONS: *Read each question or statement below. Please visit the online portion of the book to record your answers.*

C 1. For curriculum development purposes, performance expectations should be stated in terms of:
   A. instructional processes that are used.
   B. subject matter content to be covered.
   C. types of learning outcomes expected.
   D. student activities to be completed.

C 2. Action verbs are the key element in any outcome. All of the following statements support this conclusion ***except***:
   A. action verbs determine the domain and level of learning.
   B. action verbs identify the type of assessment and level of question required.
   C. action verbs describe the method and organization of content coverage.
   D. action verbs define observable and measurable performance expectations.

A 3. Which of the following is ***not*** a characteristic of a well-written performance expectation or outcome?
   A. Defines a learning activity
   B. Is clear, concise, and precise
   C. Is student oriented
   D. Describes a measurable performance

C 4. Most curriculum developers would consider learning targets and/or competencies to be what types of outcomes?
   A. Life
   B. Discipline
   C. Unit
   D. Daily

C 5. The purpose of the Taxonomy of Educational Objectives is to:
   A. define and classify various types of educational standards.
   B. determine minimum educational outcomes for each student.
   C. arrange outcomes of education in the order of their complexity.
   D. provide criteria standards for evaluation purposes.

A 6. Bloom's taxonomy describes the cognitive domain of learning. Which of the following is the *most* descriptive of the cognitive domain?
   A. Domain of knowing
   B. Domain of doing
   C. Domain of interests
   D. Domain of feeling

T (F) 7. According to most curriculum developers, competencies or performance expectations must be written at the understanding level at a minimum in order to be performance based.

B 8. Which of the following is an example of a psychomotor domain performance expectation?
   A. Solve a story problem using the Pythagorean Theorem
   B. Measure the dimensions of the classroom using a meter stick
   C. Analyze how the science of physics affects everyday life
   D. Follow safety guidelines in the chemistry laboratory

____ 9. Which of the following phrases *best* describes the process of analysis?
A. Rote memorization
B. Use of abstraction in particular situations
C. Breakdown into constituent parts
D. Producing or creating something unique

____ 10. Which of the following outcomes would indicate the *highest* level of learning for a student?
A. Explains the law of supply and demand
B. Analyzes the law of supply and demand
C. Applies the law of supply and demand
D. Gives an example of the law of supply and demand

____ 11. There are several ways in which a performance expectation or outcome may not be clear, concise, or precise. Which of the following *best* describes not being precise?
A. The verbs in the outcome are not observable and measurable
B. The intent of the outcome is higher level, but it is written at a lower level
C. The outcome contains multiple verbs—more than one performance term
D. The outcome is too wordy or contains excess verbiage

____ 12. The student will develop the ability to analyze short story elements. What is the *primary* fault of this performance expectation?
A. Economy of phrasing
B. Taxonomic misrepresentation
C. Multiple performances
D. Product clarity

____ 13. The student will identify the differences among elements, compounds, and mixtures. What is the *primary* fault of this performance expectation?
A. Economy of phrasing
B. Taxonomic misrepresentation
C. Multiple performances
D. Product clarity

____ 14. Where would you draw the line between levels of the affective domain to differentiate application or doing?
A. Receiving and responding
B. Responding and valuing
C. Valuing and organization
D. Organizing and characterizing

T F 15. One of the primary differences between the "old" and "new" Bloom's taxonomy is that the evaluating and creating levels have been switched around.

T F 16. In standards-led education reform, the emphasis is placed on the "input" side of the equation.

____ 17. Which of the following factors contributed the ***least*** to the development of the standards movement?
A. Declining test scores and poor international comparisons
B. Perceived lack of discipline in our public schools
C. Employer dissatisfaction with the skill level of graduates
D. Philosophical beliefs of politicians and the public concerning accountability

___ 18. Which of the following statements *best* describes standards-based (versus standards-referenced) curriculum?
A. Completing a checklist of what standards where covered in the course
B. Matching the standards to course performance expectations
C. Identifying what students ought to be able to know, do, and care about
D. Identifying the KSUDs in each standard and then aligning to outcomes, activities, and tasks

___ 19. Compared to most state's original sets of standards, the new CCSS in Mathematics and English Language Arts are considered:
A. fewer, clearer, higher, and different.
B. fewer, complex, higher, and different.
C. more, clearer, higher, and different.
D. fewer, clearer, higher, and similar.

___ 20. Which of the following is ***not*** a way to increase the complexity of the standards as we move up the grade levels?
A. Increase the level of learning (i.e., verb)
B. Expand the depth and breadth of content coverage
C. Enhance the connections and integration of concepts
D. Analyze the learning progressions

DIRECTIONS: *Read each scenario below. Write a brief response.*

1. Defend/reject the statement that teachers who use performance expectations or outcomes are more successful in generating student learning than those who do not. Justify your answer.
2. Discuss the relationship between unpacking and aligning standards. Please describe the process you would use to unpack and align a standard in your discipline. How do unpacking and aligning contribute to standards-based or standards-led educational reform?

Works Cited and Suggested Readings

Ainsworth, Larry. (2003). *Power Standards: Identifying the Standards that Matter the Most*. Englewood, CA; Advanced Learning Press.

Anderson, Lorin. W. & Krathwohl, David. (Eds.). (2001). *A Taxonomy for Learning, Teaching, and Assessing: A Revision of Bloom's Taxonomy of Educational Objectives*. Boston, MA: Allyn & Bacon (Pearson Education Group).

Armstrong, David. (1989). *Developing and Documenting the Curriculum*. Needham Heights, MA: Allyn and Bacon.

Association for Supervision and Curriculum Development. (2015). *Educator Advocates*, Alexandria, VA: Author.

Aseltine, James, Faryniarz, Judith, & Rigazio-DiGilio, Anthony. (2006). *Supervision for Learning*. Alexandria, VA: Association for Supervision and Curriculum Development (ASCD).

Bloom, Benjamin (Ed.). (1956). *Taxonomy of Educational Objectives: The Classification of Educational Goals: Handbook I: Cognitive Domain*. White Plains, NY: Longman.

Carr, Judy & Harris, Douglas. (2001). *Succeeding with Standards: Linking Curriculum, Assessment, and Action Planning*. Alexandria, VA: Association for Supervision and Curriculum Development (ASCD).

Clark, Leonard & Starr, Irving. (1986). *Secondary and Middle School Teaching Methods* (5th Ed.). New York, NY: Macmillan.

Commission on the Reorganization of Secondary Education. (1918). Cardinal Principles of Secondary Education. *Bureau of Education Bulletin 1918*, No. 35. Washington, DC: US Government Printing Office.

Darling-Hammond, Linda. (2013). *Getting Teacher Evaluation Right: What Really Matters for Effectiveness and Improvement.* New York, NY: Teachers College Press.

Doll, Ronald C. (1989). *Curriculum Development: Decision Making and Process* (7th ed.). Boston, MA: Allyn and Bacon.

Guskey, Thomas & Jung, Lee Ann. (2013). *Answers to Essential Questions About Standards, Assessments, Grading, and Reporting.* Thousand Oaks, CA: Corwin Press.

Harrow, Anita. (1972). *A Taxonomy of the Psychomotor Domain: A Guide for Developing Behavioral Objectives.* White Plains, NY: Longman.

Heinich, Robert, Molenda, Michael, Russell, James, & Smaldino, Sharon. (2001). *Instructional Media and Technologies for Learning,* (7th ed.). Englewood Cliffs, CA: Prentice Hall, Inc.

Henson, Kenneth. (2001). *Curriculum Planning Integrating Multiculturalism, Constructivism, and Educational Reform* (2nd ed.). New York, NY: McGraw-Hill Higher Education.

Hess, Karen. (2008). *Developing and Using Learning Progressions as a Schema for Measuring Progress.* Paper presented at 2008 CCSSO Student Assessment Conference, Orlando, FL. Retrieved from: http://www.nciea.org/publications/CCSSO2_KH08.pdf

Hunkins, Francis P. (1980). *Curriculum Development: Program Improvement.* Columbus, OH: Charles Merrill Publishing Company.

Kindsvatter, Richard, Wilen, William, & Ishler, Margaret. (1992). *Dynamics of Effective Teaching* (2nd ed.). White Plains: NY: Longman Publishing Group.

Krathwohl, David. (2002). A Revision of Bloom's Taxonomy: An Overview. *Theory into Practice, (41)*4, Columbus, OH: The Ohio State University, College of Education. Retrieved from: http://www.unco.edu/cetl/sir/stating_outcome/documents/Krathwohl.pdf

Krathwohl, David, Bloom, Benjamin, & Masia, Bertram. (1964). *Taxonomy of Educational Objectives: The Classification of Educational Goals: Handbook II: Affective Domain.* White Plains, NY: Longman.

Kryspin, William. J & Feldhusen, John F. (1974). *Writing Behavioral Objectives: A Guide to Planning Instruction.* Minneapolis, MN: Burgess Publishing Company.

Mager, Robert. (1962). *Preparing Instructional Objectives* (2nd ed.). Belmont, CA: Fearon Publishers.

Marzano, Robert & Kendall, John. (2007). *The New Taxonomy of Educational Objectives* (2nd ed.). Thousand Oaks, CA: Corwin Press.

National Governor's Association and the Council of Chief State School Officers. (2010). *Common Core State Standards.* Washington, DC: Author. Retrieved from: http://www.corestandards.org

No Child Left Behind Act of 2001, P.L. 107–110, 20 U.S.C. § 6319 (2002).

Olivia, Peter F. (1988). *Developing the Curriculum* (2nd ed.). Statesboro, GA: Georgia Southern College.

Pasch, Marvin, Sparks-Langer, Georgea, Gardner, Trevor, Stako, Alane, & Moody, Christella. (1991). *Teaching as Decision Making: Instructional Practices for the Successful Teacher.* White Plains: NY: Longman Publishing Group.

Popham, James W. (1987). Instructional Objectives 1960–1970. *Performance and Instruction, (26)*2, 11–14.

Popham, James W. (1971). Practical Ways of Improving Curriculum via Measurable Objectives. *Bulletin of the National Association of Secondary School Principals* (55)355, 76–90.

Popham, James W. (1969). *Instructional Objectives*. Chicago, IL: Rand McNally.

Reeves, Douglas. (2002). *Making Standards Work: How to Implement Standards-Based Assessments in the Classroom, School, and District*. Denver, CO: Advanced Learning Center.

Rutherford, Paula. (2002). *Instruction for All Students*. Alexandria, VA: Just Ask Publications.

Saylor, Galen, Alexander, William, & Lewis, Arthur. (1981). *Curriculum Planning for Better Teaching and Learning* (4th ed.). New York, NY: Holt, Rinehart, and Winston.

Savage, Tom & Armstrong, David. (1987). *Effective Teaching in Elementary Social Studies*. New York, NY: Macmillan Company.

Simpson, Elizabeth. (1972). The Classification of Educational Objectives in the Psychomotor Domain. *The Psychomotor Domain* (3). Washington, DC: Gryphon House.

Taylor, Ray. (2005), Life in the Pinball Machine—Looking Back with Bob Mager. *Performance Improvement*, (*44*)9, 5–8.

Tyler, Ralph W. (1949). *Basic Principles of Curriculum and Instruction*. Chicago, IL: University of Chicago Press.

Zais, Robert. (1976). *Curriculum Principles and Foundation*. New York, NY: Thomas Y. Crowell Company.

Shutterstock.com

Shutterstock.com

Source: Shutterstock.com

Source: Shutterstock.com

Chapter 7
Designing Dynamic and Quality Curriculum

"Curriculum is concerned not with what students will do in the learning situation, but with what they will learn as a consequence of what they do. Curriculum is concerned with results."
Daniel Tanner and Laurel Tanner

Anticipatory Set: Developing a Curriculum Template

DIRECTIONS: *In this activity your team will construct a sample curriculum template. There are several potential elements that might be found in a typical district's curriculum guide. Each element contains sample data (not complete) from an English Language Arts Unit on Short Stories designed for an upper elementary classroom. At the end of the anticipatory set, you will go online for these elements. Print and cut out the pieces and follow the directions outlined below in order to build your sample template. Summarize each step by completing the Template Table.*

Source: Thinkstock/Getty

#	Element
1.	First determine whether the element would be included in your template. Keep those elements that you want to include and discard the others. In the Template Table, check those elements that your team decided to keep.
2.	Are there any elements missing? If your team determines that additional elements are needed, use the blank(s) to create the missing element(s). Also include sample data to support the Short Story Unit. Add the missing element(s) to the Template Table.
3.	Next decide if each element is labeled correctly. If your team is happy with the label, move to step four. If it is not labeled correctly, choose a label that would be more appropriate or more familiar to your district colleagues. Cross out the old label and replace it with the new one. Also write in the new label on the Template Table.
4.	Are there any modifications you would like to make within each element? For example, should it be subdivided into two or more elements? Should parts of it be deleted or changed? Should two or more elements be merged? Please make those modifications on each element and record your changes in the Template Table.
5.	What is the purpose or function of each element in the curriculum? Briefly discuss among team members and record your comments in the Template Table.
6.	What curriculum development component (Curriculum, Assessment, or Instruction) does each element primarily support? Label each element—C, A, or I—on both the element itself and on the Template Table.
7.	Arrange all of the selected elements into a template. The template can be vertical or horizontal in nature. It may contain sections or additional features that your team would like to include. Glue or tape the elements in place and add any appropriate "finishing touches."
8.	Be prepared to share your final template with the whole group. Make sure to highlight its unique features.

The Template Table is also available in the online portion of the book, along with the curricular elements in Building a Curricular Template.

Template Table					
Element	**Included (✓)**	**New Label**	**Modifications**	**Purpose**	**C, A, or I**
Performance Expectations					
Content					
Standards					
Resources					
Enabling Activities					
Evidence of Student Mastery					
Enduring Understandings					
Philosophy Statement					
Essential Questions					
Other					

Example: Building a Curricular Template

Visit the online book to view and print elements that might be found in a typical district's curriculum guide. This is required for the anticipatory assignment.

Chapter Overview

The game of Checkers has been around for centuries. It remains a childhood favorite. Checkers is a lot like designing quality curriculum. One aspect of curriculum design is made up of three components which are enduring understanding, six facets of learning, and essential questions. Enduring understanding is like the "big idea." In curricular design, the big idea is an important concept or component central to a content area discipline. The big idea of the game of checkers is to capture all of your opponent's checkers or position your pieces so that your opponent has no available moves. Curricular design is made up of six facets of learning: explain, interpret, apply, perspective, empathy, and self-knowledge. While teachers need to incorporate these in the curricular design plan and daily instruction, these are also facets of any challenging board game. In Checkers, players are continually interpreting others' moves, relying on their self-knowledge, may need to explain their moves, and often show empathy when they are winning! Essential questions are also a vital component to curricular design, as these questions spark prior knowledge, help students think of alternatives and rethink conceptions. Just as in Checkers, players continually think, rethink, plan for alternatives. Every move opens untold possibilities and closes down untold more, therefore the players need to keep on their toes. That is game strategy. Checkers also has similarities to the UBD model. Teachers plan with the end in mind, identifying desired results first. Checker players also have the end in mind–how to capture all of their opponent's checkers! Players then make strategic moves, keeping the very end in mind.

The role of decision making in curriculum development, improvement, and change in general has been central concern of the first six chapters in this book. The act of making decisions, both product and process, is also a critical aspect of planning a specific curriculum. In this chapter, teachers will examine the curriculum design process in more detail. Two approaches, Curriculum Mapping and Understanding by Design® (UbD™), will be analyzed. Additionally, a sample case study, simulating the curriculum development process, is also presented.

Performance Expectations

DIRECTIONS: *How well do you know the performance expectations? Rate your knowledge of each expectation using this Likert scale. You will rate yourself again at the end of the chapter. This is for your information to assess your own learning. Visit the online book to record your answers.*

1 = I do not have any knowledge of this concept.

2 = I have minimal knowledge of this concept.

3 = I have some understanding of this concept.

4 = I have a satisfactory understanding of this concept.

5 = I am confident in my understanding of this concept.

Source: Thinkstock/Getty

This chapter should prepare you to:

Rating	#	Performance Expectations
	1.	Investigate the planning considerations associated with the curriculum decision making process.
	2.	Summarize the findings of Stake & Easley.
	3.	Explain the rationale for developing and using unit or lesson plans. What types of product and process decisions would teachers consider?
	4.	Analyze the curriculum mapping process, including the decisions and tasks that teachers often complete with maps.
	5.	Summarize the components that are typically found on a curriculum map.
	6.	Describe the purpose and benefits of using the curriculum mapping process.
	7.	Explain the "big ideas" associated with the Understanding by Design (UbD™) model.
	8.	Discuss how UbD™ avoids the "twin sins" of traditional design and how the term "backward" is used to develop the model.
	9.	Analyze the characteristics and components associated with each step of the Understanding By Design (UbD™) model.
	10.	Discuss the six Facets of Understanding.
	11.	Develop enduring understandings and essential questions for your discipline.
	12.	Explain the concept of "opportunity to learn."
	13.	Use the curriculum mapping or understanding by design model to develop curriculum in your subject area.
	14.	Compare and contrast the three stages of UbD, DeFours' PLC questions, PBI principles, and the Triad of Elements.

7.1 Curriculum Planning

John Gardner once said, "Planning is attending to the goals we ought to be thinking about and never do, the facts we do not like to face, and the questions we lack the courage to ask" (In Smith, 1969, p. 38). Planning is a process, not an event! Planning of all sorts often addresses the question of: "Where are we now?"; "Where do we want to go?"; and "How will we get there?".

If curriculum is perceived as a plan for providing sets of learning opportunities under the direction of the school (Saylor, Alexander, & Lewis, 1981), the process for developing that plan is known as curriculum development. Curriculum development is a cyclical process that includes analysis, design, implementation, and evaluation. Curriculum planning is part of the design phase of curriculum development, when curriculum leaders make **product** and **process** decisions and take actions to establish the plan those teachers and students will implement. Specifically, curriculum developers try to answer the following questions:

- What do students need to know, do, and care about? (Effective Curriculum)
- How will they learn it? (Effective Instruction)
- How will we know if they've learned it? (Effective Assessment)
- What will we do if they don't learn it? (Effective Interventions)
- What will we do if they already know it? (Effective Enrichment)

Far too often, the textbook dictates curriculum planning and development. Fifty years ago, Stake & Easley (1978) reported that 90 percent of all science teachers use the textbook, 90 percent of the time for curriculum and instruction. Although we have made some progress and publishers have gotten much more creative, the fact remains many classrooms are textbook dependent. If this is indeed the case, the curriculum plan (if one could really call it that) follows a predictable format (1) adopt the goals and objectives of the author; (2) align the scope and sequence with the topics outlined in the table of contents; (3) use whatever instructional strategies and resources that are in the accompanying teacher's manual; and (4) base evaluation solely on a series of tests that are also sometimes produced by the publisher (Saylor et al., 1981). Ignored in this approach is the type of curriculum planning advocated in this book that supports the philosophy of "teacher as decision maker." This approach also ignores the standards.

Selecting a curriculum design is not as simple as saying, "I'll take this one." Each design grows out of a series of questions and answers and curriculum planners are always making choices throughout the process. Regardless of the design followed and the template chosen, the curriculum plan should generally include a description of the learners, performance expectations or outcomes, aligned standards, types of differentiated learning experiences to be provided, general time and space allocations, formative and summative assessment procedures, and the roles of participants. All of these activities are guided by data concerning the nature of the learner, the structure of the discipline, the society served, and the KSUDs found in the standards.

Effective curriculum, instruction, and assessment require and reflect careful planning. Often the end product of this systematic curriculum planning or development process is the unit plan. A unit consists of a series of lessons whose specific outcomes and activities work together to achieve a broad purpose or goal. Units consist of lessons or learning activities that are strategies and tasks that students perform in order to achieve unit outcomes (Pasch et al, 1991). The teaching unit furnishes the instructor with a valid framework for the conduct of his or her teaching over time (Hunkins, 1980). Without the unit plan to aid in selecting and organizing ideas and approaches, teaching is likely to lack cohesiveness, continuity, and relevance (Kindsvatter, Wilen, & Ishler, 1992).

Lesson and unit plans come in many sizes and varieties, and their length and style does not make one plan better than another. A good lesson plan should challenge and engage students throughout the entire class period with activities that involve every student. Although there are many variations of unit and lesson plans and templates available, we have chosen to discuss two of the most commonly used by local school districts.

7.2 Curriculum Mapping

A curriculum map is a working document that illustrates exactly what is taking place in classrooms. Maps reveal what is being taught over the course of a year, within a unit of study, and even down to a specific lesson. Curriculum mapping is a procedure for collecting and recording data about the actual curriculum in a school district using the school calendar as an organizer. Data are gathered in a format that allows each teacher to present an overview of his or her students' actual learning experiences. The map usually identifies core skills and content taught, processes employed, and assessments used for each subject area and grade level. Curriculum mapping is an extremely useful tool for creating a "big picture" for curriculum decision making (Jacobs, 2004; Jacobs, 1997).

The fundamental purpose of curriculum mapping is communication. The purpose of a curriculum map is to document the relationship between every component of the curriculum. Truesdale, Thompson, & Lucas (2004) compared the tools of curriculum mapping to the tools on a carpenter's work belt. "The belt is the calendar that organizes the tools. The belt buckle allows for adjustable pacing throughout the school year. The content hammers in the standards—the nails. The mapping tool drills in essential questions for authentic probing and learning. The pliers (skills) hold the content, standards, and assessments together. The screwdriver turns content into knowledge. The measuring tape can be used to assess student buildings (products)" (pp. 11–12).

Found in Figure 1 is a sample curriculum map of algebra. Note that the map is organized by the calendar year, which is a feature many teachers like immensely. For each section of content, essential questions, concepts (content), performance expectations, and assessments are listed.

Sample Curriculum Map for Algebra

	Essential Questions	Content	Performance Expectations	Assessments
January	• How can we use algebra to solve real-world problems? • What is a mathematical system? • Why collect and plot data? • What does the slope of an object tell you? • When would you use the slope concept in real life?	• Plotting data • Slopes • Lines • Exponents • Powers *Terms:* slope, slope-intercept formula, quadrants	• Explains real-world algebra applications • Collects and plots data • Writes an equation for and uses a line of best fit • Writes an equation in standard form given a real-life situation • Converts back and forth from standard form and slope-intercept form • Graphs linear inequalities from situations • Uses the properties of exponents	• Uses of algebra paper • Daily assignments • Notebook • Slope project • True/False quiz • Chapter test
February	• What are variables and what can they represent? • How does the GCF help you factor polynomials? • Why is it important to know the order of operations? • How can we solve for the unknown? • When would you use systems of equations and inequalities in real-life situations?	• Variables • Factoring • Polynomials • Linear systems • Greatest common factor (GCF) *Terms:* variable, polynomial, linear, proportion, greatest common factor	• Defines and gives an example of a variable • Performs all operations on polynomials • States the rules for the order of operations • Factors out a greatest common factor from a polynomial • Factors trinomials and difference of squares • Classifies polynomials by degree and number of terms • Uses polynomials in real-life situations • Solves systems of two linear equations	• Vocabulary log • Daily assignments • Reflective journal • Short answer quiz • Chapter test

Figure 1: Algebra Curriculum Map

Mapping Components

- Essential questions
- Content
- Performance expectations
- Assessments

There are many benefits associated with curriculum mapping process. Curriculum mapping brings teachers and administrators together to examine the entire span of a curriculum as it is taught within a discipline, grade level, or school building. Educators can use mapping to direct the course of their curriculum cooperatively, instead of operating alone or in isolation from each other. Maps may be used to identify curricular gaps, overlaps, redundancies, and/or potential content areas for integration. Maps may also be used to align standards to performance expectations and classroom assessments (Jacobs, 2004; Jacobs, 1997).

Check for Understanding: Curricular Mapping

DIRECTIONS: *Read the three questions online about curricular mapping and be prepared to share your answers and ideas in the next class. We will be using the strategy "**Mix-Freeze-Group**" to pair students in sharing answers. The students will get up and "mix" around the room. The instructor will say, "freeze" and with the nearest "group" of two or three students, you will share your answers to #1. After two minutes, the class will remix for the next questions. This strategy is modified from Spencer Kagan (2009). Visit the online book to complete the activity.*

7.3 Understanding by Design® (UbD™)

Understanding by Design® (UbD™) is a framework for improving student achievement developed by Grant Wiggins & Jay McTighe. Their framework emphasizes the teacher's critical role as a designer of student learning. Wiggins & McTighe (2012) have used the UbD framework to provide a way to move from "covering the curriculum" to "creating a curriculum that is responsive to the needs of the learners it serves." UbD™ works within the standards-driven curriculum to help teachers clarify learning goals, devise revealing assessments of student understanding, and craft effective and engaging learning activities.

The UbD™ Framework is published by the Association for Supervision and Curriculum Development (ASCD) and is based on eight big ideas:

- UbD™ is a way of thinking purposefully about curricular planning and school reform, a set of helpful design tools, and design standards—not a program or recipe.
- The end goal of UbD™ is understanding and the ability to transfer learnings—to appropriately connect, make sense of, and use discrete knowledge and skills in context.
- Educators are coaches of understanding, not mere purveyors of content or activity.
- Planning is best done "backward" from the desired results and the transfer tasks that embody the goals.
- UbD™ transforms content standards and other goals into focused learning targets based on "big ideas" and transfer tasks.
- Evidence of understanding is revealed through performance—when learners transfer knowledge and skills effectively, using one or more "facets" (explain, interpret, apply, shift perspective, empathize, and self-assess).
- Design standards guide self-assessment and peer reviews of curriculum, instruction, and assessment for quality control.

- UbD™ reflects a "continuous improvement" approach to design and learning. The results of our curriculum designs (e.g., assessment results, quality of student work, degree of learner engagement) inform needed adjustments (Wiggins, 2005, p. 14).

By incorporating these big ideas, Wiggins & McTighe (2012) contend that UbD™ avoids the "twin sins" of traditional design. First, UbD™ averts the error of activity-oriented design, which is sometimes called "hands on without being minds on." These types of learning experiences lead only accidentally, if at all, to insight or achievement. These activities, though fun and interesting, lack an explicit focus on important ideas and do not often provide appropriate evidence of learning. A second form of aimlessness goes by the name of "coverage," an approach in which students march through a textbook, page by page (or teachers through lecture notes) in a valiant attempt to traverse all the factual material within a prescribed time. In this approach, students are exposed to lots of information, but often retain very little (Wiggins & McTighe, 2016).

In the UbD™ framework, the term "backward" is used in two ways. First, the term means "plan with the end in mind" by first clarifying the learning you seek—the learning results (Stage 1). The second use of the term refers to the fact that this approach is backward to the way many educators plan. For years, we have observed that curriculum planning often follows a cycle that begins with curriculum, followed by instruction, and then ends with assessment. In the UbD™ framework, curriculum is followed by assessment, and finally then teachers select their instructional activities. A major change from common practice occurs, as designers must begin to think about assessment before deciding how they will teach. Many teachers have commented that the UbD™ planning process makes sense, but feels awkward because it requires a break from comfortable planning habits (Wiggins & McTighe, 2012).

In lay terms, UbD™ is like planning a vacation. You typically plan where you will go first, then work "backward" to plan the details. Once you know where you are headed, you can make the multitude of other decisions such as fly or drive, hotel or camp, take in scenic spots or go directly to the destination, how much money is needed for spending, etc. This type of planning is similar to UbD™, starting with the end first and then working back to the beginning.

Article: Why Backward is Best

DIRECTIONS: *Read the article "Why Backward is Best." As you read, reflect on one concept in which you agree and one concept you do not agree. In the next class, you will be paired with a classmate to discuss your "**agree and disagree**" comments. To get into pairs, each student will get a card. The cards are **things that go together** (comb and brush, bacon and eggs). When learning, teachers need to mix students up randomly. This serves several purposes: students get to know each other better, students will not worry about how to find a partner, and it deepens thinking as it creates accountability. Visit the online book to read the article.*

7.4 The UbD™ Model and Template

The UbD™ framework offers a three-stage backward design process for curriculum planning that is illustrated in Figure 2. For backward design to work, curriculum developers need to identify desired results, analyze multiple sources of data (i.e., determine acceptable evidence), and determine appropriate action plans (McTighe & Thomas, 2003). Each stage of the design process involves teachers focusing on a different question:

- Stage 1: What is worthy and requiring of understanding?
- Stage 2: What is evidence of understanding?
- Stage 3: What learning experiences and teaching promote understanding, interest, and excellence?

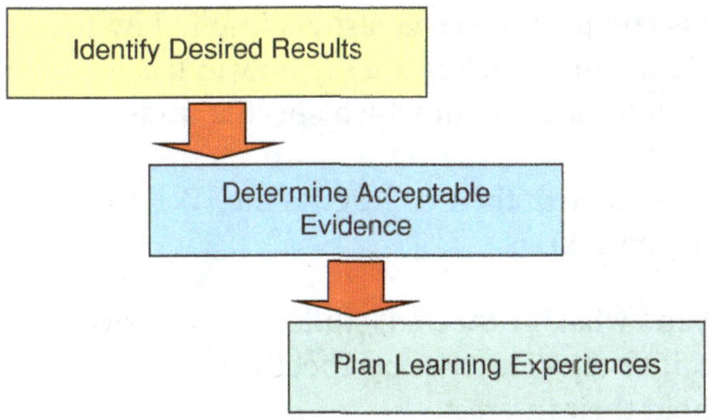

Source: J. Redman

Figure 2: The Three Stages of Understanding by Design®

An example of an UbD™ template is found in Figure 3. In **Stage 1, Identify Desired Results**, curriculum developers consider goals, align standards (national, state, or district), and review performance expectations. Additionally, they are encouraged to identify enduring understandings and develop essential questions. All of these elements are intended to answer the "what" question from different perspectives: What should students know, understand, and be able to do?

Because typically we have more content than we can reasonably address within the available time, we must make choices. Curriculum planners must narrow the content and establish priorities. Wiggins & McTighe (2005) provide a useful process for progressively focusing in on the most valuable content, by suggesting teachers answer three questions:

1. What should participants hear, read, view, explore, or otherwise encounter? This knowledge is "*worth being familiar with.*"
2. What knowledge and skills should participants master? Sharpen your choices by considering what is "*important to know and do*" for your students. What facts, concepts, and principles should they know? What processes, strategies, and methods should they learn to use?
3. What are big ideas and important understandings participants should retain? These choices are the "*enduring understandings*" that you want students to remember after they've forgotten the details of the course.

Answering each of these questions will help curriculum developers determine the most important content for their course and create observable and measurable learning outcomes for their students.

In **Stage 2, Determine Acceptable Evidence**, curriculum planners begin to think about how to determine if their students are starting to master the knowledge and skills you want them to gain. What data can you collect that will serve as acceptable evidence that students are making progress toward each performance expectation? When planning how you will collect this evidence, consider a wide range of formative and summative assessment methods. Quizzes and tests, performance tasks, projects, papers, homework assignments, checks for understanding, problems to solve, and journaling are just a few of your assessment options. Self- and peer assessments also work well. In addition, the scoring criteria (or rubric) should be developed and shared with the students.

In **Stage 3, Plan Learning Experiences**, curriculum developers and decision makers move to select the instructional strategies and design the learning activities. Finally, after having decided what results you want and how you will know that you've achieved them, you can now start planning how you're going to teach. What are the best exercises, problems, or questions for developing your students' ability to meet your performance expectations? How can they practice using new knowledge to gain the skills you want them to learn? How can they apply or transfer their learning? How can you provide opportunities for differentiation? What materials and resources are best suited to accomplish these goals? As implied by the name of the model, the focus of this approach is understanding. Remember, we cannot say how to teach for understanding or which material and activities to use until we are quite clear about which specific understandings we are after and what such understandings look like in practice.

Some curriculum developers share with their colleagues the "WHERETO" strategy when planning learning experiences (Wiggins & McTighe, 2005):

W = Where the unit is going and what is expected (student perspective)? Or where the students are coming from (prior knowledge, interests—teacher perspective);
H = Hook all students and hold their interest;
E = Equip students, help them experience the key ideas, and explore the issues;
R = Provide opportunities to rethink and revise their understandings and work;
E = Allow students to evaluate their work and its implications;
T = Be tailored (personalized) to the different needs, interests, abilities of learners; and
O = Be organized to maximize initial and sustained engagement as well as effective learning.

<table>
<tr><th colspan="3">Stage 1—Identify Desired Results</th></tr>
<tr><th>Unit Tile:</th><th>Grade Level:</th><th>Time Frame:</th></tr>
<tr><td colspan="3">Established Goal(s): Design with the end in mind—What is your terminal outcome? Write as a performance (outcome) statement. If possible, write one to three goals at the most.
• What should students be able to do at the end of this unit?</td></tr>
<tr><td colspan="2">Enduring Understanding(s):
Students will understand that . . .
• What are the "big ideas"?
• What concepts will endure the test of time?
• What misunderstandings are predictable?
• What specific facets of understanding are desired?</td><td>Essential Question(s):
• What provocative questions will foster inquiry, understanding, and transfer of learning?
• What questions will give meaning, relevance, and definition to the unit?</td></tr>
<tr><td colspan="3">Content Standards: Cite specific standards to your content to be used in this unit. List the standard number.
• What KSUDs are identified in the standards?</td></tr>
<tr><td colspan="3">Performance Expectations or Learning Targets: Specify at least one outcome in each domain of learning. Separate outcomes in the "knowing," "doing," and "caring" categories. Write each expectation in outcome equation format—adhere to the rules of well-written outcomes.</td></tr>
<tr><td>Students will know:
•
•
•</td><td>Students will be able to do:
•
•
•</td><td>Students will care about:
•
•
•</td></tr>
</table>

<table>
<tr><th colspan="2">Stage 2—Determine Acceptable Evidence</th></tr>
<tr><td>Performance Task(s):
• Serves as your culminating demonstration of learning for your unit.
• Through what authentic performance task(s) will students demonstrate the desired understandings?</td><td>Other Evidence:
• Through what other evidence (e.g., quizzes, tests, academic prompts, observations, homework, and journals) will students demonstrate achievement of the desired results?
• Identify formative checks for understanding, guided practice, or independent practice (homework).
• How will students reflect upon and self-assess their learning?
• Describe the nature of your final test.</td></tr>
<tr><td colspan="2">Key Evaluative Criteria (Use to create rubric or scoring guide):
• By what criteria will "performances of understanding" be judged?
• What criteria should be used to assess work related to the desired results?</td></tr>
<tr><th colspan="2">Stage 3—Plan Learning Experiences</th></tr>
<tr><td colspan="2">• Description of Activities: This is a summary of the learning activities. Organize the activities by the day of the unit. For each instructional component, briefly describe that activity. (For example, use a KWL Chart to assess prior knowledge on ______.)
• What learning experiences will help "uncover" the big ideas in the standard?
• What instruction is needed to equip students to meet this standard?
• What activities will engage students and help them better grasp the essence and the value of this topic/content?
• What instruction and learning activities will most effectively help to develop, refine, and make automatic this skill/process?
• What kinds of complex and interesting challenges can make the skill's value more apparent and meaningful?
• How will you differentiate instruction to meet individual student needs and interests?</td></tr>
</table>

Figure 3: Example of a UbD™ Template

Three UbD™ Stages

- **Stage One: Identify desired results**
- **Stage Two: Determine acceptable evidence**
- **Stage Three: Plan learning experiences**

7.5 Three Special UbD™ Elements

Three special elements (1) enduring understandings, (2) six facets of understanding, and (3) essential questions are found within the UbD™ model and template. **Enduring understandings** are generalizations about the "big ideas" within a content area. They are statements summarizing important ideas and core processes that are central to a discipline and have lasting value beyond the classroom. They synthesize what students should understand—not just know or do—as a result of studying a particular subject area. Enduring understandings often require "uncoverage" and further explanation. They are not simple facts that are easily understood and may be areas where students struggle to gain understanding due to their previously learned misconceptions.

Video: Twin Sins and Enduring Understandings

DIRECTIONS: *View the five-minute YouTube video. This video is about twin sins and enduring understanding. While you view the video, generate ideas for the following: Why are the twin sins considered "sins?" and reflect upon a personal assignment you have completed or planned. What made for the understanding to be enduring? For the next class, you will complete a "**pairs compare**" with classmates about this video. In pairs compare, partners will first compare their ideas and make a list. After three minutes, two pairs of students will then combine their lists to make a longer list, which will create deep discussions. This strategy is modified from Spencer Kagan (2009). Visit the online book to view the video.*

The "**Six Facets of Understanding**" enhances enduring understandings. The facets were conceived as six equal and suggestive indicators of understanding and thus are used to develop, select, or critique assessment tasks and prompts. They were never intended to be a hierarchy. Rather, one selects the appropriate facet(s) depending on the nature of the content and the desired understandings about it (Wiggins & McTighe, 2012). The six facets that demonstrate understanding are (1) can explain; (2) can interpret; (3) can apply; (4) has perspective; (5) has empathy; and (6) has self-knowledge. Figure 4 has more information on the descriptions of each facet.

Source: Thinkstock/Getty

Facets of Understanding		
Facet	**Description**	**Criteria**
Explanation	To ensure that students understand an answer or justify why an approach is the correct one—provide reasons and rationale for decisions; describe or clarify phenomena, facts, data; or justify why a course of action was correct.	Accurate
Interpretation	To ensure students avoid the drawbacks of looking for the "one right answer" and offering as many different viewpoints or alternatives as possible—Tell meaningful stories or offer proper translations; provide an enlightening historical or personal dimension to ideas and events; or make subjects personal through anecdotes, analogies, and models.	Meaningful
Application	To ensure that the learners' responses and performances are overt, conscious, explicit, and authentic—Effectively use and adapt what they know in diverse contexts; design, develop, test, and revise a solution; or analyze a product by taking it apart to see how it works.	Effective
Perspective	To ensure that students know the significance or see the importance of an idea—Ask yourself of what value is this knowledge or how important is this idea? Appreciate differing points of view; employ critical eyes and ears to reveal different perspectives; and grasp the big picture.	Credible
Empathy	To ensure that students view the world from different lenses in order to understand the diversity of thought and appreciate varying opinions—Find value in what others might find odd, unique, or implausible; defend thoughts on why you agree or disagree with a certain idea or viewpoint; or thoughtfully perceive and reflect upon ideas based on past experiences.	Sensitive
Self-knowledge	To ensure that students are deeply aware of their own and others personal boundaries and understandings—Acknowledge the personal style, prejudices, projections, and habits of mind that both shape and impede our own understanding; recognize what you do not understand and why understanding is so hard; or exhibit integrity and be willing to act on what one understands.	Self-awareness

Figure 4: Six Facets of Understanding

Video: The Six Facets of Understanding

DIRECTIONS: *For more information on the six facets of understanding, view the five-minute YouTube video. Visit the online book to view the video.*

UbD™ Elements

- Backward design
- Facets of understanding
- Enduring understandings
- Essential questions

Essential questions (EQ) develop foundational understandings. Essential questions frame a unit of study as a problem to be solved. They provide the fundamental organizing principles that are inherent in an inquiry approach and guide the development of authentic tasks. Essential questions give meaning, relevance, and definition to a unit of instruction. Often EQ spark meaningful connections with prior learning and personal experiences.

According to Wiggins (2007), a question is essential when it:

1. Causes genuine and relevant inquiry into big-picture ideas and core content;
2. Provokes deep thought, lively discussion, sustained inquiry, and new understanding as well as more questions;
3. Requires students to consider alternatives, weigh evidence, support their ideas, and justify their answers;
4. Stimulates vital, ongoing rethinking of big ideas, assumptions, and prior lessons;
5. Sparks meaningful connections with prior learning and personal experience; and
6. Naturally reoccurs, creating opportunities for transfer to other situations and subjects.

Developing essential questions is a key design strategy for engaging student inquiry, uncovering subtle ideas, and enhancing understanding. Essential questions help in designing a curriculum that is more coherent, making the student's role more inquisitive, and in focusing the teacher's priorities. Wiggins & McTighe suggest that students who have complete and mature understandings are able to explain, interpret, and apply concepts while showing insight from perspective, empathy and self-knowledge. In other words, when generating possible essential questions, it is helpful to take the six facets of understanding into consideration.

Video: Essential Questions

DIRECTIONS: *View the five-minute YouTube video. While you are watching the Essential Questions video, jot down why essential questions are vital. Bring your jots to class and we will share using the strategy "**Until the Well Runs Dry.**" In this strategy, each student takes a turn sharing one reason EQs are vital. Instead of repeating a reason, if a student does not have a "new" reason, they would say, "My well is dry." The class continues until everyone's well is dry. This strategy promotes active listening and a wide range of ideas for all to digest. Visit the online book to view the video.*

A list of essential question examples from various disciplines is found in Figure 5.

Sample Essential Questions

Math

1. When should I multiply? When can't I multiply? When is multiplication most useful?
2. How is geometry used in the real world?
3. How would you explain, demonstrate, or draw the ________ process?

Social Studies

1. How have ancient Greeks affected our society?
2. Why would the Europeans want to come to the colonies?
3. How does the economy of a society depend on the geography of the region?

Language Arts

1. What is the connection between reading and writing?
2. Do stories need a beginning, middle, and end? Why?
3. What do the "Bernstein Bears" teach us about life?

Science

1. How do chemicals benefit society?
2. What must a scientist do in order to research something?
3. Are animals essential for man's survival? Which ones or why not?

Physical Education

1. Why should you spend time stretching before and after an athletic event?
2. What are the top three rules in basketball? Why?
3. How can advertising effect a teen's choices?

Art

1. How do people express themselves through art today?
2. How has art changed through time?
3. What choices must a painter make before beginning a work?

Foreign Language

1. How is Spanish/French like and unlike English?
2. In what ways would learning a foreign language be beneficial?

Technology

1. How can the computer be used as a tool?
2. How would our culture be different without computers?
3. What are your top ten priorities when producing a news video?

Figure 5: Essential Questions in Various Disciplines

Figure 6 gives enduring understanding and essential question examples from government and geography.

Social Studies Curriculum on Government	
Enduring Understanding	*Essential Question*
• Governments exist to provide order and services to a nation. • Each government has its own unique power and structure. • People develop systems to manage, conflict, and create order. • Conflict resolution can involve aggression, compromise, cooperation, and change. • Democratic societies must balance the rights and responsibilities of individuals with the common good.	• For what purposes do governments exist? • How are governments created, structured, and maintained? • What does a government need to survive? • What happens in the absence of government? • What is power and where does power to govern come from? • How is power gained, used, and justified? • How do competing interests influence how power is distributed and exercised? • Why do we have rules and laws? What would happen if we did not? • What are the roles and responsibilities of citizens and government in a democratic society? • What effect does a democratic government have on society?

Figure 6: Enduring Understandings and Essential Questions

Check for Understanding: UbD™

DIRECTIONS: *In "Understanding by Design," Wiggins and McTighe lay out a conceptual framework for instructional designers. Unlike many instructional design models that come from a training background, the Wiggins and McTighe model is well suited for the academic community.*

Consider the vignette and what it suggests about understanding and the design of curriculum, instruction, and assessments using the Understanding by Design (UbD™) model. For the next class, will discuss the vignette and reflect upon the teaching and learning that is described. The class will use the strategy ***Inside-Outside Circle****. Inside and outside circles of students face each other. With each pair of facing students, they discuss the questions and comments they had about the vignette. The circles may rotate for new partners. Visit the online book to read the vignette.*

7.6 Opportunity to Learn (OTL)

Opportunity to learn (OTL) was originally defined as the overlap between the information students were taught and the information on which they were tested. What K-12 curricula should a district employ to determine what scope and sequence students should follow to succeed on tests, as well as, in college, or the workplace? Robert Marzano (2003) suggests that the school-level variable with the strongest link to student success is "opportunity to learn (OTL)." OTL is defined as the extent to which a school (1) clearly articulates its curriculum, (2) monitors the extent to which teachers cover the curriculum, and (3) aligns its curriculum with assessments used to measure student achievement. Of the three variables, aligning curriculum to assessments appears to have the strongest link with student achievement. Additionally, Goodwin (2010) cites two principles that emerge from his research (1) providing all students with high expectations curricula and (2) providing all students with personalized learning opportunities.

Instructional validity is essentially another term for opportunity to learn. In legal cases (e.g., *Can Johnny Read?*) involving a student's OTL and testing, instructional validity is an important standard when one considers the nature of high stakes testing in today's reform efforts. Phillips (1993) notes however, "A pure instructional validity standard would be unattainable," because it would be impossible to show that every student in every classroom had been taught all the skills that were tested. Hence the less stringent curricular validity standard would be a reasonable compromise incorporating elements of the match of the test content to both written materials and teacher judgments. The documented curriculum is the best evidence a district or teacher can present that the curriculum was taught.

Opportunity to learn equals instructional validity, which in essence equals curricular validity. When a district or teacher is confronted with a legal challenge, the courts will examine the documented curriculum (i.e., curricular validity). Additionally, they anticipate that the "official" or documented curriculum will be or has been what is taught (i.e., instructional validity). Thus the higher standard of instructional validity is met by the lower standard of curricular validity.

7.7 A Summary: Redson Curriculum Development Process

All teachers plan. According to Doll (1989), teachers are charged with three task related to curriculum (1) working and planning with pupils; (2) engaging students in individual study, and (3) communicating curriculum-related experiences with colleagues. Curriculum development at the local school district level should be an ongoing and dynamic process. The process should yield a workable, usable, student-centered product.

Curriculum deveopers make numerous product and process choices during the design phase. Past experiences have taught these authors that many teachers have not even known the questions, yet alone the options available, to make the choices. This book has hopefully provided insight into the curriculum development process under the guise "teacher as decision maker!"

As a wrap-up to this section on curriculum, the authors have provided a thorough example of curriculum development process that you would find in most districts. This example is from the fictitious school district, Redson School District. Figure 7 delineates the product and process recommendations. Figure 8 is the curriculum template. Figure 9 delineates the sample philosophy and power standards for Mathematics.

Source: Thinkstock/Getty

Section 1: Product and process recommendations or the process decisions

Redson Curriculum Development Process

Product Recommendations

- The Redson School District (RSD) identified a Curriculum Leadership Team (CLT) that participated in three one-day professional development activities on curriculum development. The CLT decided that Redson would utilize the curriculum mapping process for developing and documenting its curriculum. A mapping template was designed by the district's CLT and will be shared with all staff for further input.
- The CLT decided to use the "unit" as the basic framework for curriculum design. A unit is defined as a block of instruction over a period of time. It is a series of lessons centered on a set of related topics, skills, and/or concepts. The unit is similar in nature to a chapter in the textbook or a group of lessons on a certain theme. Some units may overlap, others may include integrated subject areas, and some units may be ongoing in nature. Teachers will complete the design template for each unit of instruction they teach.
- The design template contains the following elements (see attached model in Section 2):
    - Unit Data = Subject, Course/Grade, Unit (Title), Starting Month, and approximate Duration.
    - State Standards = Alignment of learning targets to appropriate discipline or related performance standards.
    - Essential Questions = Questions that help students make sense of important ideas, knowledge, and know-how.
    - Power Standards = K-12 outcomes established by a departmental committee (i.e., "ten big things" that students should be able to know or do in each discipline or subject area).
    - Concepts = Bulleted listing of content, or KSUDs taught in a unit of instruction (i.e., these should be short, concise phrases).
    - Learning Targets = Final expected unit outcomes (i.e., grade level or course expectations that students should be able to know or do at the end of a unit).
    - Resources = Listing of appropriate resources, for example, Web sites, text references, source documents, books, labs (no requirement to identify teaching strategies as it is a matter of academic freedom).
    - Differentiation = Listing of remediation and/or enrichment strategies that are used for differentiating instruction to meet the needs of all students.
    - Evaluation Tools = Listing of formative and summative assessment strategies; be specific—more than a "laundry list"—include tests, tasks, and rubric tools.
    - Teacher Notes = A place for teachers to record personal notes and reminders on such things as ordering materials, safety considerations, challenging concepts, effective strategies, and student groupings.
- On the template, the three elements of curriculum, instruction, and assessment will be identified and labeled. Each element will also be defined by a question:
    - Curriculum = What should students know and be able to do?
    - Instruction = How do you deliver the content?
    - Assessment = How will you measure student progress?

- Concerning the template:
  - The "content" component of the curriculum will be represented using four different methods: (1) Concepts; (2) Learning targets; (3) Essential questions, and (4) Alignment of standards.
  - The CLT decided not to use a coding system (i.e. I = Introduce, D = Develop, and M = Master) for scope and sequence.
  - Two types of learning targets will be developed: district standards (i.e., discipline outcomes) and objectives (i.e., course or grade-level unit outcomes). Each outcome should begin with an action verb that is observable and measurable.
  - For consistency purposes, all items should be bulleted in each template component area.
- It is recommended that the district use a "design-down, deliver-up" process for outcome development and curricular alignment. Power standards and learning targets will be aligned to the state standards in each discipline and/or related disciplines.

Process Recommendations

- The curriculum development process involves the work of several teams in order to have a rigorous, relevant, dynamic, and usable curriculum. Redson School District has identified the following teams and responsibilities:
  - Curriculum Leadership Team (CLT) = Develop template; Identify product and process recommendations; establish timelines; select curriculum software.
  - Discipline Teams = Develop philosophy and identify power goals; analyze scope and sequence, and identify gaps and overlaps.
  - Classroom teachers = Complete template for units taught; align standards.
- Redson School District has adopted a philosophy of "bringing everyone along together, rather than the traditional discipline (i.e., mathematics) per year approach." Additionally, they recommended professional development opportunities should be scheduled to support the curriculum development process where needed.
- The district has purchased a curriculum software package to compliment the template. The CLT viewed and recommended the purchase of the ECLIPSE software. The software will allow the district to analyze its curriculum and to produce hits charts indicating strengths, overlaps, and gaps in alignment. Curriculum leaders will work with ECLIPSE to put the Redson template into an electronic format.
- Redson will utilize a four-year cycle. Teachers will be expected to complete specific components of the template each year for <u>all</u> the courses they teach. Teachers who teach similar courses (e.g., elementary math) will work together on those courses.
  - Year One = Curriculum components (District standards, Concepts, Objectives, State standards, and (attempt) Essential questions)
  - Year Two = Assessment components (Essential questions and Evaluation tools)
  - Year Three = Instruction components (Resources and Differentiation)
  - Year Four = Curriculum Analysis (Gaps and Overlaps)
- The district has decided to identify power standards or district standards. Curriculum teams in each subject area (i.e., Reading/English Language Arts, Mathematics, Science, Social Studies, Career & Technical Education, and the "Specials") will work collaboratively with CLT to write a brief philosophy statement and then develop 6–12 discipline outcomes or district standards. Three dates are tentatively set as the dates for this professional development activity.

- Part of the beginning of the year in-service plan (tentatively scheduled for August) will involve presenting the curriculum template and a demonstration of the curriculum software. Leadership team representatives will discuss the "process of how we arrived at this point" and "rationale for our product and process recommendations." Staff will also be provided "hands-on time" to practice with the software.
- Individual faculty will be required to complete the template for the courses they teach. Teachers who teach the same courses will work together on this process. The CLT recommends that the most efficient and effective method to complete the template is right after you have taught that unit and it is fresh in your mind.
- Faculty is encouraged to attempt to write some essential questions as part of completing the curriculum components in year one. In year two, professional development opportunities will be provided on essential questions to enhance each instructor's ability to write these types of questions.
- Four early releases for the school year are scheduled for curriculum activities:
    - November: CLT will review philosophies and district standards;
    - January: Teachers input curriculum individually or in teams;
    - March: Administrative progress check on work to date;
    - May: State Test Item Analysis.
- The CLT and the Administration will also propose to the School Board that two additional nonstudent contact days will be inserted into the school calendar to be used for curriculum work. The dates identified are in November and April. During these two days, teacher will be expected to enter their curriculum, and CLT will be available to answer questions.
- Concerning the approval process, completed templates will be turned into administration as part of "the end of the year check out process."
- Completed curriculums will be posted to the district Web site.

Figure 7: Product and Process Recommendations

Shutterstock.com

Source: Shutterstock.com

Redson Curriculum Template

Subject:	Course/Grade:	Unit:	Starting Month:	Duration:

State Standards:

Essential Questions:	**Power Standards:**

Curriculum: What should students know, do, and care about?

Concepts: • • • •	**Learning Targets:**

Instruction: How do you deliver the content?

Resources:	**Differentiation:**

Assessment: How will you measure student progress and achievement?

Formative Assessments:	**Summative Assessments:**

Teacher Notes:

Figure 8: Curriculum Template

Redson School District

Mathematics Program Philosophy and Power Standards

Redson's mathematics curriculum empowers students to develop and apply mathematical knowledge, skills, and strategies. The K-12 curriculum emphasizes oral and written communication, logical reasoning, and problem solving. Mathematical knowledge and skills are enhanced through the appropriate use of manipulatives and modern technologies. Multiple strategies are used to develop and enrich mathematical competence. In summary, Redson's mathematics curriculum strives to make our students effective problem solvers for today's world.

1. Use numbers effectively for various purposes, such as counting, measuring, estimating, calculating, and problem solving.
2. Master basic facts and math properties by using a variety of strategies.
3. Use geometric concepts, relationships, and procedures to interpret, represent, and solve problems.
4. Use appropriate tools and techniques of measurement directly and indirectly.
5. Use statistics and probability for data collection, analysis, interpretation, and prediction.
6. Investigate algebraic patterns, relations, functions, expressions, and properties.
7. Analyze mathematical problems to define variables, describe relationships, solve equations and inequalities, and graph solutions.
8. Apply knowledge of appropriate strategies, logical reasoning, and analytical thinking skills to solve mathematical problems.
9. Use oral and written communications to explain and/or justify their mathematical processes, decisions, and conclusions.
10. Use various manipulatives, models, and forms of technology to expand and enhance their knowledge of mathematics.
11. Use multiple problem solving strategies and financial literacy skills to make informed, real-world decisions.

Figure 9: Sample Philosophy and Power Standards

A Fable: Bell the Cat

DIRECTIONS: *Read the Curriculum fable. Think about the connection between the fable and the curriculum concepts presented in this chapter. In class with a small group, you will come to consensus on the moral of the fable. Be prepared to share. View the online book to read the article.*

Check for Mastery: Performance Expectations

DIRECTIONS: *You rated yourself on performance expectations at the start of this chapter. Have you now mastered each performance expectation? Rate yourself using the Likert scale online. Compare this to how you rated yourself at the beginning of this chapter. If you do not know an expectation, go back to the text and re-read the information.*

Summary Learning Activity: Crossword Puzzle

***DIRECTIONS:** Crossword puzzles are a fun activity to complete. The following puzzle serves as a check for understanding of your knowledge of curriculum terminology and concepts. Read each clue and fill in the appropriate word(s) in each puzzle box.*

Across

3. Synonym for outcome
8. Method of presenting content that illustrates relationships
10. Type of architecture in which concepts are revisited at successive grade-levels
11. Contextualization of an outcome
14. Culminating demonstration of learning
16. Curriculum development stage in which the plan is developed
17. Process of aligning curricular elements
19. Curriculum process advocated by Heidi Hayes Jacobs
20. Order of the curriculum
21. Type of performance standard
23. Curriculum development stage for monitoring progress and validating achievement
24. Six Facets of _____ in UbD
25. Method of presenting content that is evidence plus topic

Down

1. Answers the "what" question
2. Breadth and depth of the curriculum
4. Curriculum development stage associated with the needs assessment process
5. Curriculum development stage that offers the greatest challenge to curriculum directors
6. Type of curriculum that results from unintended outcomes
7. Structure of the _______
9. Father of curriculum development
12. Philosophy of education and Psychology of learning
13. Students, _____, subject, and standards
15. Verb + _____ = Outcome
18. Design with the _____ in mind in UbD
22. _____ is more and different is better!

Supplemental Learning Exercises

1. ABC School District has been in operation for 75 years. A long time superintendent recently retired. During her regime, only occasional and sporadic activities to improve the curriculum occurred. The additional facts have also become evident:
   - Few of the 276 teachers have taken any in-service courses within the last three years;
   - The community has recently voted, resulting in two failed referendums;
   - The teaching staff like to think of themselves as a collection of individuals;
   - A local resident petitioned the school board to eliminate the presence of controversial trade books in the school library;
   - Teacher concerns are directed largely to improving reading scores;
   - John Dewey's name is largely despised in the school; and
   - An evaluation committee from the local teacher's college has found that the school district is significantly behind the times.

   Assume that you have been hired as the new curriculum director. Assume that the new superintendent is a forward-thinking person and has given you free reign and his full support. What would you do to remedy the situation?
2. Create a lesson from your discipline using either the curriculum mapping or UbD™ approach. Design your own template and complete it for a content topic in your subject area. Include examples of essential questions and enduring understandings.
3. As we finish our study of curriculum some "A HA!" connections should be apparent. Complete the following chart illustrating those connections. Then identify at least three similarities among all the different components.

Triad of Elements	PLC Question	UbD™ Phase	PBI Characteristics
Tool Kit	**Environment**	**Curriculum Platform**	**Philosophy**
Curriculum	?	Identify desired results	?
Assessment	?	?	Performance tasks and rubrics
Instruction	What do I do if they do not know or already know?	?	?

4. Grant Wiggins and Jay McTighe advocate a "backward design" in their UbD™ model. In this model, teachers design curriculum with the end in mind. A key concept in this process is making sure students understand what they have learned. Their model emphasizes the Six Facets of Understanding. What does it mean to "understand" something? Consider the various ways we use the term in the following examples. Then identify various summary connotations of the term "understand" that emerge from your discussion.

Sample Statements

- "Men just don't understand women!"
- "He knows the historical facts but doesn't understand what they mean."
- "I can understand the British point of view."
- "I didn't really understand it until I had to use it."
- "Does anyone here understand French?"
- "I understood exactly what she needed to hear at that moment."
- "She knows the answer but doesn't understand why it is correct."
- "Grandfather's stories about the Depression helped us to understand the importance of saving."
- "I now understand that I was mistaken."

Final Test

DIRECTIONS: *Read each question or statement below. Select the appropriate answer or write the correct answer in the blank provided.*

_____ 1. What curriculum model, developed by Heidi Hayes Jacobs, often provides a monthly chronological listing of topics, expectations, and assessments?
   A. Performance-Based Instruction
   B. Rigor, Relevance, and Relationships
   C. Curriculum Mapping
   D. Understanding by Design

_____ 2. According to Stake and Easley, what often dictates the curriculum found in a subject area?
   A. The selection of textbooks
   B. Scores on standardized tests
   C. Unpacking of standards
   D. Methods of instruction

T F 3. The curriculum development process typically involves making several product and process decisions.

_____ 4. Which of the following is ***not*** typically found on a curriculum map?
   A. Content topic and concepts
   B. Performance expectations
   C. Enduring understandings
   D. Methods of assessment

T F 5. The fundamental purpose curriculum mapping is communication and documenting the relationships between curricular components.

_____ 6. Which of the following is ***not*** a "big idea" associated with UBD?
   A. Content standards are transformed into focused learning targets.
   B. Educators are mere purveyors of content or activity.
   C. Curricular planning is best done in a backwards design.
   D. Evidence of understanding is revealed through performance.

C 7. Listed below are the three phases of UBD. What is the correct order of those phases?

1. Determine acceptable evidence
2. Plan learning experiences
3. Identify desired results

A. 1, 2, 3
B. 3, 2, 1
C. 3, 1, 2
D. 1, 3, 2

B 8. Which of the following is ***not*** associated with the lesson plan template for the Identifying Desired Results stage of UbD?
A. Enduring understandings
B. Essential questions
C. Knowing and doing outcomes
D. Performance tasks

B 9. Which of the PLC questions is associated with the Determine Acceptable Evidence stage of UbD?
A. What do we want each student to learn?
B. How will we know when each student has learned it?
C. How will we respond when they already know it?
D. How will we respond when a student experiences difficulty in learning?

A 10. What UbD term describes the "big ideas" within a content area?
A. Enduring understandings
B. Essential questions
C. Power standards
D. Essential learnings

D 11. Which of the following is the *best* stated essential question?
A. Identify the parts of the microscope.
B. Who invented the microscope?
C. How do you properly adjust the lenses on a microscope?
D. What advances in science has the microscope led scientists to discover?

B 12. If called upon by the courts to prove opportunity-to-learn, the burden of proof can often be demonstrated through
A. instructional validity.
B. curricular validity.
C. differentiated instruction.
D. reflective journals.

C 13. When comparing the Triad of Elements, Performance-based Instruction, Understanding by Design, and Professional Learning Communities, you will note several similarities. Which of the following is ***not*** one of those similarities?
A. They are all student-centered.
B. They are all driven by standards.
C. They all follow a C, I, A approach.
D. They all move from knowing to doing.

Questions 14–15 refer to the learning plans below.

Learning Plan A

1. Attend a lecture on the writing process.
2. Complete assigned textbook reading.
3. Review the handouts on the writing process.
4. Review sample essays.
5. Develop a five-paragraph essay on a current event topic.

Learning Plan B

1. Discuss the steps you currently use when you write with a small group.
2. Listen to an overview of the writing process.
3. Compare the writing process to the steps you listed in your small group discussion.
4. Listen to a description of Step One: Brainstorming.
5. Work with a small peer group to practice brainstorming ideas for a five-paragraph essay on a current event topic.
6. Obtain feedback on your work from your instructor.
7. Listen to a description of Step Two: Organizing.

____ 14. The two essential elements of planning are:
   A. reviewing textbook materials and identifying content topics.
   B. deciding what one hopes to accomplish and how to accomplish it.
   C. aligning standards and developing assessments.
   D. determining classroom teaching strategies and providing corresponding resources.

____ 15. Which of the following statements is *true* about the lesson plans?
   A. Lesson Plan A is better structured and has better practice activities than Lesson Plan B.
   B. Lesson Plan B is better structured and has better practice activities than Lesson Plan A.
   C. Lesson Plan A and Lesson Plan B are equivalent in terms of structure and practice activities.
   D. One cannot conclude which Lesson Plan is better structured and which one has better practice activities.

***DIRECTIONS:** Write a brief response.*

1. Discuss the Wiggins and McTighe's six Facets of Understanding. What are the six facets? How did they evolve? What are they used for?
2. List and describe the "twin sins" of traditional design. Explain how the UbD™ model avoids those sins.

Works Cited and Suggested Readings

Armstrong, David. (1989). *Developing and Documenting the Curriculum.* Needham Heights, MA: Allyn and Bacon.

Doll, Ronald C. (1989). *Curriculum Development: Decision Making and Process* (7th ed.). Boston, MA: Allyn and Bacon.

Goodwin, Bryan. (2010). *Changing the Odds for Student Success: What Matters Most.* (A Special Issue of "Changing Schools"). Mid-continent Research for Education and Learning (McREL).

Henson, Kenneth. (2001). *Curriculum Planning Integrating Multiculturalism, Constructivism, and Educational Reform* (2nd ed.). New York, NY: McGraw-Hill Higher Education.

Hunkins, Francis P. (1980). *Curriculum Development: Program Improvement.* Columbus, OH: Charles Merrill Publishing Company.

Jacobs, Heidi Hayes (Ed.). (2004). *Getting Results with Curriculum Mapping.* Alexandria, VA: Association for Supervision and Curriculum Development (ASCD).

Jacobs, Heidi Hayes. (1997). *Mapping the Big Picture: Integrating Curriculum and Assessment K-12.* Alexandria, VA: Association for Supervision and Curriculum Development (ASCD).

Kagan, Spencer & Kagan, Miguel. (2009). *Kagan Cooperative Learning.* San Clemente, CA: Kagan Publishing.

Kindsvatter, Richard, Wilen, William, & Ishler, Margaret. (1992). *Dynamics of Effective Teaching* (2nd ed.). White Plains: NY: Longman Publishing Group.

Linde, Sharon. (2016). *Types of Curriculum Models.* (Video Lesson from Psychology Course, Chapter 8, Lesson 74). Retrieved from: http://study.com/academy/lesson/types-of-curriculum-models.html.

Marzano, Robert J. (2003). *What Works in Schools: Translating Research into Action.* Alexandria, VA: Association for Supervision and Curriculum Development (ASCD).

McTighe, Jay & Thomas, Ronald. (2003). Backward Design for Forward Action. *Educational Leadership,* (*60*)5, 52–55.

Olivia, Peter F. (1988). *Developing the Curriculum* (2nd ed.). Statesboro, GA: Georgia Southern College.

Pasch, Marvin, Sparks-Langer, Georgea, Gardner, Trevor, Stako, Alane, & Moody, Christella. (1991). *Teaching as Decision Making: Instructional Practices for the Successful Teacher.* White Plains: NY: Longman Publishing Group.

Phillips, Elizabeth. (1993). *Legal Implications of High Stakes Assessment: What States Should Know.* Learning Point Associates: North Central Regional Educational Laboratory.

Saylor, Galen, Alexander, William, & Lewis, Authur. (1981). *Curriculum Planning for Better Teaching and Learning* (4th ed.). New York, NY: Holt, Rinehart, and Winston.

Stake, Robert, & Easley, Jack. (1978). *Case Studies in Science Education* (*2*). Washington DC: National Science Foundation, Directorate for Science Education, Office of Program Integration.

Smith, Robert. (1969). College and University Planning. *Report on a Joint Study by Colgate University and American Foundation of Management Research.* Washington DC: US Department of Health, Education & Welfare.

Truesdale, Valerie, Claire Thompson, Claire, & Lucas, Michael. (2004). Use of Curriculum Mapping to Build a Learning Community. In Heidi Hayes Jacobs (Ed.), *Getting Results with Curriculum Mapping.* Alexandria, VA: Association for Supervision and Curriculum Development (ASCD).

Wiggins, Grant & McTighe, Jay. (2016). Backward Design: Why Backward is Best. *Edutopia, What Works in Education.* George Lucas Foundation. Retrieved from: http://www.edutopia.org/pdfs/resources/wiggins-mctighe-backward-design-why-backward-is-best.pdf.

Wiggins, Grant & McTighe, Jay. (2012). *What is UbD™ Framework?* Alexandria, VA: Association for Supervision and Curriculum Development (ASCD). Retrieved from: http://www.ascd.org/ASCD/pdf/siteASCD/publications/UbD_WhitePaper0312.pdf.

Wiggins, Grant & McTighe, Jay. (2005). *Understanding By Design®* (2nd ed.) Alexandria, VA: Association for Supervision and Curriculum Development (ASCD).

Wiggins, Grant. (2007). *What is an Essential Question?* Hopewell, NJ: Authentic Education. Retrieved from: http://www.authenticeducation.org/ae_bigideas/article.lasso?artid=53.

Wiggins, Grant. (2005). *Overview of UbD™ and the Design Template.* Alexandria, VA: Association for Supervision and Curriculum Development (ASCD). Retrieved from: http://www.grantwiggins.org/documents/UbDQuikvue1005.pdf.